The
UPPER
Elementary
Years

To Holly and Leslie for giving me
another chance to experience these years.

The UPPER Elementary Years

Ensuring Success in Grades 3–6

Christine Finnan

For information:

Corwin Press
A SAGE Company
2455 Teller Road
Thousand Oaks, California 91320
www.corwinpress.com

SAGE Ltd.
1 Oliver's Yard
55 City Road
London, EC1Y 1SP
United Kingdom

SAGE India Pvt. Ltd.
B 1/I 1 Mohan Cooperative
Industrial Area
Mathura Road, New Delhi 110 044
India

SAGE Asia-Pacific
Pte. Ltd.
33 Pekin Street #02-01
Far East Square
Singapore 048763

Printed in the United States of America

Library of Congress Cataloging-in-Publication Data

Finnan, Christine R.
The upper elementary years : ensuring success in grades 3–6 /
Christine Finnan.
p. cm.
Includes bibliographical references and index.
ISBN 978-1-4129-4098-6 (cloth)—
ISBN 978-1-4129-4099-3 (pbk.)
1. Education, Elementary—United States. 2. Academic achievement—United States. 3. Effective teaching—United States. I. Title.

LA219.F56 2009
372.24'20973—dc22

2008031917

This book is printed on acid-free paper.

08 09 10 11 12 10 9 8 7 6 5 4 3 2 1

Acquisitions Editor: Cathy Hernandez
Editorial Assistant: Sarah Bartlett
Production Editor: Appingo Publishing Services
Cover Designer: Monique Hahn
Graphic Designer: Anthony Paular

Contents

Preface

In an ideal world, teachers would be teaching children. They would figure out who these kids are, how they like to learn, what they are really like as people. They would capitalize on the kids' interests and strengths instead of delivering content the same way to all students based on the teachers' guide. They would accept any reasonable answer from students that might take them in a different direction.

—National Board-certified teacher,
Middle Childhood/Generalist

PURPOSE AND AUDIENCE

This teacher summarizes the essence of this book: Upper elementary teachers need encouragement and support in finding the balance between teaching children and teaching the content we want them to learn. Because accountability for student learning has been the focus of districts, states, and the federal government, the scale has tipped heavily toward a concern about teaching content. I am not proposing that teachers abandon their responsibility for facilitating student learning of academic content; this is critically important. However, I am suggesting that too much emphasis on skills acquisition and students' standing on benchmark or high-stakes tests makes it difficult to create school and classroom environments that allow students to develop a sense of accomplishment, to experience belonging, and community, and to be intellectually, socially, and physically engaged as learners. Most teachers choose to teach upper elementary grades primarily because they enjoy children in this age span and believe that they can make a difference in their lives. This book encourages teachers to keep these ideals alive and work with others in their school to find a better balance between teaching students as whole and complex people and teaching the content that we want them to know and be able to use.

All teachers struggle to keep an appropriate balance between concern about learners and concern about what they learn, but it is especially problematic for upper elementary teachers (i.e., those who teach third through sixth grade) because these teachers have so few supports targeted specifically toward them. In addition, policies and practices—in particular, high-stakes testing and accountability—start in these grades, resulting in more scrutiny of upper elementary teachers' practices. Ask yourself the following questions:

- Do you sometimes wonder if, in the quest for making adequate yearly progress (AYP) and moving students from one achievement band to another, we lose sight of developmentally appropriate teaching for the students whose test scores become so important?
- Are you supported professionally as an upper elementary teacher (e.g., through specialized journals and books, conferences, and networks)?
- Do you ever look at the resources and programs available to young children and to adolescents and wonder why so few resources are targeted toward meeting the specific needs of upper elementary children?

These questions are at the heart of this book. By examining the developmental characteristics of upper elementary children (8- to 12-year-olds), the characteristics of schools and classrooms, and the teaching and learning process, this book proposes a balance that lets teachers' knowledge of students work to achieve the goal of increased academic accomplishment. Through voices of teachers, children, and administrators; examples from actual classrooms; and examination of current research, the book presents an argument that

- children would benefit from a clear definition of developmentally appropriate practice for the upper elementary grades;
- upper elementary teachers would benefit from targeted professional supports (e.g., professional organizations, journals, networks, conferences); and
- children and teachers would benefit from focusing, consolidating, and disseminating research and best practice and from a critical examination of current policies and practices affecting upper elementary students.

This book is written primarily for people teaching third through sixth grade. It will resonate with veteran teachers by both confirming and calling into question accepted practices and policies. For new and prospective teachers, it provides ideas, resources, and discussion of issues they face or anticipate. Although not its primary audience, principals, district office personnel, policymakers, and teacher education faculty are an important audience because they are in a position to provide or advocate for the increased professional resources, policy examination, and research called for in the following pages. Parents are also likely to find the book useful, given the description of upper elementary child development and insights into upper elementary students' life in schools and classrooms. Given its focus on children, it places teaching and learning in the context of the complex lives of 8- to 12-year-olds, a context we too often forget in the press for improving academic achievement.

I hope that this book inspires teachers to use existing resources while pressing for targeted networking and professional development opportunities. It is also my goal that administrators see the importance of examining the specific needs of these grades and for teacher education faculty and policymakers to conduct, consolidate, and disseminate relevant research and to use that research to revise and make policy. Most important, it should stimulate increased discussion about creating learning environments for upper elementary children that balance child development and academic achievement. It advocates for environments that

- encourage children to experience authentic accomplishment by mastering what they otherwise thought unattainable;
- support their sense of belonging as people who are cared for and who care for others; and
- engage students academically, socially, and physically.

BACKGROUND

The idea to write this book grew out of my personal frustration. I have taught future teachers at the College of Charleston in Charleston, South Carolina, for many years, and it finally dawned on me that an important group of students and teachers has been overlooked. This group has been overlooked in terms of advocacy. In South Carolina I saw how the lack of advocacy for upper elementary students and teachers stands in stark contrast to the effectiveness of lobbyists for specific early childhood and middle grades teacher certification requirements and for targeted services for young children and young adolescents. This age and grade span also benefits from few targeted academic resources. In preparing to teach preservice courses, I searched in vain for readings about upper elementary grades that parallel those available about early childhood and middle grades (Bredekamp & Kopple, 1997; Driscoll & Nagel, 2005; Knowles & Brown, 2000; Powell, 2005; Warner & Sower, 2005). Finally, no organization defines best practice for upper elementary grades. The organizations that do so for early childhood and middle grades ensure that teachers are prepared to balance knowledge of students and content. A formal discussion of how best to teach 8- to 12-year-olds either has not occurred or has not been disseminated widely.

ORGANIZATION OF THE BOOK

The organization of this book reflects its primary emphasis: It balances knowledge of students and their lives with knowledge of their learning environments and the teaching and learning process. Chapter 1 clarifies the need for a focus on upper elementary students and grades and identifies key issues that are developed in subsequent chapters. Chapters 2 through 4 examine all aspects of upper elementary student development, focusing on development as learners, members of society, and physical beings. These chapters explore general developmental trends of all 8- to 12-year-olds (Chapter 2), general trends by group affiliation (Chapter 3), and individual differences across all children (Chapter 4). Chapters 5 through 7 examine environments in which children develop, working from the assumption that children flourish in environments that develop their sense of accomplishment, belonging, and engagement. Chapter 5 explores influences outside of school, and Chapters 6 and 7 shift the focus to schools (Chapter 6) and classrooms (Chapter 7). Chapter 8 targets the primary classroom purpose, teaching and learning, examining the influence of teaching and assessment on students' growing sense of accomplishment, belonging, and engagement. Chapter 9 serves as a call to action. It proposes a framework for upper elementary developmentally appropriate practice, calls for targeted supports for upper elementary teacher professionalism, and advocates for a concerted examination of research and policy to best meet the needs of upper elementary children.

DATA SOURCES AND COLLECTION

The data for this book draw from many sources, including a review of the literature, interviews with teachers, observations in classrooms, informal conversations with children, student essays, future teacher essays, and conversations with colleagues. Largely, the book is shaped by my experiences working with schools and future teachers and as a parent. I spent twenty years working with a major school reform model, Accelerated Schools plus (see www.acceleratedschools.net). This involvement gave me access to schools across the country that are committed to improving students' lives; I have taught hundreds of future teachers in a variety of teacher education courses, and I raised two daughters who reminded me of the joy of this time in our lives.

The most enjoyable part of gathering information for this book has been talking directly with teachers, students, parents, future teachers, and colleagues, as well as in observing classrooms across the country. In several schools students wrote to writing prompts that had been developed by students in a fifth-grade class. These prompts (What makes you special? Why do you like to go to school? What makes a teacher fun?) provide much of the student voice in this book. I also collected data from future teachers by asking them to share their memories of being in upper elementary grades and their reasons for wanting to teach upper elementary children. Finally, every chance I had, I talked with friends who either are teachers or have children this age; I interviewed National Board Certified Teachers and people who have been involved in educational policy development at the state and national levels. Foremost, I have been an avid "kid-watcher" and question-asker.

Acknowledgments

To those who made this possible. I want to thank College of Charleston for granting me a sabbatical; this was an undertaking that I could not have completed without time away from my usual obligations. I want to express special thanks to my dean, Dr. Frances Welch, and department chair, Dr. Linda Fitzharris, for encouraging the sabbatical and respecting my time away. Very special thanks extend to my colleague Jinny Bartel and former student Melanie Knight for helping me develop the paper that served as the basis for this book. Jinny and other colleagues (Brian Lanahan, Judy Dellicolli, Diana Treahy) opened their classes to me, and their students graciously agreed to let me use their voices throughout this book. Other friends and colleagues—Diane Cudahy, Candy Jaruszewicz, Julie Swanson, Nancy Sorenson, Paula Egelson, and William Veal—listened to endless talk about upper elementary children.

My entry into a national network of elementary schools came through Accelerated Schools colleagues, especially Gene Chasin. Gene not only helped provide access to schools but also provided insights from his experience with Accelerated Schools, as a former superintendent and principal and as a father of a 12-year-old. To the many people in schools who supported the research, I am deeply indebted. I want to thank several principals and teachers who helped coordinate visits and interviews: Reggie Bright, Dolores Gribouski, Rima Meecham, Jayne Cardin, Melanie Low, Laurie Biggers, and June Gingrich. I cannot name all of the many teachers who welcomed me into their rooms and took time for interviews. Special thanks to teachers who helped with the student writing project, especially Tracy Pinnell, Chad Hunt, Chris Littleton, Trey Wiseman, and Renee Jannuzzi. Special thanks to the National Board Certified Teachers who agreed to interviews: Brooke McGuire, Renee Jannuzzi, Trey Wiseman, and Ellen Mintz.

A special group of friends and colleagues served as early reviewers and provided needed critical comments. Dr. Lorin Anderson's suggestions weave through the entire book. I am indebted to him for conceptual insights (e.g., the importance of balance and basic environmental supports to encourage children's sense of accomplishment, belonging, and engagement) and guidance on the best ways to frame points. Dr. Belinda Williams confirmed my portrayal of upper elementary student development and social and cultural influences. Ruth Cohen, Anne Gutshall, and Tysa Austin read early drafts with the perspective of an elementary school principal, guidance counselor, and teacher. I also want to thank people who willingly provided state and national perspectives on issues this book raises, especially Jerry Bullock, Tom Carroll, David Mandel, Janice Poda, and Suzanne Wilson.

Writing a book is one thing, but making it readable is another. Special thanks extend to Caroline McPartland whose attention to detail and perseverance helped immensely. The editorial staff at Corwin Press provided invaluable support. Final thanks are extended to Cathy Hernandez, Corwin Press Acquisitions Editor. Cathy saw the potential in a short paper and took the chance that a full manuscript would emerge.

Families are always happy at the end of major projects because writers become very self- or project absorbed. With love and appreciation to my husband George for many long conversations over dinner and for recognizing my need to be single minded. To my daughters Holly and Leslie, thanks for your support and encouragement; and to Leslie's friend, Aubrey Wade, for Spanish translation; and to my mother Bernice Robinson for always believing in me.

PUBLISHER'S ACKNOWLEDGMENTS

Corwin Press gratefully acknowledges the contributions of the following reviewers:

Rebecca S. Compton
Professor, Elementary Education
Director, Graduate Reading Program
East Central University
Ada, OK

Diana Coyl
Assistant Professor, Child Development
California State University, Chico
Chico, CA

Jessie Fries-Kraemer
Fifth-Grade Teacher
Eubank Academy of Literacy and Fine Arts
Albuquerque, NM

Linda Huber
Assistant Professor of Elementary Education
Ball State University
Muncie, IN

Patti Palmer
Sixth-Grade Teacher
Wynford Elementary School
Bucyrus, OH

Sandi Phair
Fifth-Grade Teacher
West Hill School
Rocky Hill, CT

Renee Ponce-Nealon
Third-Grade Teacher
McDowell Elementary School
Petaluma, CA

About the Author

Christine Finnan holds a joint position as an associate professor in the Teacher Education Department and the Sociology and Anthropology Department at the College of Charleston in Charleston, South Carolina. Before assuming this position, she was an associate professor in the Early Childhood, Elementary and Middle Grades Department. In this capacity she helped develop curriculum for a B.S. in elementary education, preparing graduates to work in second- through sixth-grade classrooms.

Dr. Finnan's joint appointment reflects her academic training and scholarship. She became interested in studying education through her research on children's play and folklore. She completed a master of arts degree from the University of Texas, Austin, in anthropology and folklore. Her research focused on the study of third-grade children's spontaneous play. Dr. Finnan completed a doctorate in education at Stanford University in 1980, focusing on anthropology and education. While at Stanford she continued to study children's play, examining how Vietnamese refugee children used play to assimilate into a new culture.

Since 1990, Dr. Finnan has been involved in school-reform initiatives, particularly the Accelerated Schools project and more recently Partners for Acceleration. Using her anthropological lens, she examines the interplay between school and classroom culture and reform models. She works closely with teachers, observing in classrooms and providing professional development.

Dr. Finnan coauthored *Accelerating the Learning of All Children: Cultivating School, Classroom and Individual Change* (Westview Press, 2000) with Julie D. Swanson, coedited *Accelerated Schools in Action: Lessons from the Field* (Corwin Press, 1996) with Ed St. John, Jane McCarthy, and Simeon Slovacek, and has published extensively in edited volumes and journals.

Dr. Finnan is the mother of two adult daughters and lives in Mt. Pleasant, South Carolina, with her husband George.

1

Why Focus on Upper Elementary Grades and Students?

I absolutely adored my fourth-grade teacher, Mrs. B. She was always so full of life, and she seemed excited every day to be with us at school and teaching us everything she knew. Along with being a role model and an adult influence, she was our friend. She was always caring and tuned into our wants and needs. She helped cultivate my love of learning at a very pivotal point in time, when grades and testing started to become a part of our regular lives in school. This period of time is one marked by a plunge in students' excitement and interest level in school and academics, but through Mrs. B's own excitement and interest, along with assignments that were fun and relevant to us, Mrs. B was able to encourage and foster our love of learning.

Mrs. B is a big reason why I want to teach. I suppose, if you ask my dad, I've always known I was going to be a teacher, even when I was only in kindergarten and would line my stuffed animals up each afternoon to teach to them. However, now I know why. Not only is it because of a deep-seated passion within me, but it's also because I know it's teachers who can truly make a difference in our children's lives, and therefore can help shape the future.

—Preservice teacher

This statement is from a young woman with a passion to teach children in the upper elementary grades. The essay she wrote describes why she wants to teach these grades rather than early childhood or middle grades. She describes some of the issues her children will face during these grades (e.g., an increased focus on grades and testing, a drop in motivation) and characteristics of a good upper elementary teacher (i.e., a teacher who knows and cares about her students and also inspires them to learn). She describes a teacher who encouraged students' accomplishments, made them feel like they belonged in the classroom, and engaged them intellectually.

Without saying so explicitly, she describes why these grades are so important in children's lives. She also alludes to why many people fondly remember this time in life. To many people it is a "grace period" between the dependence of early childhood and the stresses of early adolescence. These upper elementary years are characterized by growing physical, academic, and social confidence as well as increased involvement in a wider world. As Borland, Laybourn, Hill, and Brown (1998) concluded:

> Middle childhood is a period when children and the other key players in their lives negotiate an increasingly complex and fast-changing world. It is a time of preparation for later life in economic, technological and environmental circumstances which are hard to predict, *but it is also a time to be cherished for its own sake* [italics added]. With the marked physical dependency of early childhood over and the transitions to economic and other forms of autonomy still some way off, it is a time when children, parents and others have to manage a range of tensions and competing principles. (p. 173)

In part because this age span is seen as relatively trouble free, few people target these grades for special attention. When we think about where we should place emphasis in schools across the country, many people suggest improving programs for young children to ensure that all children are ready for school and are able to read, write, and understand basic mathematics to progress in school. Others focus on the special needs of adolescents, students who are at the critical point in their lives when they are making decisions that will affect their future careers and lives.

Both of these stages in children's lives are critical, and special attention should be paid to them. But too often, by focusing on the needs of young children or adolescents, we overlook children in grades that are becoming increasingly challenging and important to children's futures. Third grade begins a phase in children's schooling dominated by the pressure of annual high-stakes testing and accountability, a shift toward acquisition of increasingly demanding academic content, and an expectation that they have mastered basic math and literacy skills. The climate in many schools, especially those serving students who are less likely to perform well on these tests, can be stressful, focusing primarily on a conception of achievement that emphasizes skills rather than understanding, facts rather than concepts (Finn & Ravitch, 2007; Pace Marshall, & Price, 2007; Perlstein, 2007). Couple this trend with a developmental trajectory that makes children more self-aware and self-critical, and we see motivation and engagement decline in these grades (Scales, Sesma, & Bolstrom, 2004). This does not have to be the case, and many teachers and schools work hard to keep the joy alive in the upper elementary grades.

Consider . . .

Creating a class book to share with substitutes and visitors.

Help substitutes and visitors get to know your class by creating a class book that is shared with them. Give the students responsibility for determining the information that they think people should know. One strategy you can use borrows from a gift a fifth-grade class gave me. Before I visited the class, the teacher asked the students what I should know about them. They created a book titled "So, You Want to Know about a Kid My Age. . . . You Should Ask These Questions, and We'll Tell You Why" with the following topics:

- Who lives at your house?
- How would you describe your life after school?
- Do you like school? Why or why not?
- Do you have any hobbies?
- What activities do you like to do?
- What kind of music do you listen to?
- What games do you play?
- Where do kids your age hang out?
- Have you ever gone on vacation? If so, where did you go?
- What famous celebrities do you RESPECT?

The teacher put each question on a separate page, passed each page around the room, and students answered the question. They then talked about each topic, and the teacher summarized the discussion on the back of the sheet. If you create this book for substitutes, include the rules and procedures the substitutes should know, but be sure to include your students in determining what substitutes should know. If the children help create this guide for substitutes, they are more likely to support the substitute when he or she follows the rules and procedures.

UPPER ELEMENTARY CHILDREN AND GRADE LEVELS

A question may arise as you begin reading this book: Why focus on children in upper elementary grades and not on all of the children in elementary school? This is a legitimate question when we think in terms of school rather than children. However, since my focus is on children in specific grade levels, I find it more useful to narrow the focus. This narrowing is supported by research on child development as well (Collins, 2005). The 8- to 12-year-old age span is typically designated as part of *middle childhood,* the time between early childhood and young adolescence (Berk, 2003; Collins, 1984; McDevitt & Ormrod, 2004). Typically, middle childhood includes children 6 to 12 years old, but research indicates that children who are 6 to 8 differ markedly from 10- to 12-year-old children cognitively, socially, and physically (Collins, 2005). And early childhood research indicates that children up to age 8 should be considered young children (Bredekamp & Copple, 1997; National Association for the Education of Young Children, 2007). Early childhood advocates question extending the definition of middle childhood to age 6 because it pushes academic and social demands down to young children, diminishing opportunities for developmentally appropriate practice in the primary grades. For this reason I focus primarily on 8- to 12-year-olds and avoid the middle childhood designation.

I use upper elementary children or upper elementary students to limit the focus to third through sixth grade. Because sixth grade is most often in middle school (Stevenson, 2006), fewer examples of it are provided. I do not use the term *tween* that has recently entered the lexicon. Tween refers to an age span from 6 to 15 years and is a Madison Avenue invention used to identify a marketing segment (Lamb & Brown, 2006; Siegel, Coffey & Livingston, 2001). The term also strengthens the image that these students are between stages because *tween* is either an abbreviation of *between* or indicates that they are not quite teens.

I acknowledge limitations in using *upper elementary* as a designation. It is not completely synonymous with the 8- to 12-year age span. Obviously, there are some 7-year-olds in third grade and some 13- and even 14-year-olds in sixth grade. This term works reasonably well in the United States but not in all other countries. Readers outside of the United States will need to translate as necessary. It also ignores the incredible variation in schools structures within the United States. In some schools third grade is considered part of the primary program. In some schools sixth grade is an upper elementary grade; more often it is in middle school. Some middle schools extend down to include fifth grade, and some elementary schools extend to eighth grade. Finally, *upper elementary* assumes a traditional school structure in which children pass from one grade to the next each year. With those caveats aside, this term is used throughout the book. At times I also refer to these children by their age. When it seems more appropriate, they are referred to as 8-year-olds or as a group, 8- to 12-year-olds.

DEFINING UPPER ELEMENTARY TEACHERS: THEIR PRACTICE AND THE PROFESSION

Developmentally Appropriate Practice

In broad strokes we know that all effective teachers understand and value the students they teach. They know the content students are expected to learn and how to teach so that students want to learn. They know how to assess so that they are sure that students have learned. Effective teachers also know how to establish a classroom environment in which all students flourish and how to work with colleagues to create an effective, welcoming school environment. In addition, they know what it means to be a professional, and they have the dispositions expected of professional teachers. At one level these characteristics of effective teachers hold whether teaching very young children, adolescents, or adults. At another level teaching is an interaction between the students, teachers, and the content taught, and it must change when any of these variables changes. A focus on children in a specific age/grade span has implications for curriculum, instruction, and assessment, and for professional expectations for teachers.

Advocates for early childhood and middle grades education have clearly articulated what they deem appropriate for young children or young adolescents. A similar articulation of developmentally appropriate practice for upper elementary students has not occurred. The early childhood community, through the National Association for the Education of Young Children (NAEYC), pioneered the idea of developmentally appropriate practice. Their Position Statement on Developmentally Appropriate Practice (ratified in July 1996) calls for all teachers of young children to have

- knowledge of child development and learning that can be used to make general predictions about what is safe, healthy, interesting, achievable, and also challenging to children;
- knowledge of individual children's strengths, interests, and needs and ability to use this knowledge to individualize learning; and
- knowledge of the social and cultural contexts of children's lives and the ability to use this knowledge to make learning relevant, meaningful, and respectful to all children and their families (Bredekamp & Copple, 1997, pp. 8–9).

The National Middle School Association (NMSA) has a number of position statements, including one on appropriate curriculum, instruction, and assessment. In this statement teachers are encouraged to

- establish learner-centered classrooms that encourage and honor student voice;
- develop standards-based curricula that integrate subject area disciplines along with students' concerns and questions;
- design instruction to meet the diverse needs of every student
- measure student progress and development with a variety of; authentic assessments; and
- guide students in discovering their aptitudes and interests (NMSA, 2005).

Examining these position statements, one sees common threads emerge. First, developmentally appropriate practice starts with knowing children who fall into the particular age span. This includes knowing about child development, social and cultural group influences, and individual variation. Second, developmentally appropriate practice involves using this knowledge of students in combination with knowledge of subject area disciplines to guide teaching, engage students, and bring out their interests and voice.

Unlike the definitions of developmentally appropriate practice put forward by early childhood and young adolescent advocates, many of the practices commonly encouraged in upper elementary teaching (e.g., an emphasis on teaching academic content, preparation for high-stakes tests) illustrate a move away from a focus on students in their family and community context toward a focus on students as academic-content learners. Throughout the following chapters, I provide the basis for a framework for upper elementary practice that starts with the children and works toward creating environments in which they can learn necessary knowledge and skills. This framework establishes developmentally appropriate practice as an interplay between actions of students and teachers, characteristics of the classroom environment, and the act of teaching and learning.

- Actions of students in which they
    - are involved in learning
    - cooperate and collaborate
    - are successful and empowered
- Actions of teachers in which they
    - understand students in their family, social, and cultural context
    - serve as learning leaders
- Characteristics of the classroom environment in which
    - there is mutual respect

  - diversity is viewed as a strength
  - students and the teacher agree on what is considered responsible behavior

- Characteristics of the teaching and learning process in which

  - learning is authentic and relates to students' lives
  - curriculum is integrated
  - instruction occurs through dialogue
  - instruction is inclusive
  - students engage in active knowledge construction
  - learning is made meaningful by focusing on larger concepts
  - connections are made within a subject

Professional Support

Teachers are part of an exciting, dynamic profession, and as professionals, recognize the importance of growing professionally and contributing to the profession. To grow and contribute, we rely on resources from professional organizations, unions, state agencies, districts offices, colleges and universities, our schools, and colleagues. Some teachers are fortunate to have many resources targeted to their specific needs. As Table 1.1 illustrates, early childhood and middle grades teachers have many more targeted professional resources than upper elementary teachers have. They enjoy professional organizations, journals, access to active Web sites, and avenues for advocacy. Upper elementary teachers, in contrast, have to cull information from more generic sources (e.g., organizations, Web sites, and journals for P–12 or P–8 teachers) and adapt resources developed for younger or older children.

The only organization that recognizes the unique challenges and strengths of upper elementary teachers is the National Board for Professional Teaching Standards (NBPTS) with its Middle Childhood/Generalist certificate. The NBPTS was established in 1987 to strengthen teaching by developing standards for accomplished teachers. NBPTS developed five core propositions defining essential characteristics of any accomplished teacher: commitment to students and their learning; knowledge of subject matter and how to teach it to students; managing and monitoring student learning; thinking systematically about practice; and being members of learning communities. The Middle Childhood/Generalist certification adapts the core propositions for teachers of 7- to 12-year-olds (National Board for Professional Teaching Standards, 2001). Teachers who have at least three years of teaching experience are eligible to participate in the lengthy process of compiling a portfolio demonstrating how they meet the exacting standards for those who teach all subjects to students in middle childhood.

Table 1.1 Comparison of Resources for Early Childhood, Upper Elementary, and Middle Grades Teachers

Resource	*Early childhood*	*Upper elementary*	*Middle grades*
Professional organizations for teachers	National Association for the Education of Young Children	None	National Middle School Association
Journals	Eight national journals	No journals specific to upper elementary grades	One national journal
Web sites	http://www.naeyc.org	None	http://nmsa.org
Focused research on upper elementary education (American Educational Research Association: AERA, 2007)	Two special interest groups	None	One special interest group
National Board for Professional Teaching Standards	Early childhood generalist	Middle childhood generalist	Early adolescence generalist
Advocacy for students	NAEYC	None	NMSA
Clearly articulated developmentally appropriate practice	Yes	No	Yes

ADVOCATING FOR UPPER ELEMENTARY STUDENTS

The upper elementary years and grades are critical not only in terms of children's future success but also as a time in their lives to be nurtured and enjoyed. I raise a number of issues in this book because, although

Consider . . .

Becoming an advocate for upper elementary grades and students in your school.

All schools have room for improvement and have issues that people may not have fully recognized. Depending on what is happening in your school, here are some suggestions.

- Join with upper elementary colleagues in your school to take stock of the resources and issues that are unique to the grades you teach.
- Meet together regularly with upper elementary colleagues to share best practices.
- Use meeting times to examine how school and district policies affect you and your students.
- Suggest cross-grade-level meetings to gain a better sense of issues and expectations in the lower grades.
- Observe in other grade levels, especially in early childhood classes, to better understand what your students have experienced and how being in the upper elementary grades is different for your students.
- Volunteer to work with preservice students to provide them good experiences in upper elementary grades.

considerable research exists on this age/grade span, it is not consolidated and used to advocate for students and to support teachers, nor does it appear to shape many of the policies that directly impact children's lives in schools and classrooms. Early childhood advocates use research to support their fight for stimulating and appropriate educational opportunities for all young children. They compile considerable evidence on brain growth (Jensen, 1998), language learning (Hart & Risley, 1995), and stimulating and nurturing learning environments (Bredekamp & Copple, 1997). Middle grades advocates use research on student disengagement and point to high school dropout rates to advocate for educational programs that will keep students engaged (Knowles & Brown, 2000; NMSA, 2007; Powell, 2005). Advocates for special needs children use research to press for the least restrictive environments for exceptional children (CEC, 2007).

Given that upper elementary children are often subjects in research studies (Collins, 2005; Cooper, et al., 2005; Kennedy, 2005; Scales, Sesma, & Bolstrom, 2004), why hasn't this research been compiled and used to advocate for these children? My best explanation for this is that a crisis has not mobilized people in support of upper elementary children. Unlike early childhood organizations that had to fight to formally educate young children, we have always educated 8- to 12-year-olds. Unlike middle grades advocates who fought to change the structure of educational delivery to young adolescents, we have not seriously questioned the structure of upper elementary grades (e.g., the curriculum, student grouping, instructional practices). Unlike parents of special needs children, exceptionalities have not kept most upper elementary children out of school.

When considering issues for upper elementary children, there appears to be a "let sleeping dogs lie" or "if it ain't broke, don't fix it" mentality. We may also have a classic "chicken-and-egg" problem. Educators and parents are less likely to raise questions and concerns related to upper elementary issues because, on the one hand, they have no organizations to turn to and, on the other hand, organizations do not develop because no one articulates common problems or concerns. This is unfortunate because, once organized, groups like NAEYC, NMSA, and the Council for Exceptional Children (CEC) continue to advocate for appropriate education for the children they serve, support journals and other publications, provide regional and national conferences, and mobilize members when issues arise.

In the following chapters the issues raised above will be addressed in more depth. The questions that recur throughout this book are the following.

- How do we create a balance between the strengths and needs of upper elementary children while ensuring that they learn the content that will engage and stimulate them and prepare them for future learning?
- How does a clearly articulated definition of developmentally appropriate practice keep an appropriate balance?
- What is involved in creating learning environments in elementary schools and upper elementary classrooms that promote student accomplishment, belonging, and engagement?
- What supports do upper elementary teachers need to develop professionally and to best serve their students?
- How can research be encouraged, compiled, and disseminated to best serve upper elementary students and teachers?
- What policies and practices need to be critically examined to support this balance?

2

Development of 8- to 12-Year-Old Children

How would I describe my fifth graders? Energetic, talkative, mobile, curious, extremely social, [pause] enormously social.

—Fifth-grade teacher

They are sponges. You can mold them, shape them. They love unconditionally, not like sixth or seventh graders. Fourth and fifth are better than third because of their thought processes. They can analyze and have critical thinking skills. Socially they conform.

—Fourth-grade teacher

In third grade they are babies compared to fifth. They want to be independent, but they lack the organization skills and thought processes to be as independent as they think they should be.

—Third-grade teacher

Although it is important to avoid overgeneralizing, finding commonalities among children helps us set developmentally appropriate expectations and identify what makes each child unique. These common expectations serve not as an ideal, but as a common point of measure. From them we can view the wide array of differences and determine how to guide each child appropriately. This chapter provides an overview of what one can reasonably expect of upper elementary children in terms of their learning, understanding of themselves in relation to others, and physical growth and development. Because this book spans five years in a child's life and four grade levels, what we expect of an 8-year-old is clearly different than what can be expected of a 12-year-old. In reading the generalizations here, assume that most 8-year-olds are acquiring the traits or abilities, whereas most 12-year-olds are refining them.

The field of child development was dominated by *stage theories* for many years. These theories neatly dissect the human experience into predictable, hierarchical stages of development. The most famous of the stage theories are Jean Piaget's (1936/1952) stages of cognitive development, Sigmund Freud's (1959) stages of psychosexual development, Erik Erikson's (1968) stages of psychosocial development, and Lawrence Kohlberg's (1969) stages of moral development. Stage theories have been criticized for being applicable primarily to children who resembled the theorists (White, middle class, male); for being too linear and assuming that later stages of development are preferable to earlier ones (James, Jenks, & Prout, 1998); for ignoring the fact that development is not always a continuous march forward (Kowaleski-Jones & Duncan, 1999); and for downplaying the importance of the physical and cultural context in which children develop (Berk, 2003; Borland, Laybourn, Hill, & Brown, 1998; James, Jenks, & Prout, 1998; McDevitt & Ormrod, 2002; Salkind, 2004). These theories are still important in drawing a broad picture of development, but they have been refined by more recent research, particularly medical research on brain development (Nelson, de Haan, & Thomas, 2006) and sociological and anthropological research on childhood (Boocock & Scott, 2005; Borland, et al., 1998; Cooper, García Coll, Bartko, Davis, & Chatman, 2005; García Coll & Szalacha, 2004; James, Jenks, & Prout, 1998).

Each of the stage theorists assigned a name for a particular stage and set an age range that should fall within it. Within several of these theoretical constructs, the stage in which upper elementary children fall is considered transitional. Terms such as *latency* (used by both Freud and Erikson) bring to mind dormancy or a rest or respite from one extreme stage of life and preparation for future trials. Upper elementary children are probably not aware of developmental stage theories, but they do recognize that they are considered in transition. This is the focus of one of their biggest complaints. When asked what could make their lives better, they suggest that adults focus more on the present and pay more attention to who they *are* now, not who they *will* be. They do not want more freedom or more empowerment; they want adults to listen and pay attention to them, to find out about what they are interested in and capable of doing (Borland, et al., 1998, p 166).

Scales, Sesma, and Bolstrom (2004) summarized some of the key developments that occur during the upper elementary years. As they state, children make some important decisions based on their here-and-now experiences—decisions that have a profound impact on their future.

> Children's academic and personal interests, sense of competence and efficacy, perceptions about the usefulness of particular subject matter, motivation, classroom goals, and belief that school is an enjoyable and accepting place become differentiated and unique. During middle childhood, these and other variables, including children's peer relationships and general social competencies, combine to either strengthen or weaken developmental trajectories favorable to strong school bonding and school performance. (p. 145)

DEVELOPMENT AS LEARNERS

> *In the third grade they are academically still in the infant stage. You may assume that they know more than they do. You need to continue to build their foundation. By fifth and sixth grade, everything is cut and dry, yes or no. They want to live in a clean yes/no world. We need to expose them to more gray.*
>
> —Elementary school Title 1 math coordinator

> *Active, lots of energy, curious, excited about learning, starting to create a self-identity, aware of what they are good at and where their challenges are, especially by end of third.*
>
> —Third-grade teacher

Learner development is primarily about change in a person's cognitive functioning. Cognitive development occurs within the brain and is influenced by experience, environment, and other biological changes. We know a lot more about this process through advances in neuroscience research, and this research continues to shed more light on cognition and its development. However, we are still burdened by common thinking about learning as a function of intelligence, or our innate capacity to learn. The concept of intelligence is burdened by its origins in the intellectual and social climate of the early twentieth century. At this time there was faith in our ability to scientifically measure human traits coupled with a belief that society would benefit from sorting people based on these tests. Stephen Murdoch (2007) in *IQ: A Smart History of a Failed Idea* paints a disturbing picture of the slapdash development of many intelligence tests (that they were developed without a definition of intelligence is only one issue) and their misuse in sorting people, especially children. I will deal with the limitations of a conception of intelligence as a single, static attribute in Chapter 4, but I raise it here because it influences our thinking about learner development. Although understanding of cognitive development was rudimentary when intelligence tests were first developed, there was a realization that in order to test what was seen as a static attribute, tests had to account for cognitive development. An 8-year-old cannot be given the same test as a 20-year-old or it would appear that intelligence develops overtime.

Cognitive Development

The focus on learner development usually emphasizes cognition, or "the inner processes and products of the mind that lead to 'knowing.' It includes all mental activity—attending, remembering, symbolizing, categorizing, planning, reasoning, problem solving, creating, and fantasizing" (Berk, 2003, p, 218). Cognition differs from intelligence in that cognition is a process that results in knowing, whereas intelligence is a person's capacity to learn. For this reason this chapter focuses on cognition because it is a process that is shared by all people, and Chapter 4 ("Individual Differences") focuses on intelligence because humans do vary in their capacity to learn.

All of the cognitive functions occur in the brain, an organ that has reached almost complete size and density by age four (Jensen, 1998). Although the brain may not grow substantially, it continues to change and develop. Through neuroscience research we now have a better idea of how the brain works and develops, and these insights have challenged old conceptions of cognitive development. It is clear that most brain growth occurs early in life (primarily before birth), but some growth in areas central to learning continues through at least the end of adolescence (Nelson, de Haan, & Thomas, 2006; Rueda, Fan, McCandliss, Halparin, Gruber, Lercari, et al., 2004). The development that occurs during the upper elementary years primarily involves *synaptogenesis* (brain wiring), *myelination* (making the brain work more efficiently), and *pruning* (sculpting away connections that are not used and refining those that are used). Researchers have noted that these processes "show dramatic, nonlinear changes from the preschool period through the end of adolescence" (Nelson, de Haan & Thomas, 2006, p. 29). Researchers have also found that the cortex (the outer layer that controls functions such as memory, planning, and reasoning) thickens during middle childhood and that rates of thickening appear to vary in relation to children's performance on tests of intelligence (Shaw, Greenstein, Lerch, Clasen, Lenroot, Gogtay, Evans, Rapoport, et al., 2006).

We will continue to refine our understanding of how the brain functions and grows as neuroscience expands and technologies become more sophisticated, but it is clear that although the brain may have reached its maximum size and density well before the upper elementary years, it continues to build connections throughout life. Children maintain and refine synaptic connections through stimulation, active engagement, and exploration (Willis, 2007). These connections are made in multiple ways: through children actively using their brains (e.g., dialogue and other forms of verbal expression, through grappling with mathematical challenges, through music, art, sports); by being supported and cared for; and through experiencing a healthy lifestyle (sufficient sleep and healthy diet) (Jensen, 1998; Nelson, de Haan, & Thomas, 2006).

Consistent with brain growth in the frontal lobe and cerebral cortex, upper elementary children are developing the cognitive functions that reside in that part of the brain. They are developing more advanced memory, reasoning, planning, and categorizing abilities. Without access to brain research, Piaget correctly designated this period as "concrete operational" (Piaget, 1952, 1969). At this point in development, children work effectively with concrete tasks that are based on experience or prior knowledge. They are good at finding patterns and determining connections and have learned or developed processes that help them categorize, plan, and remember. Their ability to do so is a blending of experience and physical changes in the brain (Wolfe & Brandt, 1998).

Upper elementary children exhibit superior ability over younger children in several cognitive processes. This does not imply that younger children are unable to do these tasks (as Piaget assumed) but that upper elementary students can do them fluidly. Classification is a prime example. Where young children can classify familiar objects or people, they struggle with those they are unfamiliar with and may not be able to create subcategories (Berk, 2003). For example, young children may know that there is a class of furniture and that furniture items they have experienced (e.g., beds, tables, chairs) fall into this class. They may not be able to place unfamiliar furniture in the class. Upper elementary children are more apt to be able to look at something unfamiliar and identify characteristics that make it "furniture" and place it in the class. They are also able to extend their classification ability to creating subclasses (i.e., placing a lounge chair, desk chair, and rocking chair into a subclass of chairs); they will be able to explain why they chose to include or not include stools in the category "chair."

Classification is enjoyable to many upper elementary students, as evidenced by their interest in building collections. It is at this point that many children spend hours sorting and classifying collections of stamps, sports cards, video games, rocks, shells, stickers, and other toys. Most children collect for the sheer enjoyment of building and organizing a collection, but for some their enjoyment of classification is enhanced by the prospect that their collection may be worth money. Many of us remember the Beanie Baby craze in the 1990s in which the small stuffed animals were purchased, sorted, classified, and treasured for their potential value as collectibles, and both children and adults continue to collect sports cards in the hope that they may possess tomorrow's Babe Ruth card.

This ability to classify further allows children to make predictions and generalizations in their problem solving. They understand and can find relationships between and among like and disparate things. By being able to categorize and find subcategories, they are able to determine hierarchical relationships. This also is evident in their ability to *serialize*, or place events or objects in descending or ascending order (Salkind, 2004). They can organize books alphabetically, arrange their stuffed animal collection by height, and determine their own categories to organize their video game collections.

Consider . . .

Helping students meet curriculum standards by providing instruction that builds on and stretches their cognitive development.

Curriculum standards guide most of what we teach, and the standards, by and large, are appropriate for children's developmental level. Given that you are held accountable to the standards, they are a given in terms of what you teach. How you teach them is up to you. Upper elementary children are concrete thinkers who like to categorize, find patterns, and think through problems logically, and they thrive on opportunities to hone these skills. Allow them to work with concrete objects (e.g., math manipulatives, plants, shells, seeds, etc.) or with familiar categories as a starting place, and give them tools such as graphic organizers and concept maps to extend their knowledge (see http://www.graphic.org/concept.html for ideas on creating concept maps). As social learners, this is best done in groups with you serving as a facilitator and model. In this way, the children discover their own patterns and systems to make sense of what they are learning.

Upper elementary children are becoming more logical in their thinking. This is evident in their understanding of conservation and ability to reverse operations. For example, where young children think a ball of clay is smaller if they flatten it, children in the concrete operational stage understand that the mass is the same but the shape changes. Where young children struggle to understand that subtraction is the reverse of addition, upper elementary children understand the relationship between addition and subtraction. Upper elementary children are also able to focus their attention more effectively than young children can, controlling distracting thoughts (Berk, 2003; McDevitt & Ormrod, 2004), and they use their ability to categorize to increase their ability to remember (Schneider & Pressley, 1989). Research indicates that there is a slump in creativity around fourth grade (Raina, 1997 in Runco, 2007) that may be explained by children's more concrete thinking as well as their better fine and gross motor control.

Although upper elementary children are capable of more logical thinking than younger children are, they also lose some of their confidence, or conceit, in their ability. As Scales, Sesma, and Bolstrom (2004) wrote, "Young children tend to begin formal schooling (i.e., kindergarten and Grade 1) with positive, even lofty beliefs, attitudes and perceptions regarding their involvement and performance in various school and academic competencies" (p. 164). But their perception of competence declines as they become more adept at comparisons with peers and as they incorporate feedback from adults into their assessment of their academic ability and into their perceptions of the value of subjects such as reading and mathematics.

These cognitive developments are attributed to physical changes in the brain, to personal experimentation, and to experiences and opportunities. By focusing on how children process information, we can see that they develop these abilities through a series of personal experiments and by exposure to learning strategies (Siegler, 1996). We have all watched children move from despair over a daunting task (e.g., memorizing state capitals, learning a complicated piece of music, finding the main point in a reading selection) to personal satisfaction when they either figure out a system to help them remember or perform or adopt a system someone suggests to them. Their ability to find strategies to make sense of material or tasks that initially appear to be random is a hallmark of upper elementary student development.

Children may experience difficulty if they are asked to perform new cognitive tasks, because their brains may have pruned the synapses needed for the task (Berk, 2003). Researchers have also found that if people are not expected to perform cognitive tasks, such as memorizing information for its own sake (a task not required in all cultures), or if they find the tasks disconnected from their daily experience, they may not develop the necessary strategies (Rogoff & Chavajay, 1995; Rogoff, Mistry, Göncü, & Mosier, 1985). For example, although memorization was rewarded at my daughter's school, she saw no value in memorizing state capitals, presidents, names of architectural features of ancient Athens, and other facts. She was happy to talk about the importance of a state capital in state government or what various presidents did, but she saw no reason to recite the names of fifty of state capitals or forty-two presidents; needless to say, she did poorly on a few tests.

The cognitive psychologist Lev Vygotsky (1978; Pass, 2004) is well known for extending our understanding of learning to include social, cultural, and other environmental influences, but his other significant contribution has been the recognition that optimal learning occurs in what he called the *zone of proximal development* (ZPD). This is the potential ability range in which students, with guidance or facilitation from a more knowledgeable person, can build on prior knowledge and experience to extend and expand their knowledge or skills. Within the ZPD adults challenge children without overwhelming them; they pose questions that are slightly beyond students' comfort zone or assign work that children have yet to experience. Some children seek the upper limits of their ZPD on their own, whereas others timidly enter into new areas. It is a teacher's challenge to keep upper elementary students within their ZPD so that they can use their developing cognitive skills to advance to more challenging levels.

Language Development

> *I want to be a third-, fourth-, or fifth-grade teacher because students and teachers can truly form an intellectual relationship. In early childhood classrooms teachers engage and facilitate students, but generally students don't challenge his or her thinking. In upper elementary classrooms, there is enough maturity from students to hold a meaningful conversation that includes such insightful questions.*
>
> —Preservice teacher

One reason why many adults like to interact with upper elementary children is that it is much easier to talk to them than it is to younger children. Our capacity to generate and understand language develops rapidly, and by the time children are in upper elementary grades, they are usually quite proficient communicators, especially verbally. Between the age of 6 and 11, most children's vocabulary increases from 10,000 words to 40,000 words (Berk, 2003). By the time they are 11 years old, most children have mastered pronunciation of commonly used words. They apply and appreciate multiple meanings of words and misleading expressions that become a large part of their humor (e.g., What do you call a setter who can't point? Disa-pointing; What animals eat with their tails? All animals eat with their tails—they can't take them off). Conversations with upper elementary students involve expression and discussion of more complex ideas and, when focused primarily on concrete topics, can be sustained. Finally, they can consider a listener's knowledge and perspective when speaking (McDevitt & Ormrod, 2002).

The ability to communicate is both a product of the developmental process and a contributor to it. Most upper elementary children are fairly sophisticated users of at least one language, and many have had the opportunity to learn multiple languages. Children who learn multiple languages when their brains are still receptive to understanding and forming unfamiliar sounds and tones are more apt to speak the languages accent-free (Nelson, de Haan, & Thomas, 2006).

As language use becomes more sophisticated, children's use and appreciation of humor develops as well. Riddles, wordplay, and formulaic jokes (e.g., knock-knock jokes) are popular among upper elementary children. No longer content to laugh uproariously over clandestine opportunities to say "bad words" out loud or to create jokes with no punch lines (or so they seem to adults), upper elementary students use their more highly developed understanding of semantics, especially in relation to words with multiple meanings, and syntax to entertain themselves, friends, and adults (McDevitt & Ormrod, 2002).

Humor, like play, serves multiple functions as children develop. It provides a safe place to experiment with developing skills and with new ideas, words, and syntactic structures. For example, when asked for favorite jokes, several fourth and fifth graders at one California elementary school said, "The telephone greens; I pink it up, and I say 'yellow.'" Additionally, humor allows children a vehicle to turn the tables on adults by using the question/answer format so ubiquitous in school. By riddling, the child asks the question and the adult has the uncomfortable experience of being unable to answer it (Bariaud, 1988). Knock-knock jokes, popular for generations, are still favorites among upper elementary students. A favorite among upper elementary children is

Knock knock.
Who's there?
Banana
Banana who?
Knock knock.
Who's there?
Banana
Banana who?
Knock knock.
Who's there?
Orange
Orange who?
Orange you glad I didn't say banana?

Humor also serves as a safety valve; as children's lives become more complex and school becomes more demanding, humor and wordplay allow them to make fun of challenging and stressful situations (McGhee, 1988).

DEVELOPMENT AS INDIVIDUALS AND MEMBERS OF SOCIETY

They love to help. At school, they like to help clean the room and run errands. They are starting to know about the world through movies and sports teams. They are starting to make friends on their own, not only the ones their parents pick. They will be friends one day and not the next.

They are very concerned about fairness. They expect it and can even accept consequences if they think it's fair. They are attracted to their teacher; they still need nurturing.

—Fifth-grade teacher

I would want to teach fifth grade because the students are capable of doing work and activities on their own more than, say, a first grader. Students have personalities by this point, and I believe it is easier to connect with them.

—Preservice teacher

The fifth-grade teacher captures many of the key aspects of upper elementary students' social and moral development. They like to be helpful and needed; their world is expanding, and they expect and are given more independence; friends are very important, but they also seek adult attention and affirmation; they understand and accept rules if they think they are fair. In addition, they retain much of the confidence in their abilities they had when they began school but are more aware of their limitations as they compare themselves to others and to adult expectations.

Motivation becomes more of an issue for upper elementary children. Where young children are motivated to learn by the sheer joy of learning, upper elementary children, especially those who tend to struggle with reading or mathematics, are becoming more motivated by extrinsic rewards or punishments (i.e., grades, rewards, sanctions) or in relation to personal passions in certain areas (e.g., horses, sports, computers). Those who retain their belief in their academic competency and in their personal efficacy are likely to remain successful students (Scales, Sesma, & Bolstrom, 2004). For many reasons this is a complex time in which children develop a sense of self as individuals while determining how to fit into an increasingly broader social world. In addition, those who believe they can be instrumental in their learning are more likely to be successful and involved than those students who believe their intelligence is static and that they cannot affect the pace of their own learning (Dweck, 2007).

Development of Sense of Self

In terms of developing self-identity, upper elementary children begin to see themselves as having both strengths and weaknesses (Harter, 1998). Children this age can list many things in which they perceive themselves to be strong or weak, whether in the domain of academics, athletics, or interpersonal relations. For example, 123 children at one California elementary school wrote about why they are special. Among these children, sixty-three mentioned academics (e.g., being smart, working hard, loving math), twenty-seven mentioned athletics (most mentioned soccer), and eighty-six mentioned interpersonal relations (e.g., relations with family, friends, and teachers; being nice, helpful, and responsible). Given the focus of the question, they did not mention weaknesses. Although many mentioned that they are smart or good athletes, more often they highlighted subjects or sports at which they excel. For example, many of these students, most of whom are second language learners, mentioned that they are good at math; fewer commented on being good readers. They are able to fine-tune their self-assessment, basing it more on comparisons to others than they did when they were younger (McDevitt & Ormrod, 2004).

The tendency to refine their sense of self based on comparisons and feedback from a wider circle of peers and adults is consistent with Erik Erikson's characterization of this stage of development as a tension of industry versus inferiority (Salkind, 2004, p. 143). The upper elementary years provide opportunities for children to refine and develop skills and knowledge (what Erikson calls *industry*), and if they fail to do so, they feel inferior, especially when they see their peers mastering the skills and knowledge they are lacking. In this stage children learn to juggle demands not only from school but also from home, friends, and extracurricular activities. If they are able to meet these multiple demands successfully, they feel good about themselves; if they struggle to find a successful balance, they may develop a sense of inferiority that is difficult to turn around.

Most upper elementary children enjoy assuming more responsibilities for themselves and others. Maccoby (1984) described the process of taking more personal responsibility as one of moving from being *other-regulated* by more mature others (a characteristic of young children) to *coregulating*, or taking on more responsibility for themselves (in Scales, Sesma, & Bolstrom, 2004, p. 47). This process of taking more responsibility occurs both in the classroom and at home. By fourth grade many teachers expect students to take responsibility for their homework and for completing class assignments properly and on time. As a fourth-grade teacher said:

> They take responsibility for their own learning. Teachers need to help nurture that and push them to take responsibility. They are expected to have time management. They can't blame mom and dad. If they don't understand, they know they are responsible to raise their hands and ask. I teach them to keep a planner, how to ask questions, how to find what they need.

Parents also increase expectations for children's responsibilities at home. Although there are marked differences across social classes in how upper elementary students spend time outside of school (Lareau, 2003), most parents expect upper elementary students to take on additional chores, complete homework on time without as much supervision as in earlier grades, help with younger siblings, care for pets, and keep track of extracurricular activities. Additionally, upper elementary children are typically allowed to venture farther from home than when they were younger because parents expect them to make good decisions outside of the home.

Consider . . .

Displaying a Student of the Week board.

Many early childhood teachers maintain Student of the Week displays and encourage the student to bring in pictures and important items from home. Upper elementary students also enjoy sharing what makes them special and enjoy the public recognition of who they are and who and what is important in their lives.

Autonomy and Relatedness

What makes me special is I am myself and I am not someone else. Another thing that I am special is that I try my best to do good at school. I am special because I am not trying to act like another person because that is what I don't want to do. I am also smart.

—Fifth-grade boy

The greater expectation for responsibility relates to growing autonomy and independence. Where Erikson focused on the tension between industry and inferiority, another tension exists between *autonomy* (being one's own self) and *relatedness* (being part of a larger whole). Upper elementary children's sense of competence reflects their ability to successfully juggle the competing desires for autonomy and relatedness (Bryant, 1994; Connell, 1990). The fifth grader's statement about being himself and not anyone else illustrates the importance of autonomy in his mind. Many of his classmates placed more emphasis on their ability to fit in with others. Although this tension does not begin in the upper elementary years, it is heightened by expectations on the part of children and adults to take on more responsibilities, experience more independence, and interact in a wider world.

As children are increasingly involved in activities outside the home, as they choose their friends rather than relying on parents to do so, and as they are expected to complete school work and chores without close supervision, they become more autonomous and competent. Most children welcome this autonomy, but not if it is at the expense of valued relationships with significant adults. Although students move toward peers as confidants and helpers, they still seek affirmation and relationships with family members, teachers, and other significant adults (Borland, Laybourn, Hill, Brown, 1998). As Scales, Sesma, and Bolstrom (2004) suggested, "In middle childhood, even though the child's striving for autonomy increases as an expected dimension of development, perhaps the healthiest 'tilt' is toward more emphasis on the child's experience of greater relatedness" (p. 46).

Relations with adults are very important, but those with other children are becoming increasingly important. Judith Harris, a developmental psychologist, challenged conventional thinking by asserting that peers are more important than parents or other adults in shaping children's futures (1995; 2006). School for most children is both a place to learn and a place to make and see friends. As a fifth-grade boy wrote:

> What makes me special is that I am smart. I am special because I am a good friend, I am very helpful, I am a nice person, I am considerate of others, and I am thoughtful.
>
> Another thing that makes me special is I am funny. I have a lot of friends to play with and they play with me too. Sometimes I make up games and let others play or someone else makes up a game and lets me play. I also like to share my nachos with others and sometimes they let me have some of theirs.

Doing What Is Right

What motivates upper elementary students to get along in their social world? Most of them have learned the cultural rules related to what is considered good and bad, right and wrong, and they try to do what is right either because they want the approval of others, especially adults, or because they fear the consequences of doing something wrong or bad (Power, Higgens, & Kohlberg, 1989). According to Kohlberg, upper elementary children are entering the level of *conventional morality*. This level is characterized by moral decisions shaped by what children consider acceptable or pleasing to others, especially important adults and popular peers. They are eager to please and to be accepted as good people. This level of moral development is also characterized by adherence to rules. Because they are still relatively powerless in relation to adults, they generally follow rules established by adults, but they are also capable of establishing and maintaining rules among themselves that are reasonably fair and consistent. Upper elementary children are often hyperaware of rules and are quick to point out when parents and teachers fail to follow them.

For example, children this age will quickly react when parents say "bad" words or violate minor traffic rules and when teachers are not following class rules or treat students unfairly.

> *I am special because I help people like my homeroom teacher. I do nice things for people without being asked. These are the reasons that I am special.*
>
> —Fifth-grade girl

In addition to wanting to do what is right and fair, children this age have a compelling concern to help those in need; they believe that caring for others is a moral imperative (Gilligan, 1982; Noddings, 1992). This is not to say that children this age cannot be cruel and uncaring, because they certainly can, but when they are, they typically understand that what they are doing is wrong and hurtful.

Consider . . .

Providing multiple opportunities for students to assume responsibility and help other children.

You can build on upper elementary children's growing sense of responsibility and their desire to help others by creating democratic classroom communities. Regular class meetings in which students set and adjust classroom rules and expectations give them ownership of the workings of the classroom and help them understand personal and group responsibilities. Guidance counselors are trained in these models and are a good resource for getting the step-by-step procedures for how to set up and maintain these meetings (also see Tollefson & Osborn, 2008).

Within the democratic classroom, you can establish a rotating set of roles (e.g., lunch counter, board wiper, material go-fer, line leader, animal feeder, etc.) that allow students to develop a sense of belonging by contributing to their classroom. They can extend their sense of community outside their classroom by adopting a primary classroom where they may read or tutor younger children or by taking responsibility for keeping one part of the school grounds clean and beautiful. In addition, they can examine and devise solutions for school-wide issues (e.g., recycling practices throughout the school, setting up and maintaining a garden). These are great opportunities for real world application of standards as well and for including all students in something meaningful.

Physical Development

While all of the changes mentioned earlier are happening within upper elementary children, their bodies are also changing. As described in relation to development as learners, changes occur in the brain that relate to their developing cognitive abilities. At the same time, children's bodies grow slowly and steadily. A defining characteristic of upper elementary students is their improved coordination and gross motor development. Where younger children enjoy running, skipping, jumping, and swinging for the sheer sake of it, upper elementary students channel their physical efforts into more organized activities. Children this age are often involved in organized sports, dance, and gymnastics; their spontaneous play on the playground is often subject to rules, often of their own device (Finnan, 1982; Smith, 1997). The organized activities require well-developed muscles and strong skeletal structures, as well as an ability to concentrate, follow a series of instructions, and work well with others.

In addition, their developing fine motor skills are evident in handwriting that is characterized by smaller, smoother letters; by drawings with more detail and accuracy; and by interest in handcrafts such as sewing and model building (McDevitt & Ormrod, 2004). Although the value of such activities is contested, many students this age hone their fine motor skills using video games and other electronic toys. Changes in upper elementary students' artwork reflect not only their improved fine motor skills but also their cognitive development. Art at this stage is detailed and realistic. Even drawings of fantasy creatures or characters are drawn with precision and accuracy; the abstraction characteristic of younger children and possible in later artistic endeavors is unusual among upper elementary students.

"Am I pretty?" "Why do I have to be so short when all the girls are getting taller?" "My teeth are a mess!" "I'm so fat!"

Upper elementary children definitely are becoming more aware of their bodies and comparing them to their peers and to celebrities they see in the media. We have been aware of this issue for girls for some time, but research indicates increased body awareness issues of preadolescent boys as well (Phares, Steinberg. & Thompson, 2004). At this stage children may become conscious of weight. Whereas obesity is a serious problem for many students in these grades, other students begin potentially destructive diets to remain or become thin. Messages about body types, weight, and physical appearance are definitely sent out constantly by the media, but they are also a part of the conversation at home and at school. Upper elementary children are susceptible to teasing from adults and peers, which is associated with low self-esteem and body image dissatisfaction (Phares, Steinberg, & Thompson). Children, especially girls, also mimic the "fat talk" (e.g., "I'm so fat." "Do these jeans make me look fat?") they hear at home and between adults at school (Lamb & Brown, 2006).

The onset of puberty becomes a factor in these grades, especially by the end of fourth grade and during fifth and sixth grades. Early signs of puberty begin as early as eight years old for girls and nine years old for boys (McDevitt & Ormrod, 2004). As children near or reach puberty, self-image and social interaction patterns change. Sigmund Freud referred to this stage of development as a *latency stage,* in which children build a reserve of psychic energy for the coming *genital stage* (adolescence) (Salkind, 2004, p. 131). Gender identity is definitely important at this time. During third grade and most of fourth grade, most children prefer to play with others of the same sex. This is what many would refer to as the *cooties stage*. Girls and boys claim to "hate" the opposite sex, but they become more aware of each other as they move through these grades. The following episode described by a teacher is not atypical:

> Variation among fifth graders is really great. Last year a girl came into fifth grade midyear. She looked like she should be in seventh grade, and she knew it. One day I was in the gym and a group of fourth-grade boys were talking. The girl walked by them slowly. All of the boys stopped talking and watched her until she was out of the gym. They resumed their conversation as if nothing happened. They probably didn't even know what had happened. This would not have happened in third grade.

REFINING THE BROAD STROKES OF GENERALIZATIONS

The next chapters address many of the "yes, buts" that may have entered your mind as you read these generalizations. Anyone who has spent time with children knows that they are not walking off a developmental assembly line. The next chapters explore how and why students in this grade span differ. Where this chapter explores broad areas in which students develop, those that follow examine how, either because of group affiliation or individual characteristics, these generalizations cannot serve as more than a broad framework to guide our understanding of students and their lives inside and outside of school.

Our understanding of the general developmental characteristics of upper elementary children shapes our expectations of them as learners, individuals within social contexts, and physically developing people. This developmental process is heavily influenced by the environments in which children live and go to school (i.e., their homes, schools, and neighborhoods, along with out-of-school activities). These environments influence all aspects of their development because development is more than a biological process. Because school, home, and community contexts vary greatly, children's development varies as well. We hope that all children grow up in environments that support basic needs for accomplishment, belonging, and engagement, but we know that some children do not. For example, when upper elementary children are in environments that foster a sense of accomplishment, they use their more advanced conceptual abilities, prior knowledge, and desire for increased responsibilities to seek more challenging accomplishments. At the same time, their tendency toward self-criticism and comparison to others helps them recognize the difference between real and contrived celebration of accomplishment.

Upper elementary children are also at a critical point in their development to benefit from environments that encourage them to develop a sense of belonging and to understand that their contributions to the group, family, or community are valued. As children juggle conflicting desires for autonomy and relatedness, supportive environments help them learn to interact with diverse people and to develop both a sense of self and a realization of the rewards and responsibilities of being a member of a group.

Finally, healthy development as learners, as individuals within a group, and as physically changing young people occurs through active engagement in supportive environments. Upper elementary children learn best by doing, by making connections, and through talking through their thinking and ideas. Through multiple opportunities for social engagement, upper elementary children develop a healthy sense of self and social skills and proclivities to interact productively with others. Similarly, upper elementary children benefit from multiple opportunities in and out of school for active physical engagement, whether developing gross motor skills through sports, dance, and theater or fine motor skills through art, crafts, and hobbies.

Consider the following questions as you think more deeply and critically about upper elementary children's general developmental trends.

- How can you use your knowledge of general developmental trends to positively influence your interactions with upper elementary children?
- What dangers do you see in relying too heavily on these generalizations?
- How can you counteract or build on environmental influences both inside and out of school that affect general developmental trends?

Most elementary schools serve young children as well as upper elementary children; how can your knowledge of general developmental trends serve to ensure that all children's development is appropriately supported?

3

Children as Members of Groups

I am a boy, because God made me one. I am Dominican because my parents were born in Dominican Republic. I am Dominican American because I was born here. I am Latino because that's what they call people here who speak Spanish. And I am White because my skin is light.

—Fourth-grade boy (in Cooper et al., 2005, p. 1)

Most upper elementary children think of themselves primarily as children who have special characteristics, but as the boy's quote indicates, they are also aware of the multiple groups (e.g., racial and/or ethnic, socioeconomic, primary language, gender, and exceptionality) that shape their sense of self and influence their experience as learners. Group affiliation would merely be one of the accepted aspects of living in a diverse society if it did not have such a profound effect on academic achievement. Student achievement data show consistent patterns. Economically disadvantaged students perform less well than economically privileged students; White and Asian American students perform better than African American, Hispanic, and American Indian students; native English speakers perform better than English-language learners; students with disabilities perform less well than students without disabilities (McCall, Hauser, Cronin, Kingsbury, & Houser, 2006; National

Center for Educational Statistics, 2006; Noguera & Wing, 2006; Rothstein, 2004; Williams, 2003).

Identifying an achievement gap between groups of children is one thing; knowing what to do about these differences and how to address their root causes is another. Group affiliations and the differences associated with them are very complex and sensitive; they are deeply rooted in our society, reflect persistent discriminatory attitudes and practices (e.g., residential segregation, unequal access to resources), and resist easy solutions (Education Trust, 2006; García Coll & Szalacha, 2004; Noguera & Wing, 2006).

The preceding chapter describes what our society considers "normal" development for upper elementary children. Given that not all children are the same, we assume that abilities fall along a normal learning curve, with most children grouping around the middle (i.e., normal). The achievement gap essentially reflects a lopsided curve, with certain children disproportionately falling below the norm (i.e., children of color, English-language learners, rural and urban children, children living in poverty, and the disabled) whereas others (i.e., White, Asian American, suburban, and middle-to upper-class children) disproportionately falling above the norm (McCall, et al., 2006; Williams, 2003). Efforts to attribute these differences to genetics have been overwhelmingly discredited (Dickens & Flynn, 2001; Fryer & Levitt, 2006; Murdoch, 2007), which leads us to explore the more complex issues of social, cultural, historical, political, and economic causes. We recognize that individual differences are inevitable, but ethnic/racial, socioeconomic, language, gender, and disability differences are not.

This chapter focuses on the thorny issues of the effect of group affiliation on learning, social interaction, and physical development. It begins with an examination of the origins of group difference and then explores how race and ethnicity, socioeconomic status, language, gender, and exceptionality influence students as learners and as social actors. All children have an identity that includes racial/ethnic origins, social class, gender, language, and ableness. For many children the combination of these traits stacks the deck against them (e.g., low-income, African American boys), but many children beat the odds and succeed in school. The chapter ends with a discussion of these resilient children.

SITUATING GROUP DIFFERENCES: BIOLOGICAL, CULTURAL, AND SOCIETAL INFLUENCES

Biological Influences

Some of the differences between groups have biological roots. For example, gender differences begin with the biological difference between males and females. Hormonal, skeletal, and muscular differences account for obvious gender differences. Recent brain research identifies significant differences in how male and female brains process information and send messages to the rest of the body (Gurian, Henley, & Trueman, 2001; James, 2007; Jensen, 1998). However, many of the differences between males and females are socially determined as well. For example, does society expect different performance and behavior of boys than of girls? Why do girls and boys tend to gravitate to some subjects and not others? Do we always apply rules equally to boys and girls?

Children with disabilities may differ from others for biological and neurological reasons, but here too there are complex social influences that shape their academic and social experience (Artiles, Klingner, & Tate, 2006; McDermott, Goldman, & Varenne, 2006; Reid & Knight, 2006). Differences in expectations for the disabled are again socially shaped. To what extent do people's disabilities influence our expectations for them? Why are so many people labeled as disabled viewed as deficient? Too often behavior resulting from cultural, linguistic, or social differences is assumed a disability, resulting in disproportionate numbers of minorities, especially minority boys, being diagnosed with disabilities (Artiles, Klingner, & Tate; Lorsen & Orfield, 2002; McDermott, Goldman, & Varenne, 2006; Reid & Knight, 2006; Spear-Swerling & Sternberg, 1996).

Cultural Influences

We recognize racial and some ethnic differences by physical attributes (i.e., skin color, hair color and texture, eye shape, facial bone structure), but these differences are genetically miniscule (Olson, 2002); there are no biological differences between people of different socioeconomic groups or between those who come to school speaking a language other than English. So what sets these groups apart from each other? Cultural differences account for much of the difference. From the day children are born, they are socialized by the cultural knowledge of those around them. For many children this knowledge differs from that expected in schools and other public institutions. Behaviors and expectations that are valued in their homes and communities may not be valued or tolerated in school.

These cultural differences can lead to misunderstandings and miscommunication. No matter what racial or ethnic group or gender we identify with, what income level we enjoy, or what language we speak, our identity and interactions are shaped largely by culture. Culture is not something that other people have; culture shapes everyone's perceptions, values, and attitudes. Culture is something that surrounds us; it gives meaning to our world and is constantly being changed and adapted as we interact with others and reflect on life (Finnan & Swanson, 2000). Culture is so ever-present in our lives that we do not realize its influence. Clyde Kluckhohn (1949), an early American anthropologist said of culture that it is like fish and water: Fish will be the last creatures to discover water because it is always there. Culture is the same; it surrounds us, invisibly sustaining and supporting our lives.

Given that culture shapes our beliefs, values, assumptions, and the actions we take, we rarely take time to think about all the aspects of our lives that are shaped by our culture. We usually do not think about culture until someone does or says something that we do not understand. Initially we are puzzled by their behavior or attitude. Upon reflection we may realize that their different cultural perspective led to the misunderstanding. However, we rarely go the next step to ponder that it was *our* cultural perspective that contributed to the problem; we rarely consider that we too are culture bearers and that our worlds are shaped by the values, beliefs, and assumptions that are learned and are not innate (Schram, 1994).

Social, Historical, and Economic Influences

In addition to bringing cultural differences to school, many groups have long histories of inequitable treatment and continue to experience discrimination and segregation in their daily lives. Children not only come to school viewing the world through different cultural lenses but also experience the world outside of school within a social structure that provides very different opportunities and resources. Today overt, intentional discriminatory practices are unacceptable, but nonetheless, practices that favor or welcome some groups over others persist (García Coll & Szalacha, 2004; Frankenberg, Lee, & Orfield, 2003). As society becomes increasingly diverse (Civil Rights Project, 2002), and because a disproportionate percentage of children live in poverty—children comprise 25 percent of the United States population but nearly 40 percent of its poor(Boocock & Scott, 2005)—social issues will not disappear.

Institutions like schools promote "mainstream" beliefs and values, those beliefs and values that perpetuate society as we know it and prepare people to assume roles in society and the workplace that are much like those held by their parents (Bowles & Gintis, 1976; Carnoy & Levin, 1985). Although we, as a society, value and promote ideals of equal opportunity for all, and we publicly celebrate diversity, most people of color, poor people, recent immigrants, and disabled people are marginalized through intentional and unintentional racism and segregation. For most racially, ethnically, or socioeconomically different upper elementary children, school is the first institution where they encounter "exclusion, devaluation, invisibility, discrimination, and racism" (García Coll & Szalacha, 2004, p. 82). How these children respond to school as an institution and to schooling as a process varies greatly, depending on the child and his family (Borman & Overman, 2004; Lewis, 2004–2005); on the school (Finnan & Swanson, 2000; Lee & Williams, 2006); and on the community (Noguera & Wing, 2006). Later I explore the influence of being a group member on upper elementary children's identity development. I conclude by addressing the interconnection between each of these group identities.

ETHNIC AND RACIAL GROUP AFFILIATION

I visited a school in an old New England mill town to observe classes and interview teachers. The school, in one of the poorest parts of the town, is a looming brick structure built in 1918. It has no playground and few resources we associate with good learning environments. The affective environment is worlds apart from the physical; it is warm, inviting, and nurturing. Each day begins with all students, often accompanied by their parents, meeting in the gym for "morning meeting." Students line up by class, and announcements are made by the principal and students. Often everyone joins together to sing or recite in unison. Morning meeting takes only a few minutes, but it illustrates the sense of community in an otherwise highly diverse school. People described the school population as a "mini-United Nations." Many of the students are first- or second-generation immigrants from countries in Asia and Africa, as well as from Albania, Jamaica, Mexico, and Puerto Rico. Statistics (30 percent White, 12 percent African American, 42 percent Hispanic, and 15 percent Asian or Pacific Islander) mask the diversity within these racial and ethnic categories. Some 29 percent are Limited English proficient, and 91.5 percent qualify for free or reduced-price lunch. About 24 percent receive special education services.

Increasingly the population of school-aged children in the United States resembles the school described earlier. The shift from a majority White population has been steady, and projections hold that non-Hispanic whites will relinquish majority status by 2050. The fastest growing segments of the population are Hispanic and Asian (Civil Rights Project, 2002). Since racial and ethnic designations have almost no biological basis (Olson, 2002), why do we base so many assumptions about people on skin color, hair texture and color, eye shape, and other physical indicators of race and ethnicity? Primarily because differences in physical characteristics frequently, but often erroneously, serve as proxies for cultural and social differences.

Whether attending schools that resemble the United Nations or schools with little racial or ethnic diversity—referred to as *apartheid schools* by the Civil Rights Project (Frankenberg, Lee, & Orfield, 2003)—we must realize that children bring to school cultural beliefs, values, and assumptions shaped by their racial or ethnic group affiliation, and they expect these beliefs, values, and assumptions to be shared at school. For most White children, this expectation is realized. For many racial and ethnic minority children, mismatches occur between their cultures and the culture that pervades schools (Cooper et al., 2005; Finnan & Swanson, 2000; Ladson-Billings, 1994; Lewis, 2003; Ogbu, 1991). Table 3.1 offers a few examples of areas in which cultural miscues can occur in the classroom. As it illustrates, miscommunications are often in the small, taken-for-granted aspects of human interaction. Once recognized it is easy for teachers to accommodate these differences. This mismatch exists for the 20 percent of students who are first- or second-generation immigrants (Portes & Rumbaut, 2001) as well as for children of minority groups with a long history of discrimination (Ogbu, 1991).

Table 3.1 Common Areas of Cultural Miscommunication

Action	*Teacher expectation*	*Student behavior*
Rewards	Each student will take one reward (e.g., candy) for himself and enjoy it in class.	Students from cultures that stress the collective over the individual (e.g., many Hispanic, African Americans, Asian, and American Indians) will take enough candy to give one to their siblings; they may wait to eat their candy until they get home.
Silence	Students will answer questions and engage in class discussions. Silence is an indicator of not knowing, not paying attention, shyness, or not caring.	Silence is valued in other cultures as a sign of respect for others (e.g., Brazilians, Peruvians, Apaches, many Asian cultures) or as a way of achieving privacy (e.g., Arabs).
Interaction with adults	Students will ask questions and express ideas and opinions that differ from those of the teacher.	Children (e.g., Mexican Americans and many Asians; some African Americans, especially in the Southeast) have been taught not to initiate discussions with adults, and some children have learned that speaking directly to adults is rude and even rebellious.
Making eye contact	Students are engaged and listening intently.	Looking an adult in the eye is disrespectful; children are taught to look down when adults talk to them (frequently seen among African American, Puerto Rican, Mexican, American Indian, and Asian cultures).
Questioning	Students have experience with a common questioning format (teacher initiates, one student responds, teacher evaluates) and expect to be asked questions calling for factual responses.	In some cultures parents do not use questioning in this way (e.g., some Mexican, American Indian, Hawaiian, African American homes). Some children, especially African American children, have more experience with more metaphorical questions (e.g., "What is that like?" rather than "What color is that?"

SOURCE: Delgado-Gaitan, 1994; Heath, 1983; Ladson-Billings, 1994; McDevitt & Ormrod, 2004.

Race and Ethnicity: Relation to Achievement

The existence of racial and ethnic group differences in achievement has received considerable attention. With mandatory state testing beginning in third grade and national testing in fourth grade through the National Assessment of Educational Progress (NAEP), information on achievement gaps between racial and ethnic groups is obvious to upper elementary school teachers. Both state and national data point to persistent gaps between racial/ethnic groups, as indicated in Figure 3.1. These data illustrate a 20 to 30 percent gap between White and Asian/Pacific Island students on one side of the achievement continuum and African American, Hispanic, and American Indian students on the other (National Center for Education Statistics, 2006). The achievement gap extends to overrepresentation of racial and ethnic minorities in grade retention and special education identification. African American and Hispanic children, especially males, are much more likely to repeat grades (Center for Mental Health in Schools at UCLA, 2006; Thompson & Cunningham, 2000), and African American and American Indian children are placed in special education at much higher rates than other children are (Artiles, Klingner, & Tate, 2006).

Figure 3.1 Achievement Differences Between Racial/Ethnic Groups

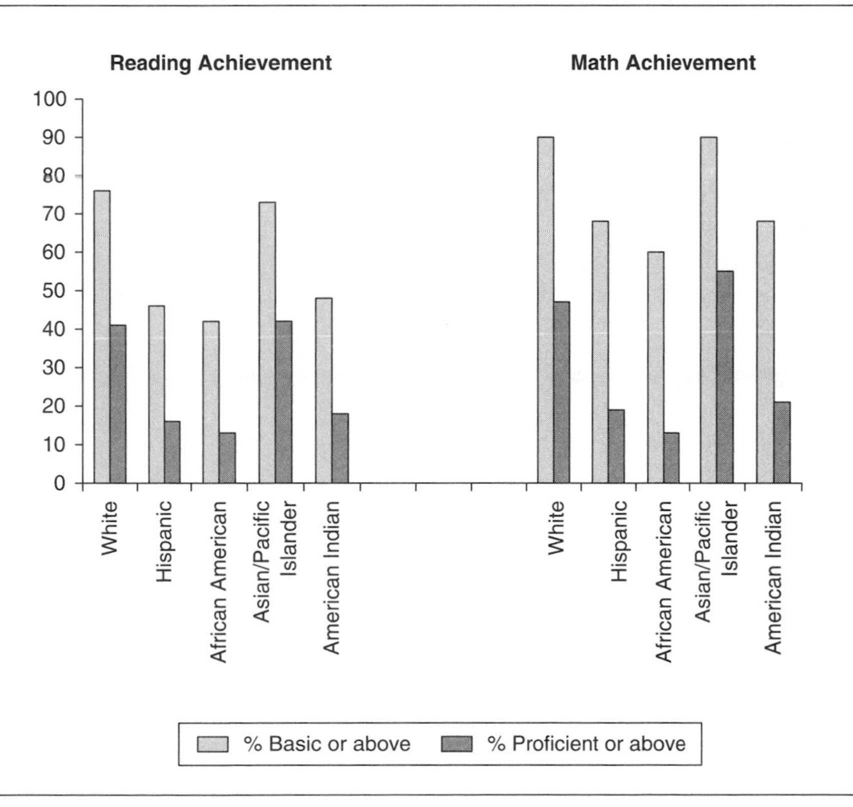

SOURCE: National Center for Educational Statistics data.

NOTE: Fourth-Grade National Assessment of Educational Progress (NAEP) Scores 2005

Given that a disproportionate percentage of underachieving children are classified as both racial/ethnic minorities and low income, explanations for this gap are complicated and multifaceted. One disturbing finding is that when socioeconomic status is held constant (i.e., low-income African American children's scores are compared to low-income White or Asian American children's scores), African American students of all income levels still perform less well than White and Asian American students (McCall et al., 2006; Williams, 1993). Because these differences are not evident in intelligence tests given before third grade, we need to consider other explanations, such as school factors, lifestyle choices within the racial or ethnic group (Ferguson, 2002), societal expectations and structures that exclude and limit certain groups (García Coll & Szalacha, 2004; Williams, 2003), or the fact that African American families may have recently joined the middle class.

Consider . . .

Becoming a cultural "boundary crosser" to help your students be cultural "boundary crossers."

Children from racial and ethnic groups that are different than the mainstream will always straddle the boundary between cultures. They will have one foot in their racial or ethnic community and the other in schools and jobs that reflect mainstream values and beliefs. We can help them be "boundary crossers" by modeling boundary crossing ourselves. Start with an exploration of your own culture and how it shapes your beliefs, values, and actions. For example, what do you think is worth learning, and how do you think people should interact with each other? Consider where you acquired these beliefs and values (e.g., home, church, school, friends, etc.) and compare them to those that underlie actions in your school (e.g., to what extent do you feel comfortable with the school's expectations about what and how children learn, about how adults interact with each other and with children, about the value of the resources in the community?). Take the time to talk with your students and their family members. Ask questions and seek to understand your commonalities and differences. Open communication and interest in their cultures demonstrates to them that you strive to understand and value their culture. To say, "I don't see color" or "to me all children are just children" assumes that the children share your cultural values and are growing up in homes similar to yours. Where their beliefs, values, and actions differ from those of the school, you need to help them understand that an important part of your job is to help students become "boundary crossers," people who are comfortable in their home culture and that of school and work.

Race and Ethnicity: Relation to Social Development

I am special because I have Mexican and El Salvador blood.

—Fourth-grade boy

The Latino kids have it the best; they have a large extended family. They are emotionally taken care of. This is also true for the Southeast Asian kids. They are all cared for by their community. The Anglo kids are the ones that have trouble. Many of them are latchkey. They see drug use. The families want to be involved, but the school needs to figure out the avenues. We don't have soccer moms here at our school. Middle-class families have a different rich experience. They travel, model academics and language. There are separate issues at home.

—Fourth-grade teacher

Upper elementary students have to consciously examine their beliefs and values when they interact in a diverse classroom environment. Even though most adults are able to think abstractly about concepts like culture, adults still struggle to avoid stereotypical and prejudicial thinking. This is even more difficult for most upper elementary students who are more concrete thinkers and tend toward seeing things in black/white, yes/no terms. When they encounter different values, beliefs, and actions, they struggle to see these differences as anything but weird or wrong.

In addition, students who are different may draw the conclusion that they are strange, less intelligent, or less capable than classmates who share their teachers' cultural understandings. Although upper elementary students' ability and interest in categorization contributes to their academic learning and helps them define who they are in relation to others, it can also result in categorizing people who do not share similar characteristics as "other" or categorizing themselves as the "other" who is less capable. Lisa Delpit (2006) illustrated this point in the following exchange with an African American child:

> I was once working with a young girl who had failed to learn multiplication. When I announced my intention to work with her on the topic, she looked at me and said, "Ms. Lisa, why are you doing this? Black people don't multiply; they just add and subtract. White people multiply." Were it not for the poignancy of her statement, it would be funny. Here is a child who set severe limits on her potential based on a misguided notion of the limits of African Americans, a notion no doubt appropriated from general American culture. (p. 224)

Lewis (2003) overheard an even more troubling statement by a African American fourth-grade boy who explained that he had to go to prison before he could go to college because "All black men go to prison" (p. 54).

She also warned that the silence of other ethnic minority students (especially Hispanic and Asian girls) can potentially be as damaging as the overt misbehavior of other students.

As described earlier, by the upper elementary grades, children are more apt to compare themselves to others and, in doing so, are more aware of both individual and group differences. They are concerned about fitting in and sometimes move away from classmates who are racially or ethnically different to form friendships with students more like themselves (Lareau, 2003). In most cases they do this not because they are prejudiced or they dislike people of other races or ethnic groups but because they just gravitate to comfortable interactions. During the upper elementary grades, students' awareness of their ethnic/racial identity grows, which also contributes to both gravitation toward peers of the same group and toward a realization that racism exists. For example, by the age of nine or ten, children cite racism as a possible explanation for negative interactions with both teachers and peers (García Coll & Szalacha, 2004). This realization is likely fed by the fact that upper elementary students are more likely to tease or reject racial and ethnic minority students (Borland et al., 1998), so although teachers may try to create respectful environments in their classrooms, social interactions outside of the class may be different.

These data highlight differences between large subgroups, but they also mask other differences. Within subgroups are major differences. Each of the major subgroups represents students from widely different backgrounds. For example, Hispanic (or Latino) includes students from the entire western hemisphere as well as Spain. Culturally, children who trace their lineage back to El Salvador, Chile, Honduras, Puerto Rico, Cuba, Mexico, or any number of countries vary greatly. Even within these countries, regional and ethnic differences exist. Couple that with the fact that some Hispanic students' ancestors were in the United States before the Mayflower sailed, whereas others have recently arrived. Similar distinctions can be made for any of the racial and ethnic subcategories used to identify the achievement gap.

These differences must be acknowledged when thinking about achievement differences and when interacting with children in the classroom and across the school. Teachers need to check assumptions at several levels. At one level we must realize that we are apt to see the world very differently than our students see it and that there is not a right or wrong way to view the world. At another level we cannot assume that all children of a certain racial or ethnic group share the same values, beliefs, assumptions, and actions. We have all been surprised when our stereotypes are shattered. For these obvious reasons, there is no easy fix to the achievement gap because not only is there no one solution for all students but there is no "African American student solution" or a "Hispanic student solution."

SOCIOECONOMIC GROUP AFFILIATION

There was one girl in my fifth-grade class who was always made fun of. She was a little overweight, considered to be in poverty, and a little slow. In my White, upper-middle class town, she did not fit in. At recess she was excluded. In class she was teased. At home she was ignored. I always tried to talk to her because I don't think she realized that people made fun of her as much as they did. She invited a bunch of people to her birthday party at the Super Sizzler, and I was the only one who showed up. So I sat at the table with her and her mom. I'll never forget the day she came to school after her aunt had a baby. She told me that she was allowed to name it, so she named it after me.

—Madison, preservice teacher

In third grade there was a Caucasian girl who came from a low socioeconomic family. Since I grew up in a middle-class neighborhood and went to school in that neighborhood, she stood out. It wasn't her low socioeconomic status that made her stand out but her fighting attitude. Her attitude only made her socioeconomic status more pronounced. She wanted to fight everyone, and no one wanted to fight her back, so no one would play with her. Therefore, she became more of an outcast to her peers. I felt this way about her also. I was afraid of her. The teachers would try to calm her and assign other children to work with her in groups, but no matter what, on the playground she would not cooperate and always walked away crying.

—Laura, preservice teacher

Madison and Laura describe situations in which low-income children struggle to be accepted by their more affluent peers. Why did these girls appear to be so different from their peers? Would their experience have been different if the schools had been more socioeconomically balanced? Children like the future teachers describe stand out in part because they come to school with different *cultural capital* (Bourdieu, 1986). In their homes and neighborhood, they learn values and skills and acquire knowledge that differs from that acquired in the middle-class homes and neighborhoods. As members of the middle class, we talk with our children, schedule our lives around their activities, talk frequently about their future and what each of us needs to do to assure a productive future. Our children see us paying bills, withdrawing money from the bank, reading books; they assume we will keep our jobs and homes. Children in poverty learn different values and skills. They learn to adapt to an insecure future, to focus on today, and to obey authority figures. They recognize that their parents' lives are complex and that they may need to fend for themselves and protect their siblings (Lareau, 2002; Payne, 2005). The problem for poor children is that the values, assumptions, skills, and knowledge that support a middle-class life are those that pervade schools.

Some of the differences between socioeconomic groups begin well before the upper elementary grades. A key difference is language use in the home. In a longitudinal study, researchers found that by the age of three, children whose parents are professionals have about 1,000 words in their vocabularies, whereas children raised in poverty have about 500 words. The children of professionals also have much higher IQ scores (illustrating the importance of language in the traditional concept of IQ). When the researchers examined the interaction patterns between parents and children, they found that professional parents direct considerably more utterances toward their children than do poor parents (487 an hour compared to 178 an hour). Additionally, the nature of these utterances differs by class. Whereas professional parents use praise and encouragement extensively (e.g., What a good girl! You made your friend very happy by sharing!), poor parents are more apt to use language to discourage and admonish (e.g., Sit down and be quiet! Close the door behind you!) (Hart & Risley, 1995; Heath, 1983). Additional studies of parent/child interactions support these findings and conclude that the extensive engagement of young children in dialogue and the encouraging and supportive behaviors exhibited by more affluent parents stimulates children's brain growth and makes them more ready for school (Tough, 2006).

Socioeconomic Influences on Achievement

The gap in size of vocabulary and children's inexperience expressing thoughts and ideas carries into the upper elementary grades. Differences in language experience, coupled with fewer educational resources (i.e., books, magazines, computers) and more television viewing among children in poverty (Huston & Wright, 1998 in García Coll & Szalacha, 2004) add to the achievement gap evident between poor upper elementary children and their more affluent peers. The 2005 NAEP reading and math scores for fourth grade documented a significant difference between children who are eligible for free/reduced price meals and those who are not. Figure 3.2 illustrates the gap between poor and more affluent children. A 31 percent gap exists in reading and a 23 percent gap in mathematics (scoring basic or above), depending on eligibility for free/reduced lunch (National Center for Educational Statistics, 2007). The gap is also reflected in disproportionate grade retention (Center for Mental Health in Schools at UCLA, 2006; Thompson & Cunningham, 2000) and special education placement (Artiles, Klingner, & Tate, 2006) for poor children. As suggested, in relation to racial and ethnic achievement differences, the achievement gap between poor children and more affluent children reflects both lifestyle (Lareau, 2003; Payne, 2005) and societal expectations and structures that exclude and limit the poor (García Coll & Szalacha, 2004; Noguera & Wing, 2006; Williams, 2003).

Figure 3.2 Achievement Differences Between Socioeconomic Groups

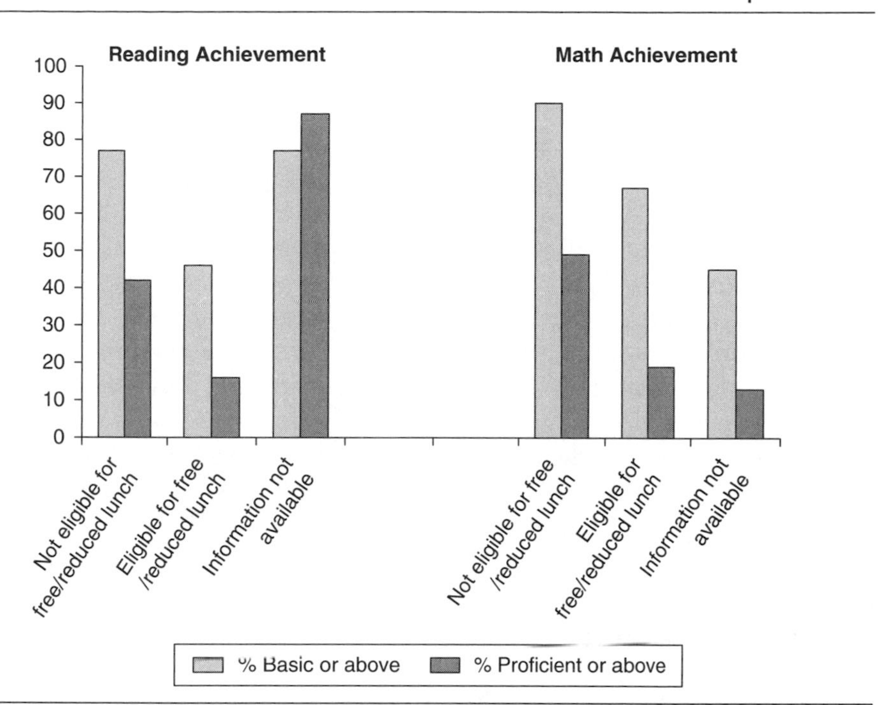

SOURCE: National Center for Educational Statistics data.

NOTE: Fourth-Grade National Assessment of Educational Progress (NAEP) Scores 2005

Becoming a dialogue facilitator to help your students build vocabulary and become comfortable expressing themselves verbally.

Children who grow up in less affluent homes often lack the vocabulary of their more affluent peers. You can help them build vocabulary and confidence expressing ideas and opinions by encouraging dialogue and self-expression. As you teach think about who uses the most words, you or the students. Adjust your teaching so that you encourage students to express ideas and explain their thinking. Model for them how you think through problems and allow them to demonstrate and explain their thinking. Doing so will likely shift the balance of talk from being teacher dominated to student dominated. Encourage them to use vivid language and vocabulary that may be new to them. At the same time, provide a print-rich environment, with books at a wide range of reading levels. Encourage them to talk to each other about the books they are reading. As they use more advanced vocabulary, it becomes a part of their normal speech.

Socioeconomic Influences on Social Development

As will be discussed in more depth in Chapter 5, upper elementary children's lives outside of school differ markedly along socioeconomic lines, significantly influencing their social development. Through considerable interaction with adults and many opportunities to develop abilities and skills through out-of-school activities, upper- and middle-class children develop the social skills expected at school, use an extensive vocabulary, interact confidently with adults, and expect to be treated as a valuable member of society. Working- and lower-class children develop different social skills because their lives are less adult-directed, and their time is not structured by organized activities. They typically have more opportunities to play unsupervised with other children, finding ways to fill free time, solve problems without adult intervention, and create and negotiate their own rules. When in adult company, working-class and poor children are usually expected to accept adult authority; questioning or challenging adult authority (i.e. "talking back") is unacceptable (Lareau, 2003). This, of course, does not hold for many poor children who live in dangerous neighborhoods where they are not allowed to play outside or they learn quickly to be tough, show no weakness, and respond quickly to real and perceived threats (America's Promise Alliance, 2006; Scales, Sesma, & Bolstrom, 2004). Often these children bring anger and frustration to school that is difficult to accommodate in the classroom (Sussman, 2006).

By third grade the socioeconomic differences in academic and social development are clear. In schools like the ones Madison and Laura attended, differences between middle class and poor children were easily evident to upper elementary children. Children this age recognize that peers from different socioeconomic groups interact differently, value different things, and spend their free time differently. They have also reached an age, especially by fourth and fifth grade, where they are very aware of clothing and other possessions. The fact that this age group watches a lot of television, in fact, more than any other age group (Roberts, Foehr, Rideout, & Brodie, 1999 in García Coll & Szalacha, 2004), makes them very aware of fashion and the latest must-have possessions. For poor children attending school with more affluent children, the inability to buy the latest fashions, spend money freely at the mall, go on trips, or enroll in after-school programs is more obvious to them than when they were younger. This can put pressure on families to spend more than they can afford.

ENGLISH-LANGUAGE LEARNERS

Lo que para mi es especial es estudiar ingles para saber ingles y entender escribir en ingles para que puedo entender. Eso es lo que para mi es

> *especial. Hay otra cosa que es especial, es que salga nos todos en mi familia a los lades y a las tiendas comerciales tan bien a los super a con pallar. A taen los alimentos para la casa, ayudar le a mi Mama, coger las camas y el mandaroro es que todos estemos juntos y sanos y fuertes. Que mi tío me saca a las yarda que está por casas y abense me con otras cosas en la yarda que incontrano y cuando mi papá trabaja con el y me compra cosas.*
>
> —Fifth-grade boy: essay, "Why I'm Special"

Obviously the boy writing here is more comfortable writing in Spanish than in English. He writes about how he is special because he is learning English; his family is reuniting in the United States, and they enjoy shopping in the United States. In his school 80 percent of the students are Hispanic, primarily from Mexico, and many upper elementary students there are learning English as they learn the required third- through sixth-grade curriculum. His classmates can help translate for him, and many of his teachers are fluent or conversant in Spanish. This boy could easily be in another school in which he is one of the few Spanish speakers among many other English-language learners, coming to school speaking languages as different as Cantonese, Albanian, Arabic, Portuguese, Cambodian, and Swahili, as well as dialects of English. Assuming that standard English is the language of school and the primary way of communicating in most classrooms, how does coming to school as a speaker of a language or dialect other than standard English influence upper elementary children's development both academically and socially? Many of the issues discussed earlier in relation to race, ethnicity, and social class also apply to English language learners because of the interconnections between culture and language. Culture cannot exist without language and language is shaped by what is recognized and valued in a culture.

Although English-language learners are considered as a group in most schools, there is great diversity among language learners. Consider the many variations that potentially exist within an upper elementary classroom in terms of language use. As Table 3.2 illustrates, all language-learning groups, including monolingual English speakers, have advantages and disadvantages in the classroom. The monolingual English speakers communicate easily with the teacher and their English-speaking peers, and they take for granted the vocabulary, concepts, and schema learned as part of English-language acquisition. They are disadvantaged by being monolingual because of all of the opportunities they miss by not learning and speaking another language.

Table 3.2 Diversity of English-Language Learners

Category of language learner	*Advantages to student*	*Disadvantages to student*
Monolingual native standard English learners (i.e., children who speak only standard English at home and at school)	No disconnect between language used at home and at school; children speak and think in English; instruction can build on concepts, schema, understandings, and skills developed in English	Children do not analyze the structure of English in relation to other languages; monolingual speakers cannot use language to more deeply explore other cultures; long-term opportunities in the global economy are limited
Native standard English learners, knowledge of additional language (e.g., children who speak English as a primary language but have learned or are learning additional languages)	All of the advantages above; opportunity to analyze structure of English; ability to use second language to explore own culture and that of people who speak the other language; long-term opportunities in global economy	None
Native speakers of English dialects, learners of standard English (e.g., children who speak African-American English, Gullah, or other dialects at home and in their community)	Opportunity to express ideas through a different language structure; connection to a culture and community different from mainstream American society	Perceptions by standard-English speakers that dialects reflect poor language learning and are inferior in structure and expressiveness to standard English; children need to know how and when to codeswitch
English-language learners continuous previous formal education in English-speaking country (e.g., children who began formal schooling in kindergarten or first grade in English-speaking countries)	Acquired literacy skills in English; ability to use concepts, schema, understandings from primary language and English; connection to culture and language other than English; long-term opportunities in a global economy	May have struggled with early literacy because of limited exposure to English; may have speaking knowledge of primary language but not reading and writing skills

Category of language learner	*Advantages to student*	*Disadvantages to student*
English-language learners who attended formal schooling for several years in their primary language and are literate in their primary language	Connection to culture and language other than English; acquisition of concepts, schema, understandings, and skills in primary language and application to English; potential long-term opportunities in a global economy	Lack of fluency in English basic vocabulary and language structure assumed for content learning in upper elementary grades; limited ability to communicate with peers and teacher; development of sense of being "other" socially
English-language learners, interrupted or no previous formal education (e.g., refugees either from areas in which schooling was not available or from preliterate tribal groups, such as the Hmong)	Resiliency, given trials associated with background; ability to speak primary language and potentially some literacy in the language	Limited acquisition of concepts, schema, understandings, and skills in primary language; trauma associated with migration experience; lack of fluency in English basic vocabulary and language structure assumed for content learning in upper elementary grades; limited ability to communicate with peers and teacher; development of sense of being "other" socially

SOURCE: Adapted from Commins & Miramontes, 2006; Delpit, 2006.

English-Language Learners and Achievement

How do English learners perform academically? When children take the NAEP test, their school designates if they are English-language learners or not. States differ in how English-language learners are defined. The category *English-language learners* does not account for students' primary language and past educational experience; *non-English-language learners* can include a wide range of students also, including students who are far from fluent in English. Figure 3.3 illustrates the gap between fourth-grade performance of English-language learners and non-English-language

Figure 3.3 Comparison of English-Language Learners and Non-English-Language Learners

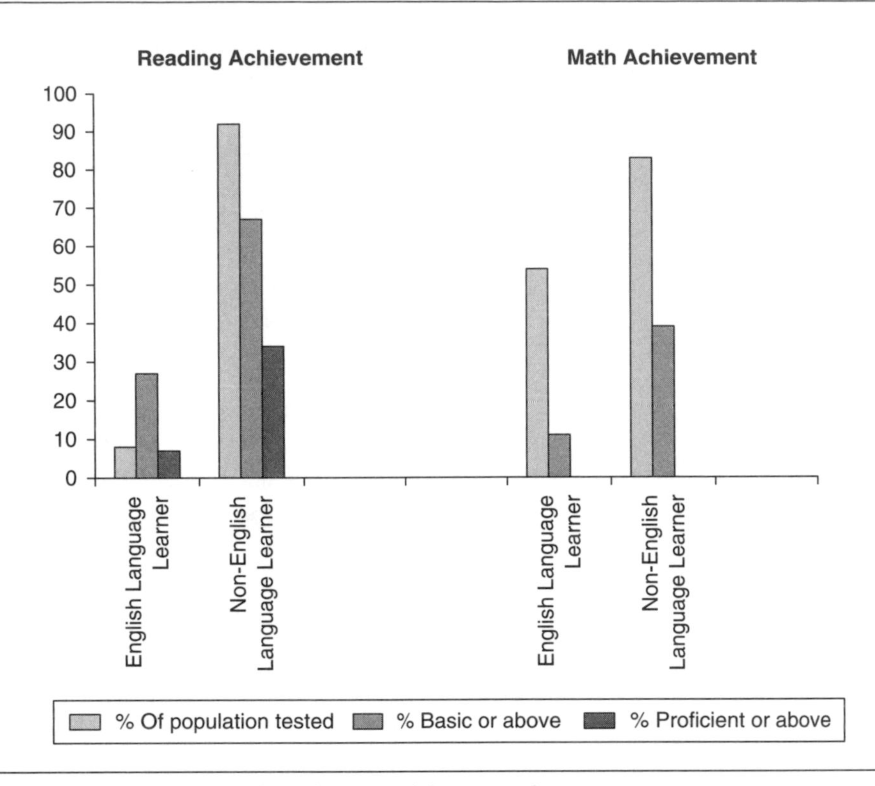

SOURCE: National Center for Educational Statistics data.

NOTE: Fourth-Grade National Assessment of Educational Progress (NAEP) Scores 2005

learners in reading and math. English-language learners fall below their peers in both reading (40 percent difference in students performing at or above basic) and math (29 percent difference). Given children's limited understanding and use of English, these data have to be used with caution. By the upper elementary grades, most children who qualify as English-language learners are recent immigrants, so they are new to our schools and the curriculum, as well as to the English language. In some cases these children arrive without literacy in their native language so they need to learn not only English but also the concepts of literacy.

English-Language Learners and Social Development

> *I have a lot of recent immigrants in my class. I have one with no English and another who came here a year ago from Ghana. When kids come in fifth grade, the language issue is so much harder. They have to learn difficult material and make friends. Fortunately, their disagreements aren't cultural.*
>
> —Fifth-grade teacher

Some of my students have language disabilities. There are a lot of second-language learners. They have social language but not academic language. I read that it takes five years to develop academic language.

—Fourth-grade/special education teacher

Although children develop social language ability more rapidly than they develop academic language, being an English-language learner influences children's social interactions. In schools in which many other children speak the same primary language, new arrivals often gravitate to others who speak their language. In schools in which children speak multiple primary languages, children as well as teachers learn to use body language and clear routines to help students who do not speak or understand much English. On the playground children with limited English often gravitate to games with clear rules that require little communication in English (Finnan, 1982). This is more difficult for girls because by the upper elementary grades, girls often socialize on the playground rather than play organized games or sports (Thorne, 1993); this either isolates the girl with limited English or reduces her to a passive observer of her peers. In the wider community, children of immigrants may take on the role of translator once they gain a degree of fluency in English. Many children are called upon to translate for their parents, especially for their mothers, at school, in stores, and with social service agencies. This places these children in adult roles that most children who grow up in English-speaking homes do not adopt.

Consider . . .

Forming a Whisper Club in your classroom.

All students enjoy talking with each other and appreciate having the opportunity to talk quietly about their work. English-language learners can use the Whisper Club to practice English in a safe environment or to talk quietly in their native language to understand directions and concepts. Place a poster on your wall such as the following:

Are You in the Whisper Club?

- Can you whisper to your partner without anyone else hearing your voice?
- Are you reading or discussing what you are supposed to read or discuss?
- BE A MEMBER TODAY!

GENDER AFFILIATION

Gender differences aren't a big deal in third grade. The boys play with the boys and the girls with the girls. Before the Christmas break they work well together. After the break, they get upset if they are "stuck" at a table with the other gender.

—Third-grade teacher

Girls like to read, and boys are more physical. Boys like math better than reading; not all of them but most. For some boys it's a struggle with behavior, getting their homework. They are more immature. A few of the boys are a year older and they are starting to look at the girls. The older boys are more of a behavior problem; they are more physical. The lack of physical activity is really hard on some of the boys especially; they don't have morning recess.

—Fifth-grade teacher

The nature/nurture debate about gender differences has raged for years. I remember presenting research on gender differences in children's play (Finnan, 1982) to one of the graduate classes I took in the mid-1970s. I had studied gender differences in second and third grade children's chase games and found consistent differences in the structure and goals of their games. One of my classmates was incensed, accusing me of sexism and perpetuating stereotypes. She had worked with preschool children and stated flatly that gender differences were all socially constructed. She believed that, left to play on their own, boys and girls showed no differences in play preferences. That her experience was with preschool children and my research was with second and third-grade children I believe contributed greatly to our difference in perception, but it also reflected different views on the role of gender in social interactions.

The debate is certainly not over. Whereas one recent report indicated that only 1 percent of genetic coding differentiates males and females (Brizendine, 2006), other reports (Gurian, Henley, & Trueman, 2001; James, 2007) have detailed significant genetic differences in brain functioning, chemical balance, and hormone levels that contribute to male and female differences from birth until death. Undeniably, social and cultural expectations for males and females profoundly influence children's gender-identity development. As parents who vigilantly attempt to eliminate gender differences in their homes learn, children have their own ways of marking their gender identity. These actions begin early (e.g., where girls are apt to choose pink and purple as favorite colors and boys turn every pointed object into a weapon) and continue into the upper elementary school grades (Gurian, Henley, & Trueman, 2001; Thorne, 1993).

Gender identity and classification influence children's academic, social, and physical development. Many of the stereotypes for males and females have been assailed (e.g., that boys do not show emotion; that girls do not do well in math and science) and some are slowly disappearing. However, most upper elementary teachers see distinct differences between boys and girls in their classes, and they work with children who are beginning to experience more mature sexual impulses and some who may be questioning their sexual orientation. Whether gender differences are biologically based or the product of social and cultural expectations is important to consider as we work with students to maximize their experience in the upper elementary grades and their future success in school and beyond.

Gender and Academic Achievement

Contrary to stereotypical expectations, upper elementary girls and boys achieve at similar levels in both reading and mathematics. As Figure 3.4 illustrates, the gap between fourth-grade reading and math scores is much less than gaps reported for other groups. In reading 6 percent more fourth-grade girls than boys scored basic or above (67 percent for girls and 61 percent for boys). The gap was even smaller in math, with only a 1 percent difference between fourth-grade boys and girls: Some 81 percent boys and 80 percent girls scored basic or above (National Center for Education Statistics, 2007). The differences in these scores, although statistically significant, certainly do not support stereotypes of male math geniuses and female supercommunicators.

Figure 3.4 Comparison of Male and Female Achievement

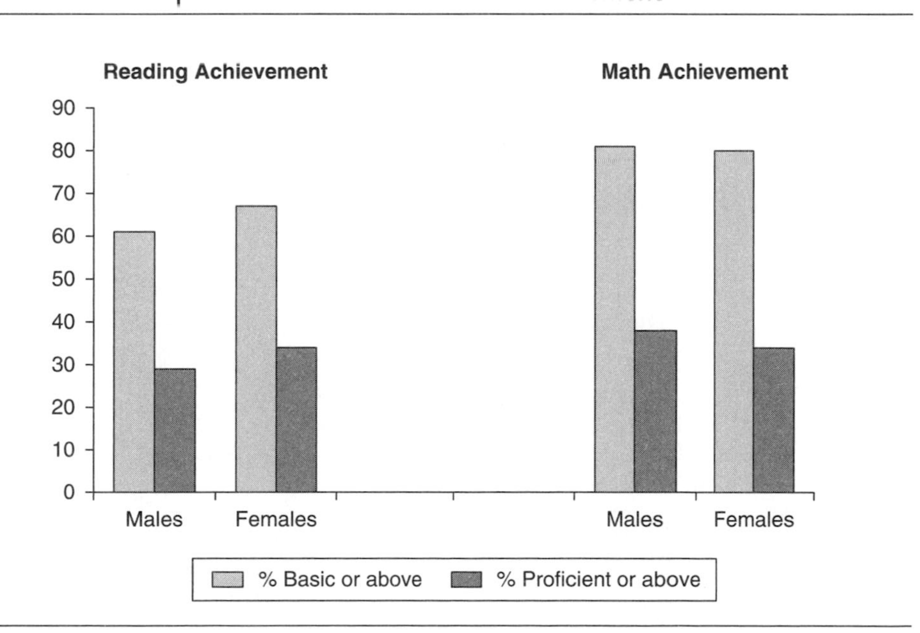

SOURCE: National Center for Educational Statistics data.

NOTE: Fourth-Grade National Assessment of Educational Progress (NAEP) Scores 2005

Teachers often notice that boys are more apt to stake out the extremes on the achievement continuum. A few boys are often the academic stars in the class, shouting out answers, asking difficult questions, and being nominated as outstanding students by their peers (Sadker & Sadker, 2002). Other boys hug the bottom of the achievement rankings, especially in reading. The NAEP data support the difference seen at the bottom but not at the top. Some 6 percent more fourth-grade boys and 10 percent more eighth-grade boys score below basic in reading than girls do, but only 1 percentage point separates girls and boys (fourth and eighth grade) in poor math performance. The gap at the top for both subjects and both grade levels is only 2 to 3 percentage points, which does not support the contention that boys dominate as top achievers, even in math. Teachers' perceptions probably reflect how students demonstrate knowledge (e.g., boys call out more frequently) and self-confidence (e.g., girls are more apt to doubt their ability and are more sensitive to negative feedback) (James, 2007; Scales, Sesma, & Bolstrom, 2004).

Although the NAEP scores show little difference between boys and girls, boys are more likely to repeat grades and be tested for special education. By high school between 7 percent and 10 percent more boys than girls have repeated a grade (Center for Mental Health in Schools at UCLA, 2006). In addition, boys are more apt than girls are to be identified as disabled. Upper elementary special education classrooms usually serve many more boys than girls (Gurian, Henley, & Trueman, 2001), "They represent 58 percent of those in classes for the mentally retarded, 71 percent of the learning disabled, and 80 percent of those in classes for the emotionally disturbed" (Sadker & Sadker, 2002, p. 195).

Gender and Social Development

The push to grow up early is more for girls than boys. Boys are more like men, or maybe more accurately, men remain like boys. They don't care as much about social things. Boys and men continue to play the same sports and video games all their lives. Boys have more freedom. Girls are thinking about boys at this age. Girls are more interested in self-image. In some cases this comes from Mom. If their mom is concerned with her appearance, especially if she is dating, this filters to the girl. Some of the negative behavior we see, some of the drama, may come from home; it definitely comes from what they watch on TV.

—Fifth-grade teacher

Socially, differences between boys and girls become more pronounced in the upper elementary grades. Clearly, there is great variation within each gender; some girls exhibit traits more commonly associated with boys and vice versa. However, some general trends are clear to teachers and parents. For example, as early as preschool and continuing through the upper elementary grades, girls typically play with girls and boys with boys when given the choice (Borland et al., 1998; Harris, 1995; Maccoby & Jacklin, 1987; Thorne, 1993). How much these same-sex choices are part of children's own construction of their gender identity (e.g., girls insisting that they dress in ways that they believe make them look more feminine) or are influenced by media (e.g., boys emulating sports idols; girls trying to look like sexy actresses), gender roles in the family or school practices (e.g., lining up for transitions in same-sex lines) is not clear.

Boys and girls play differently in the upper elementary grades (Finnan, 1982; Thorne, 1993) and interact differently in the classroom (James, 2007). In broad strokes the playground is where boys rule and find comfort; they can run, play sports, and interact physically. In contrast, the classroom is a more female domain. Since women comprise 90 percent of elementary school teachers, classrooms tend to favor female social interaction patterns. Sitting in place, quietly doing work, helping students in need are characteristics commonly attributed to upper elementary girls and are traits that are rewarded in the classroom (Gurian, Henley, & Trueman, 2001; Sadker & Sadker, 2002). Typically, because boys are more physical and active, they may be seen as acting up, but they also receive disproportionate attention, both positive and negative. As Sadker and Sadker (p. 183) described, boys play starring roles as either heroes (e.g., the boy who always knows the answer) or the villains (e.g., the boy who disrupts the class).

Social development of girls and boys differs; each having issues that impact on their school experience in the upper elementary grades. Most boys and girls understand and follow rules, take responsibility for themselves, and take pride in accomplishing tasks. Boys, however, are more frequently disciplined for misconduct in the classroom and are less likely to complete homework and keep their space orderly (Gurian, Henley, & Trueman, 2001; Sadker & Sadker, 2002). These problems may reflect boys' slower development socially but more likely they reflect one of many other issues, such as boys' greater need for physical activity, frustration over doing poorly in school, inability to resolve problems that originated outside of school, a mismatch between the expectations for appropriate classroom behavior of a largely female teaching profession and boys' social development, or hormonal and neurological differences (Gurian, Henley, & Trueman; Sadker & Sadker). The aggressive and disruptive behaviors that often accompany boys' entry into puberty are less likely to occur in upper elementary classrooms. However, some boys, especially those who have repeated grades, may begin to show such behaviors (Gurian, Henley, & Trueman,).

Upper elementary girls are entering a difficult time in their social development. On the whole they want very much to do the right thing, behave properly, take responsibility, and be caring friends, students, and daughters. Girls and boys are very concerned about friends, but girls' friendship circles are ever changing. Best friends are very important, and breakups between best friends preview breakups they are soon likely to have with boys. Girls' friendships focus heavily on emotions that trigger some of their interpersonal issues (Borland et al., 1998). The following questions posted to a page on the Girl Scouts' Web site represent concerns girls have about making and keeping friends:

- I have three best friends and they all want to know who my best best friend is. What do I do?
  —11-year-old from Wisconsin
- I got mad at my friend because she was talking about me behind my back. Now, she is trying to be my friend, but she still talks about me. What should I do?
  —10-year-old from Indiana
- One of my friends is hanging out with me too much. It's making my other best friend feel bad. I don't want to hurt their feelings. What should I do?
  —10-year-old from Ohio

Consider . . .

Being an advocate for extending childhood.

Boys and girls mature at different rates and face different issues in the upper elementary grades, but both benefit from encouragement to remain children as long as possible. On the one hand, the media encourages children, especially girls, to emulate teenagers and to shape their interests and spending patterns in line with adolescents; on the other hand, upper elementary children continue to enjoy the pleasures of younger children. Most upper elementary children, even the most precocious girl in your class, vacillate between playing as they did when they were little children and taking on the mannerisms and interests of teens. While you cannot compete against the power of the media, provide opportunities in the classroom and the playground for children to retain behaviors they enjoyed when they were younger. For example, encourage girls to continue to jump rope, play hopscotch, and engage in fantasy play on the playground. In the classroom have stuffed animals and dolls in the reading corner; include books they enjoyed reading in primary grades. On rainy days play games they may have played when they were younger. In addition, engage students in an analysis of why advertisers have targeted their age group, and encourage them to discuss the pros and cons of media messages.

- I am sad, but I don't know why. On the outside, I'm happy, but inside I'm sad. There's nobody making me sad, but I don't have friends. That's the problem. I don't know what to do. Help me.
  —10-year-old from Texas (Girls Only, 2007)

Upper elementary girls are more apt to express interest in boys than vice versa. Even if they are not interested in the boys in their school, many have crushes on young men they see on television, in movies, or in music videos. The media caters heavily to girls this age and pushes them toward clothing styles, lifestyle choices, and conversations that were considered by many people to be inappropriate for teens a generation ago (Girls, Inc., 2007; Lambs & Brown, 2006; Mitchell & Reid-Walsh, 2005).

Gender and Physical Development

Onset of puberty heavily influences gender differences in the upper elementary grades. Although neuroscience indicates that male and female brains function differently throughout life (Gurian, Henley, & Trueman, 2001, see pp. 20–26 in particular), the bodily changes associated with the onset of puberty exacerbate these differences. Some of the social issues mentioned earlier reflect girls' changing hormonal balance. By third grade quite a few girls (48 percent of African American and 17 percent of White girls) are beginning to show signs of the onset of puberty (Zuckerman, 2001). On average, girls begin to show signs of puberty at 10 years, whereas for boys it is around 11½ years (McDevitt & Ormrod, 2004). Childhood obesity appears to play a role in girls' early maturation. Because of these changes, and the social pressures to grow up quickly, many upper elementary girls are orienting more toward adult sexuality, whereas most boys are still focused on childhood activities and interests (e.g., sports, collections). By the middle of third grade, boys and girls appear to live in different worlds. Girls find their male peers immature and silly, and boys do not understand what has happened to the girls they once knew.

EXCEPTIONAL LEARNERS

During the upper elementary grades, many children are tested and labeled as "exceptional." Those who "by virtue of outstanding abilities are capable of high performance" may be labeled as "gifted" (Council on Exceptional Children, 2006). Others who cannot perform at a "normal" level receive labels indicating a disability. Although all children vary physically, socially, and academically and have widely divergent interests, some have differences that lead to a process of identification, testing, and specialized services. These children, by definition, comprise a group considered exceptional.

The practice of identifying children as exceptional is highly contested; it assumes "normalcy as a regime of truth" (Davis, 1997, in Reid & Knight, 2006). As described earlier the concept of normal is very problematic because normalcy is definitely in the eyes of the beholder. By assuming there is a normal, we relegate those who look, think, and act differently to a category of "other." A disproportionate number of ethnic and racial minorities, students living in poverty, and language learners are labeled as disabled and a disproportionate number of Asian and White students are labeled as gifted, calling to question the objectivity of this labeling process (McDermott, Goldman, & Varenne, 2006; Reid & Knight, 2006). Even more problematic, the high incident disability labels (e.g., learning disabled, mentally retarded, and emotionally disabled) are the most subjectively defined and are most disproportionately applied to poor and minority students (McDermott, Goldman, & Varenne, 2006).

Achievement of Exceptional Learners

It is probably not surprising that fourth-grade students identified as disabled perform at lower levels in both reading and math. Figure 3.5 illustrates that a 33 percent gap exists in reading (percentage of students scoring basic or above) and a 26 percent gap exists in math scores between students who are identified as disabled and those who are not. Given that performance on standardized tests is one of the primary tools used for identification as either disabled or gifted, it is not surprising that such gaps exist. Being identified and classified as exceptional has a profound impact on students' sense of themselves as learners. On the one hand, children identified with learning disabilities may be relieved that they have an explanation for why they struggle to learn and welcome interventions by professionals trained to help them accommodate their disability. Similarly, many children identified as gifted are thrilled to carry such a label, especially in schools in which academics are valued by both adults and children. On the other hand, any label that identifies children as different or "other" is not a characterization most children seek by the upper elementary grades.

Social Development of Exceptional Children

In terms of social development, exceptional children often differ from their peers and from adult expectations. It is difficult to generalize about how exceptional children develop socially because the conditions that make them exceptional vary so greatly, but often their learning and

Figure 3.5 Comparison of Students With Disabilities to Students Without Disabilities

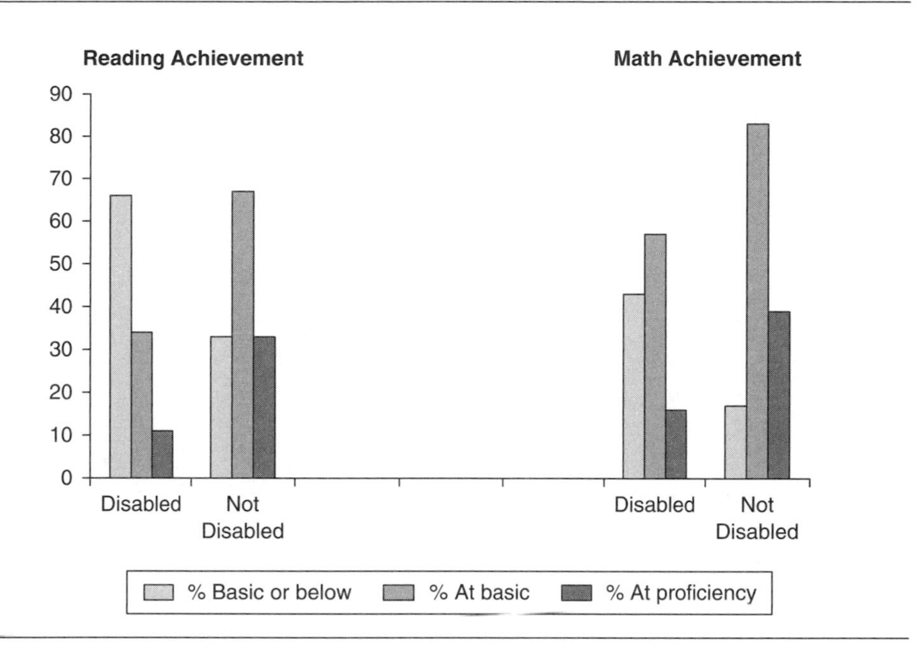

SOURCE: National Center for Educational Statistics data.

NOTE: Fourth-Grade National Assessment of Educational Progress (NAEP) Scores 2005

communication differences result in uncomfortable interaction patterns with their peers and with adults. Most children who are identified as gifted and talented have good social and communication skills. In some cases though, their vocabulary and easy grasp of concepts and abstractions can alienate them from other children; they can lose patience with others who learn more slowly or be viewed as strange or conceited by others. If not stimulated in the classroom, gifted children can turn their intelligence toward classroom disruption (Davis & Rimm, 2004). Children identified with mental retardation often have the social skills associated with much younger children. Some disabilities such as autism and attention-deficit/hyperactivity disorder involve information processing that can influence their ability to communicate and interact as expected in the classroom (Levine, 2002; McDevitt & Ormrod, 2004). Clearly, children diagnosed with emotional disabilities have special challenges in their social development.

Most exceptional children want very much to be accepted socially by their peers and to do the things expected of children their age. For example, in *Adventures in the Darkness: Memoirs of an Eleven-Year-Old Blind Boy*, Tom Sullivan (2007) provided a vivid account of how he, blind since birth, sought to do and experience life as any bright, energetic boy would do. He sees blindness as just one of many of his characteristics; it is definitely not his defining characteristic. Although Sullivan is extraordinary in his accomplishments, his desire for ordinary social interactions is common among disabled children. His aversion to being known primarily as a blind man and secondarily for his other attributes is shared by many disabled people.

As has been mentioned in the discussion of other groups, most upper elementary children are at the developmental stage where they like to sort and categorize. In the case of exceptional children, school practices and programs provide ready categories and labels for them. Upper elementary children are certainly aware of what labels such as "LD," "MR," or "ADD" mean, and they apply them to each other (as well as applying more crude and cruel labels). In many schools classification as exceptional often occurs in the upper elementary grades. Many children with learning disabilities are monitored in the primary grades but are not formally identified until the upper elementary grades. Children considered "slow learners" are often subject to multiple rounds of testing to determine causes and possible treatments for their weaknesses, usually in reading, even though they may never be formally identified with a disability (Spear-Swerling & Sternberg, 1996). At the other end of the continuum, children who perform well in literacy and mathematics are most apt to be identified as gifted and talented (Renzulli, 1986); formal identification is often made in second and third grade. Most school districts begin offering special services to gifted students during the upper elementary grades. In fact, in more than half of the states, districts begin serving gifted students in third or fourth grade (National Association for Gifted Children, 2005, p. 133). By providing services to exceptional children, we draw attention to their differences and potentially influence their social interactions and self-image.

THE HOLISTIC CHILD: MIXING GROUP IDENTITIES

Patterns definitely emerge from the previous discussion. Without a doubt, expectations for academic and social development advantage certain groups. For example, White, middle-class, English-speaking, and normal tend to be rewarded in school. Schools' academic and social expectations were established with these children in mind, and academically and socially these children do reasonably well in school. That most elementary school teachers are White, middle class, and female also makes school a comfortable place for these children. Test scores, special education placement rates, and grade retention patterns all indicate that certain children move relatively easily through the upper elementary years.

Whereas some children are multiply advantaged by group memberships, others have multiple risk factors. Racial and ethnic minorities are much more likely to live in poverty (Borman & Overman, 2004; García Coll & Szalacha, 2004; Ladson-Billings, 2006a). Although poverty and race are not synonymous, poverty for African American children is more likely to be a permanent state, whereas for White children it is transitory (Huston, 1994 in James, Jenks, & Prout, 1998). Poor minority children are more likely to be identified as disabled and repeat a grade (Center for Mental Health in Schools at UCLA, 2006; García Coll & Szalacha, 2004; Lorsen & Orfield, 2002); they are also more likely to receive exclusionary disciplinary actions (Fenning & Rose, 2007). One explanation for this is that the cultural beliefs, values, and assumptions they bring to school often collide with those perpetuated in the school. Through poverty, residential segregation, and limited access to public and private services, their lives outside of school are a far cry from those of their more privileged peers.

Data clearly show that poor African American boys are most at risk of school failure. They are most often likely to score below basic on achievement tests, to repeat grades, to be suspended or expelled (Fenning & Rose, 2007), and to be identified as disabled. The literature addressing African American boys' social and academic issues is rich and challenging (Fashola, 2005; Ferguson, 2000; Noguera, 2002). It explores historic, cultural, social, political, psychological, and economic reasons why poor African American boys struggle to find a place in most classrooms and schools. Consider Eddy, a lanky 15-year-old African American boy I interviewed in a special program for children who have repeated grades. Eddy bounced around from one apartment to another much of his life. When asked about his elementary school experience, he looked down at his hands, shook his head from side to side, and chuckled to himself. He said that in the elementary school where he went to third, fourth, and part of fifth grades (an all African American school in an impoverished neighborhood), "It was cool to be bad." When he was in fourth grade, he described himself as "a complete pain in the neck. It was so crazy. I had to do something to get them laughing. I'd do something and get sent to the behavior room. I'd slam the door to the room to make them laugh but also because I was mad. I didn't want to go to the behavior room. I was one of the 'bad boys' that the teacher was always ready to pounce on. She just wanted to get us out of the class." Fortunately for Eddy, his mom moved to another neighborhood, and he finished fifth grade in a school where the teachers gave him special help, had children do projects of their choice, and where his classmates were calm and focused on their work. As Eddy said, "It was a nice school that didn't have people like the home boys at my old school."

Each child comes to school with multiple identities, multiple affiliations. Some, like gender, have a biological basis, but all of them are shaped by cultural, social, economic, and historical influences. Within each child this unique blend of identities—racial, ethnic, socioeconomic, language, gender, and able/disabled—merge and interact. For some children the accident of birth bestows advantages. This is not to say that they do not have to work hard, will not struggle, but the odds are in their favor. Others do not have such advantages; the odds are not in their favor. However, they too can and do succeed. Consider the following questions in examining how group affiliation affects upper elementary children in your school.

- How can you balance high expectations for all children while simultaneously accounting for cultural, social, historical, and economic differences among groups of children?
- How can you acknowledge differences while avoiding stereotypes?
- How does your school use data on subgroups to better serve all children?
- What can be done in your school and classroom to turn around negative trends for groups of children, especially for low-income African American boys?

4

Individual Developmental Differences

I am special because I was born by Brian Craft. I'm the only Nick J. Craft in the world. I'm also special because I have a great family.

—Fourth-grade boy

I am special because I am great in different areas in school, like reading, and I try my best to do great in school. I am good at volleyball and homework. I am unique.

—Fourth-grade girl

I'm special because I am a good friend. I am different than everybody else, so nobody is the same as me.

—Fourth-grade girl

I am special because my parents are a different color than me. But my little sister is not. I like being different.

—Fourth-grade girl

These students are all in the same fourth-grade class, are the same age, live in the same community, and most share common ethnic and socioeconomic group affiliations, but their statements of what makes them special illustrate that they are proud to be unlike anyone else. As their statements reflect, upper elementary children are willing to identify things that make them different and unique. For some it is their academic or athletic interests and abilities (e.g., "I'm good at math" or "I play soccer"); for others it is their interpersonal relationships with family, friends, and teachers. Others stress personal characteristics of being responsible, kind, nice, and well behaved; others identify themselves being unique or different; and still others mention being members of ethnic groups or being bilingual. In their own words, students indicate pride in both individual characteristics that set them apart from others and how membership in groups makes them different.

The focus of Chapter 2 is on what is reasonable to expect of all upper elementary students in relation to being learners, individuals within a larger society, and physically developing young people. There is not only a profound change from third grade through sixth grade in terms of development in these domains but also considerable variation at each grade level. Some of this variation is individual; as children are quick to notice and parents and teachers marvel at, each child, even within a family, develops very differently. As described in Chapter 3, other variation is influenced by racial and ethnic group identification, social-class status, primary language, gender identification, and being identified as exceptional. Too often we try to simplify our understanding of this variation and focus exclusively on either individual differences or group characteristics; in the first case, we potentially shortchange children; in the second case, we stand to perpetuate stereotypes. When the focus is on only individual differences, children can be blamed or rewarded for performance that is shaped by factors out of their control (e.g., when considerations of the ill effects of poverty and the positive effects of affluence are ignored in examinations of academic performance). However, focusing too much on group characteristics can result in stereotyping that is equally damaging (e.g., assuming that all Asian American students are quick to master mathematics or that girls are not as athletic as boys).

This chapter focuses on individual differences, how the developmental process varies for each child. As in the previous chapter, it questions the emphasis on normalcy that outdated definitions of intelligence and stage theories of development encourage (Davis, 1997, in Reid & Knight, 2006). Because we assume that most children of a certain age are developmentally normal, we structure how children progress through school based on age, and we assume that all students in a given grade should reach academic proficiency at the same time. James, Jenks, and Prout (1998) explained why too much focus on defining normalcy and establishing school structures and practices based on this sense of normal is shortsighted and potentially damaging to children:

> None the less, Piaget's genetic epistemology has, through its measuring, grading, ranking and assessing of children, instilled a

> deep-seated positivism and rigid empiricism into our contemporary understandings of the child. Under the hegemony of developmental stage monitoring it is not just iniquitous comparison with their peers which children suffer through testing and league tables, but also a constant evaluation against a "gold standard" of the normal child. For those who fail to meet that standard, whether in education, bodily development or welfare, the repercussions and sanctions are strong. (p.19)

This focus on normalcy makes two false assumptions. First, that, depending on what is measured (academic ability, social skills, physical development), children can be distributed along a bell curve, with most children falling into the midcategory of normal and a certain percentage falling below the norm and another percentage falling above. If we lived in a truly egalitarian society, and all children had similar experiences and opportunities at home, in the community, and at school, a bell curve might help explain the natural variation that occurs among individuals in relation to their learning, social interactions, and physical development (Rothstein, Jacobsen, & Wilder, 2006; Williams, 2003). However, all things are not equal in society, at home, in the community, and at school. Additionally, determinations of where children fall on these bell curves are typically made based on a limited number of measures (typically one test), measures that are frequently found to be biased (Haney, 1993; Roscigno & Ainsworth-Darnell, 1999).

The focus on identifying normal is flawed for a second reason. Considerations of what is normal are based on a dominant group's social and cultural assumption. In the United States, developmental patterns of White, middle-class, physically able, English-speaking people shape our expectations for learning and development. By establishing an expectation for what is normal and a structure to move so-called normal children through an educational system, we marginalize those who are different, often labeling them as deficient, damaged, or at risk in some way (James, Jenks, & Prout, 1998; McDermott, Goldman, & Varenne, 2006).

This chapter begins with a focus on individual differences in learning, exploring variation in learning and focusing on how broader conceptualizations of intelligence provide a more nuanced understanding of learner differences in the upper elementary years. This discussion includes variables, such as creativity and motivation, which contribute to individual learning differences. The chapter then moves to the social domain and considers individual differences in identity development and social-interaction preferences. The focus on individual variation ends with a discussion of physical differences, emphasizing differences in students' appearance and onset of puberty.

INDIVIDUALS AS LEARNERS

> *I'm special by trying. What makes me special is my effort. That's why I'm special. My parents are happy because I try my best. I mostly try my best on some stuff that I don't get. Last time we did a multiplication test and I tried my best and I got a good grade. My parents never put me down when I get a bad grade, but they only say good try.*
>
> —Fifth-grade girl

> *What makes me special is that I am smart because being smart you could go to Challenge [the school's program for gifted students]; then you could get smarter. I like to be smart because then my homework could be so easy then I could play my Nintendo 64 because it is so fun, and I bought it with my own money. I want to go to Challenge because it is so cool, and you might live with your friend. I would go anywhere I want.*
>
> —Fifth-grade boy

The focus of Chapter 2 on commonalities among learners examines brain growth and cognitive and language development. Upper elementary learners are characterized as *concrete learners* who are gaining proficiency in their ability to make distinctions, categorize, serialize, and reverse operations. Obviously, a natural variation exists among children in when and to what extent they master these competencies. Although some children struggle to meet grade level expectations in these skills, others are capable of much more abstract thinking than is typically expected of upper elementary children. Within an individual child, cognitive development varies, depending on the task. For example, a child may be able to work at an abstract level in mathematics but struggle to understand symbolism in a short story.

Chapters 2 and 3 provide general discussions of language development in upper elementary students, focusing on their increased vocabulary and ability to play with language meaning and syntax and on differences commonly found between groups of students. Here too children vary greatly and may defy standard expectations. Some enter third grade with extensive vocabularies and a comfort level in spoken and written language that exceeds expectations for elementary age children. Others have very limited language skills and struggle to express themselves. Variation in language and cognitive development are heavily influenced by experiences outside of school, social and cultural factors, and physiology.

Each individual approaches the learning process differently. The first child quoted earlier focuses on aspects of intelligence that, although not measured in traditional intelligence tests, are critical to academic learning: motivation and effort. Her comments point to the importance of viewing intelligence as more than a score on an IQ test or a single static trait

(Dweck, 2002, 2006; Gardner, 1983/1993, 1999; Levine, 2002; Renzulli, 1986; Sternberg, 1985, 1997). When we think of variation in student learning, we often focus primarily on differences in test scores and reading levels. For example, when asked to talk about student academic differences, teachers are quick to make comments such as, "I have a range from first to third grade. They have different learning styles." Or, "Most of my kids are below grade level. I have students who can't write a sentence to others who can write essays. They span from first to sixth grade." Most teachers face similar challenges trying to help all students meet grade-level expectations that, given individual and group differences, are difficult for some students to meet and not challenging enough for others.

Why are children at such different levels? Clearly, not all children have the same opportunities to achieve at high levels in school, and they develop as learners in very different contexts. Aside from considerations of opportunity and context, individual students vary in terms of effort or commitment, how their brain is wired (Levine, 2006); how they apply or manifest intelligence (Gardner, 1983/1993, 1999; Sternberg, 1997); and how they express creativity (Renzulli, 1986).

Variation in Cognition and Intelligence

We know that certain functions are taking place in upper elementary children's brains, and we also know that great variation exists between children in terms of how their brains work. These differences account for much of the variation we see in learners. As pediatrician Mel Levine (2002) wrote:

> Some children end up paying an exorbitant price for having the kind of mind they were born with. Through no fault of their own, they are the owners of brains that somehow don't quite mesh with the demands they come up against, requirements like the need to spell accurately, write legibly, read quickly, work efficiently, or recall multiplication facts automatically. When they grow up, they will be able to practice their brain's specialties; in childhood they will be evaluated ruthlessly on how well they do everything. (p. 14)

Children also differ in terms of how they are intelligent. Most educators are familiar with challenges to the traditional conceptualization of intelligence. Howard Gardner's (1993, 1999) theory of multiple intelligences emphasizes the importance of abilities other than linguistic and mathematical in lives of successful adults. Robert Sternberg (1997; Sternberg et al., 2006; Sternberg & Subotnik, 2006) extended theories of intelligence to focus on the multiple factors that make people successful at school and in life. To Sternberg intelligence involves one's ability to capitalize on strengths while compensating for weaknesses; to adapt to the environment or adapt the environment to oneself to demonstrate motivation and willingness to overcome difficulties; and to balance analytical, creative, and practical abilities.

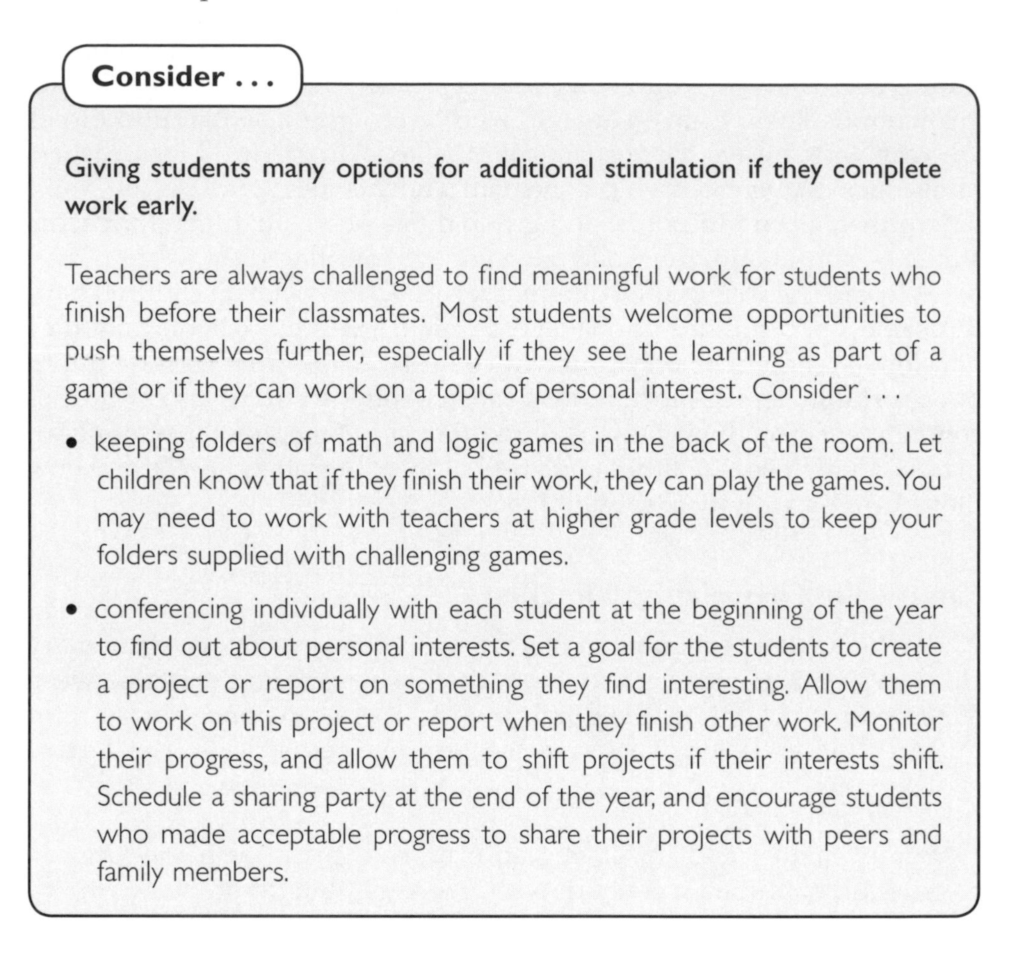

Consider . . .

Giving students many options for additional stimulation if they complete work early.

Teachers are always challenged to find meaningful work for students who finish before their classmates. Most students welcome opportunities to push themselves further, especially if they see the learning as part of a game or if they can work on a topic of personal interest. Consider . . .

- keeping folders of math and logic games in the back of the room. Let children know that if they finish their work, they can play the games. You may need to work with teachers at higher grade levels to keep your folders supplied with challenging games.
- conferencing individually with each student at the beginning of the year to find out about personal interests. Set a goal for the students to create a project or report on something they find interesting. Allow them to work on this project or report when they finish other work. Monitor their progress, and allow them to shift projects if their interests shift. Schedule a sharing party at the end of the year, and encourage students who made acceptable progress to share their projects with peers and family members.

Variation in Motivation to Learn

Differences in motivation (both intrinsic and extrinsic) and task commitment become more pronounced during these years. During the upper elementary years, children are less optimistic about their capacities than they were when they were younger. Through a series of successes and failures, they compare themselves to their peers and to their teachers' and parents' expectations; this can be seen as a process of becoming more realistic about their strengths and weaknesses, but it also begins a negative pattern for many children if they are repeatedly unsuccessful. Their interests also become more stable and tied to what they can do well and to what is expected of them. Where young children are easily interested in many things and assume they can master most anything they attempt, upper elementary children show a definite preference for doing what they enjoy and are successful at. In addition, intrinsic motivation to learn for its own sake begins to wane in third grade as concern about grades and rewards and punishments for achievement become more important in their minds. (McDevitt & Ormrod, 2004).

Research shows a link between motivation and concepts of intelligence (Dweck, 2002, 2006). How often have you caught yourself telling a child, "You are SO smart!" when she performed well on a task? It turns out that this kind of praise may have unintended consequences if the child views intelligence as a fixed trait, something she either has or hasn't. Mueller and Dweck (1998) found that preadolescents who are praised for their effort rather than their intelligence are motivated to persevere when tasks become more difficult, and they enjoy tackling increasingly difficult tasks. In contrast, those praised for their intelligence on an initial task become discouraged when the task becomes more difficult and often give up or determine that the task is worthless. They believe that having to work hard on a task indicates that they are not smart, so if they do not try, they can continue to see themselves as intelligent.

Consider . . .

Becoming an advocate for hard work and group rewards.

We can help children maintain their motivation to learn if we emphasize effort and reward group accomplishments in addition to individual accomplishments. Establish systems within your classroom that encourage students to work collectively toward a reward (e.g., extended recess time, a pizza party, no-homework nights). Reward hard work and persistence because all children are capable of hard work. Many children are motivated to work harder if they are part of a team; as team members, "stars" and "losers" do not always win and lose. Children who might otherwise give up or put in minimal effort have the incentive to stretch themselves. Being part of a team also minimizes the personal risk for students who fear failure.

Consider the following system used by a fourth-grade teacher I observed. She wears three plastic wrist bands (the expandable ones that hold keys) on her left arm. If students remain well behaved, she keeps them on her left arm. If students or a student misbehaves, she moves one band to her right arm. If she has any bands left on her left arm at the end of a designated time (e.g., before they leave for special area or before lunch) they add a link (made from a pipe cleaner) to their Success Chain. If she had to move all bands to her right arm, they do not receive a link, but they start over once they return to the room. In this way, even if they were not good in the morning, they can still be successful later in the day. When the Success Chain has 20 links, they earn a group treat, such as a pizza party.

Variation in Expressions of Creativity

A final area in which children exhibit individual differences as learners is in their creativity. Creativity involves originality, flexibility, and fluency in ideas. Additionally, it involves not only problem solving but also problem finding. The creative child is often inclined toward divergent thinking, offering novel or unexpected analyses, explanations, or representations of ideas. This does not mean that they are incapable of convergent thinking (ability to offer the "right" answer to a question or prompt), but they excel when able to range freely in their thinking. They are often nonconformists and may even be rebellious (Runco, 2007). As described earlier upper elementary children are more aware of their strengths and weaknesses, and they are apt to channel their creativity into areas they enjoy. For example, the child who dabbled in art lessons, ballet, gymnastics, and music lessons as a young child may decide that piano is not for her but becomes passionate about ballet.

Exceptional Variation

Variation in learners is most obvious for those who are considered exceptional. Within most "regular" upper elementary classrooms are students who have been identified as exceptional learners. Some of these students are exceptionally gifted academically or artistically. Others, for any number of reasons, struggle to learn. Returning to Levine's contention that human's brains are wired differently, this difference is most pronounced in exceptional children. The disabilities most often seen in upper elementary classrooms—learning disabilities, attention-deficit/hyperactivity disorder (ADHD), and forms of autism—may be the result of some kind of brain abnormality, but the fact that poor African American and Hispanic boys are disproportionately identified as mentally retarded, learning disabled, ADHD, and emotionally disabled calls to question the methods used to identify disabilities and the role of social and cultural expectations in labeling some children as disabled (McDermott, Goldman, & Varenne, 2006; Reid & Knight, 2006).

Whereas these disabilities are evident in the primary grades, they may not be diagnosed until the upper elementary grades because the independent skills needed for assignments that expose the discrepancy between performance and ability in students are not routinely in place until the upper elementary grades. In addition, teachers and parents are reluctant to label children as disabled so may put off testing hoping children will acquire needed skills. Throughout the elementary grades, children with learning disabilities are slow to learn one or more skills (often reading), have trouble focusing on their work, and may appear to lack motivation to learn. As a result of years of frustration with learning, behavioral problems often begin to arise in the upper elementary years (McDevitt & Ormrod, 2002).

Variation in Development of Self-Concept and Social Competency

They [fifth-grade students] struggle with their maturity level. Their home life, culture. Society made them older than they are, but they are really still kids. In private some of them still play with Barbies, but they don't want their friends to know. This is the beginning of the time of discovery of who they are and where they fit in. This is pretty well determined by the time they get to middle school. In fifth grade they know where they are both academically and socially.

—Fifth-grade teachers

In my current class, one child is an only child who shares nothing; things are hers and hers alone. Others treat each other like they would brothers and sisters. They fight and then love each other. Some want their hands held; others take off on their own.

—Third-grade teacher

I am special because I am me and just me.

—Third-grade girl

In Chapter 2 I describe key aspects of upper elementary children's development of a sense of self in relation to others. During these years most children become more responsible and independent; they are responsive to rules, have a desire for fairness, and are peer focused (while retaining a need and desire for adult relationships). Obviously, children vary in their development of social interaction skills and self-concept. As the fifth-grade teachers quoted earlier note, children's sense of self shifts frequently; one day they want to be seen as mature individuals; the next they behave like much younger children. Additionally, there is great variation between children in how they manifest their sense of self and relate to others. The upper elementary grades highlight individual differences between children, especially since adults and other children expect a level of responsibility and autonomy that some children do not possess. Children who are unsuccessful academically or in peer relations begin a spiral of low self–esteem, which negatively impacts on motivation and initiative. As described earlier this becomes more evident in the upper elementary grades when there is more pressure to perform at grade level and when children are more apt to make judgments of their worth based on comparisons to each other.

There was a girl in my fifth-grade class who was significantly larger than the other students. She was both tall and overweight. She was clearly insecure about her physical appearance. She had one really close friend, but other peers in the class constantly made fun of her. There was a group of boys that seemed to make fun of her the most. She usually made fun of herself along with the class, but occasionally she would get really upset by the comments either lashing out or crying. The teacher intervened when possible, but there was no way she could catch all that was said or done. She was constantly reminding us about how to treat others.

—Preservice teacher

There was a young boy who had been rejected by his peers for most of elementary school. He really enjoyed subjects like math and science. Most of my peers, myself included, chose to ignore him. He was usually very vulgar and rude to adults and other students. He was awkward looking with greasy blonde hair and dirty clothes. He often spoke about hunting and dead things. There was one group of coed students that chose to tease him. They would initiate conversations about hunting and science to intrigue the boy. Then the group of students would tease him, which made the boy really angry. This is when he would get defensive and threaten us as students. My fifth-grade teacher usually ignored these episodes, assuming that it was normal behavior for 11-year-olds. She actually used to pinpoint him for disrupting class or would send him to the main office. These actions, I feel, made his behavior even worse because it was not always his behavior that was causing the disruptions. This enforced the idea of teacher expectations, and the boy would respond by being disrespectful to the teacher in his own defense.

—Preservice teacher

These essays are painful to read because we can all remember the dynamics of peer acceptance and rejection in the upper elementary grades. It is in these grades that peer relationships become more solidified. Children tend to fall into social categories that are likely to stay with them into middle school. Popularity is very important; cliques form, and as the aforementioned essays from college students illustrate, students who do not fit in are ostracized and ridiculed. Many of us remember specific social groups or cliques in high school (e.g., nerds, jocks, druggies, techies, etc.), but these groups had their origins long before high school.

By the upper elementary grades, a clear social hierarchy exists in most classrooms. The names of groups may vary but usually there are "popular" children who carry considerable influence in the classroom. These students are often good looking, are either good students or good athletes, and have highly desirable material possessions. They may use their popularity to wield power over others, especially the "wannabes" who hang on the edges of the popular group. At the opposite end of the hierarchy are the rejected children who are often aggressive, immature, disruptive, and difficult to interact with. As both essays illustrate, this aggressive behavior is often due to complex interplay between the rejected child and his or her peers. Hidden by these more extreme groups are the average children who are often quiet and do not create drama in the classroom (Adler & Adler, 1998; McDevitt & Ormrod, 2002).

Some of these differences relate to the degree to which upper elementary children seek autonomy and relationships. Some children may intentionally seek smaller social groups or enjoy time alone. Upper elementary children are becoming increasingly able to self-regulate their behavior, which may involve intentionally removing themselves from social situations. For example, a child may move himself from a group table to a single desk because he "got up on the wrong side of the bed" and does not want to interact with his classmates that day. Some children choose to make such requests permanent, preferring to work alone when possible.

Consider . . .

That you cannot like all children equally.

Children come in all shapes and sizes; their personalities are even more varied. It is your job to be fair and caring to all students, but you have to accept the reality that you have to work harder to like some students. Make a "lunch date" with a child who rubs you wrong and get to know him better. Find the things that make him excited and happy, and encourage those interests. If he happens to be a child who struggles to get along with others, your one-on-one attention can help him develop confidence and better interpersonal skills. If problems persist, do not hesitate to use the services of your school counselor, psychologist, or social worker to better understand the issues the child is facing.

Physical Variation

Although dramatic growth spurts are not a characteristic of this age, students become increasingly aware of differences in their physical appearance and are becoming more aware of gender differences. By the end of the upper elementary grade/age span, some of the dramatic differences one sees in middle schools are evident. This is especially obvious in children who have been retained one or more years. Being especially small or large for one's age can cause great discomfort for children. For example, a fifth-grade boys' autobiographical essay consisted of one photograph taken when he was an infant and a single sentence: "When I was born I was a normal size." This boy is reminded daily that he is "not normal" by the fact that he does not fit into the elementary school furniture, that his hands are larger than everyone else's, that he is clumsy on the playground, and that he towers over his classmates. A college student reflected on children who did not fit in when she was in fifth grade and wrote about a boy who was much smaller than others his age.

At my school, fifth grade was the first year of middle school, which was located at a different campus across town than lower school. Given this, you were surrounded by nothing but older, taller, and bigger kids, and if you showed any fear or uneasiness, you were in trouble. There was a boy in my grade who was much shorter than any other student in fifth grade, and in turn shorter than all of the older students. He was very self-conscious about his height and was very quiet and by himself a lot. Because he was so small, older bigger boys would never pick on him for sports; they called him names like "shorty," or they threw him in lockers or trashcans. Our guidance counselor would talk to him and reassure him he would grow, and she would scold and punish the other students who picked on him.

—Preservice teacher

Upper elementary students are gaining more individuality in physical appearance. Gone are chubby cheeks and baby fat of earlier years. With large permanent teeth, usually yet to be straightened if needed or affordable, upper elementary children's faces are in transition. In addition, children are becoming more aware of their own appearance and of that of their peers. This is difficult for less attractive children because children treat attractive peers more favorably and adults give attractive children more positive attention and support (Zebrowitz, Hall, Murphy, & Rhodes, 2002).

Physical differences related to onset of puberty are discussed in Chapter 3, but individual differences related to puberty are evident in upper elementary years. Most notable are issues early-developing girls face as they become heavier and develop curves that set them apart from their peers. Reactions vary, but some girls begin a cycle of potentially dangerous weight control. A fifth-grade teacher mentioned this as a serious problem among some of the girls in her class.

There are a lot of changes in their bodies, especially related to hormones. Some of my girls don't eat the free breakfast or lunch. I'm afraid that it is a weight thing. In Mexico it is a term of endearment to comment on chubby cheeks or other references to weight. These girls are so influenced by the media, that they want to be superthin women. They are already avoiding food to achieve these unreal body images.

—Fifth-grade teacher

Other girls attract unwanted attention from peers, especially boys, as illustrated in the following essay:

I was the "fat kid" that everyone made fun of in fourth grade. The boys would snap my bra because I was the only girl in the class that needed to wear one. In health, they would giggle and laugh at me and tell me I needed to stop eating food, period, because I was overweight. I would cry because the boys all laughed at me and my self-esteem was really low. The teacher would discipline the boys, but it still hurt, and they still made fun. The next three years (throughout middle school) I lost the baby fat; the boys apologized, eventually, and I became one of the popular kids.

—Preservice teacher

Fortunately, things worked out for this girl, and she did not spiral into unhealthy behavior, but research indicates that early maturation for girls is tied to engagement in more risky behavior than for later maturing girls (McDevitt & Ormrod, 2002).

SUMMARY

To return to the fourth graders quoted earlier: All children are unique and will retain characteristics that set them apart from others. As learners each student's brain is wired a little differently due to physiological and environmental differences. They vary in how they like to learn and how their intelligence is manifested. Upper elementary children differ in their motivation to learn, their levels of creativity, and how they manifest creativity. Differences also exist in how students develop socially, in how they treat and are treated by their peers and adults, and in their physical development and their acceptance of themselves physically.

These individual children tend to share characteristics with others depending on their group affiliation. As described at the end of Chapter 3, group affiliations too often work against low-income, African American, Hispanic, and American Indian students, resulting in poor academic performance and disproportionate numbers of suspensions and expulsions. However, many children who apparently have the deck stacked against them do succeed in school. Despite multiple risk factors—poverty, single-parent family, grade retention, being a male and a racial minority—many children overcome the odds and succeed in school. A growing body of literature on resilient children points to the intersection of individual children's characteristics, the classroom environment facilitated by the teacher, and the overall school environment (America's Promise Alliance, 2006; Borman & Overman, 2004; Lewis, 2004–2005; Scales, Sesma, & Bolstrom, 2004).

Resilient children tend to retain their intrinsic motivation to learn, which typically drops for all students the longer they are in school (Finn & Rock, 1997; Skinner & Belmont, 1993). They have greater engagement in academic activities, stronger belief that they can learn the subject matter, enjoy attending school, and have higher self-esteem (Borman & Overman, 2004). Although resiliency is an individual characteristic, it is clear that something in resilient children's environment—whether outside of school, in school, or in the classroom—helps them perform better than others with similar group characteristics. The following three chapters turn the focus from children to the environments in which they grow and learn. All three environments—outside of school (Chapter 5), in school (Chapter 6), and in classrooms (Chapter 7)—include people, structures, and activities that encourage or discourage development of these important traits.

Before moving to an examination of environmental influences on children, consider the following questions about upper elementary children as individuals.

- How do you treat each child as a unique individual while being held accountable for all children meeting standards?
- What can be done at the school and classroom levels to counteract decreases in student motivation and creativity in the upper elementary grades?
- What can you do to encourage greater resiliency in students?
- How can you ensure that the school and classroom are safe places for students who might otherwise be marginalized by their peers?

5

Children's Lives Outside of School

In fourth grade you could always find me with my best friend, Liz. After school, we'd walk to meet each other half way between our houses. From there we'd go exploring or go over to my tree house or Liz's backyard. We loved to read, and both of us had vivid imaginations. One day we'd be in Terebithia and the next we'd be hanging out with the BFG. In the summer we'd make tents from old picnic blankets in Liz's backyard and lay in the cool grass reading our beloved chapter books. When the day got too hot, we'd walk to the neighborhood pool where games of Sharks & Minnows were always underway. When we were lucky, our moms would take us to the movies, and we would sit in the air-conditioned darkness soaking up the latest PG movie while gorging ourselves on popcorn and M&M's. Nothing could compare to those fabulous days at the movies! In fourth grade, Liz and I truly blossomed.

—Rebecca, preservice teacher

From this description, Rebecca and Liz's life outside of school was idyllic when they were in the upper elementary grades. They clearly had multiple opportunities to develop a sense of accomplishment, whether in their play or with their families. They lived in homes and a neighborhood that enveloped them in a sense of belonging, and they were intellectually, socially, and physically engaged in safe, age-appropriate activities. How representative are the lives of Rebecca and her friend Liz of those of upper elementary children in the United States? Consider the follow statistics for 6- to 11-year-olds drawn from a study of thousands of parents and children across the country (America's Promise Alliance, 2006):

- 90 percent have caring adults.
- 31 percent have safe places to live and play.
- 49 percent receive proper health care.
- 79 percent receive effective education.
- 55 percent have opportunities to help each other.

Beneath these statistics are stories of real children and families living very different lives. When children cannot count on having these basic needs met, it is hard for them to develop a sense of accomplishment, belonging, and engagement in or out of school. Consider statements from teachers in three schools in different corners of the country. The commonality of the schools is that they all serve populations in which the majority of children live in poverty.

> *I just had parent conferences, so this is fresh in my mind. So many kids have to deal with things they shouldn't have to deal with: drugs, siblings making bad choices, guns, not being safe. They see things I never saw. They do have tight families. They are very family oriented. There are lots of family members in the area, lots of aunts and uncles. Some have dads who travel a lot for work. I do have problem families. Three or four kids have someone (mom's boyfriend, mom, dad) in prison. Some don't know where they will live. Probably quite a few are illegal, so they don't go to the authorities. Many have a hard life.*
>
> —Fifth-grade teacher

> *There are two groups in this school. In one group there is always an adult available after school, either at home, at a relative's house, or after school program. The parent or parents could be working multiple jobs, but they make sure kids are taken care of. These same parents are involved at the school in whatever ways they can. On weekends they do things together that require family interaction, like picnics. The other group brings themselves up. Some third graders are responsible for their younger siblings. These are the "worker bees" in class. They eagerly do the chores, but they are often behind academically; often their homework doesn't get done. On the weekends this group either does nothing or plays outside. TV and video games are a big deal. Besides TV and video games, I can't think of anything they do other than sleep.*
>
> —Third-grade teacher

The kids in the housing project don't have the things many other kids have. They may go to the pool, but that's about it. They make up stories about riding bikes and going to Six Flags. In fact, they watch a lot of TV. Some do go to camp in the summer.

—Fourth-grade teacher

Between Rebecca's reminiscence, America's Promise Alliance statistics, and the teacher comments, students clearly bring different experiences to the classroom. This chapter examines the contexts of children's lives outside of schools, focusing on how their experience in their homes, with their friends, in their neighborhoods and in afterschool and summer activities contribute to their development of a sense of accomplishment, belonging, and engagement.

In addition to examining the multiple contexts in which upper elementary children interact and the ways they spend their time, the chapter also provides a larger picture of upper elementary children as active agents in shaping their own lives. This view of children will also frame later descriptions of upper elementary students in the context of school and the classroom. Anthropologists (Ladson-Billings, 2006a; Spindler, 1997), sociologists (Boocock & Scott, 2005; James, Jenks, & Prout, 1998; Lareau, 2003), and cultural psychologists (Cole, 1996; Vygotsky, 1978) encourage us to recognize that children are active participants in the social and cultural contexts in which they live; they are not merely passive observers or recipients of adult edicts or actions. Upper elementary students are definitely shaped by their community, family, key other places, and peer circle, but they are also active agents in all of these interactions (Boocock & Scott, 2005; James, Jenks, & Prout, 1998).

THE MULTIPLE CONTEXTS OF CHILDREN'S LIVES

Upper elementary children's worlds become much larger as they gain more independence, identify specific interests, take on more responsibilities, and seek increased interaction with peers and nonfamily adults. As their involvement in multiple contexts expands, they interact with a variety of nonfamily adults; have encounters with children in many different contexts; roam further from home in their neighborhoods and communities; and participate in a wide variety of organizations, teams, and clubs. In this expanded environment, new and different opportunities are available that influence their developing sense of accomplishment, belonging, and engagement. Additionally, involvement in multiple contexts gives children the opportunity to negotiate different relationships, which potentially expands and deepens their self-image (Boocock & Scott, 2005).

Family and Home

Family and home provide the first and most enduring opportunities for children to develop a sense of accomplishment, belonging, and engagement. As Alice and Peter Rossi (1990) explained:

> No other human relationship has as long a history as that between a parent and child, [and] no other adult figures are as important to the qualities children will bring to their adulthood as parents are, from the shared genes to personality characteristics, status attainment, basic values, and perhaps, the parenting styles the children bring to the raising of their own children. (p. 252 in Boocock & Scott, 2005)

This relationship exists in a wide variety of family structures: for example, married parents with children; mother or father only; unmarried biological families; biological parent with a stepparent or partner; same-sex parents; grandparents or other extended family; and nonfamily, such as foster care (Boocock & Scott, 2005). For many of us, some of these arrangements seem quite complicated. Where there are alternative family structures, there are often blended families and families that expand and contract as children move between parents (cocustodial or custodial/noncustodial). For many children the extended family lives together or in close proximity, and children spend considerable time with grandparents, aunts, uncles, and cousins. Their definition of family extends far beyond mother, father, and siblings, and these family members extend a wider web of belonging.

Assuming that both change and stability are givens in families, upper elementary children's sense of belonging can be rocked by family events. On one level family and stability are nearly synonymous. Family is usually the most reliable source of help and support; family provides the ultimate sense of belonging. Family members have long histories together and are a constant in our lives, whereas friends and neighbors change. However, change, at many levels, constantly affects families. Depending on the type of change, most upper elementary students take family changes (e.g., parental job change, new babies, siblings leaving for college or moving out, pets dying) in stride. Although these changes bring some stress, negative effects are short-lived. In contrast, changes related to death and divorce result in strong emotional responses that differ for each individual and are likely to influence school performance. Long-term negative effects of divorce are well documented (Hetherington, Stanley-Hagan, & Anderson, 1989) and are exacerbated by the fact that divorce (as well as death of a parent) can also trigger relocation, new romantic relations for parents, and remarriage, which challenge children's sense of belonging (Harris, 1995; McLanahan & Booth, 1989).

Building a sense of belonging in a family involves mutual nurture and support, especially once children are in the upper elementary grades. Most parents nurture and support their children; let's hope they are there to kiss scraped knees, to encourage children when their performance at school is disappointing, and to cheer them on at sporting events or other performances. Upper elementary children also provide nurture and support; they are keenly aware of parental moods and stresses and easily see when mom or dad has had a bad day. Upper elementary children are well aware of how to "push a parent's button" and how to provide support. When asked, upper elementary children can provide detailed descriptions of warning signs that parents are in a bad mood and suggestions on how to turn moods around: for example, doing chores without being asked, being cheerful, or keeping younger siblings occupied (Boocock & Scott, 2005; Borland, et al. 1998).

How the family creates an environment of belonging, accomplishment, and engagement is influenced by adults' parenting styles. Adults who see their role as authoritative (i.e., having more knowledge and experience than their children have) offer a high level of support to their children. They are warm and caring; they monitor their children's activities they are firm, fair, and flexible. These parents understand that giving their upper elementary children more decision-making opportunities does not diminish their role as parents as long as they communicate openly with their children and step in with noncoercive discipline when needed. Children are less apt to develop a sense of belonging, accomplishment, and engagement when parents are either extremely authoritarian or permissive. Extremely authoritarian parents are inflexible, rarely seek children's opinions, and may be harsh in their discipline. Children in these homes may be fearful of adults in general and abusive with peers. They are likely to question their value as family members and diminish their own accomplishments. Children of extremely permissive parents also have trouble developing a sense of belonging, accomplishment, and engagement because they are allowed too much freedom. With little discipline and haphazard guidance, children struggle to accept rules and compromises. Many children of permissive parents struggle with feelings of belonging because they fear that adults do not care about them; they long for limits their parents are unable or unwilling to offer (Baumrind, 2005) In addition, erratic or neglectful parents prove to be inconsistent, strict one day and lenient another. Children never know what to expect and are often on edge, never knowing whether their actions will be acceptable (Maccoby, 1992).

Parent/child relationships have to be understood in a broader social, cultural, and economic context. For example, in *Unequal Childhoods* Annette Lareau (2003) vividly described how social class shapes differences in how families interact and spend time. She found that in both African American and White middle-class families, children are encouraged to engage in discussions and to negotiate with their parents. Decisions are frequently made jointly, and children's schedules override parents' nonwork obligations. She describes this process as *concerted cultivation* because middle-class parents know that this kind of interaction will prepare their children to advance their ideas and advocate for themselves. These families conform to most educators' ideas of appropriate ways to encourage accomplishment, belonging, and engagement. In contrast, in both African American and White working-class and poverty-level families, children and adults coexist quite differently. Parents do not seek their children's opinions, view negotiation as disobedience, and expect their children to amuse themselves (a process Lareau calls *natural growth*). These children develop a sense of accomplishment, belonging, and engagement but in very different ways than do their middle-class peers.

Although Lareau found similar patterns between African American and White families who share the same socioeconomic level, she did not study Hispanic or immigrant families. Given that family interactions are heavily influenced by culture, how families encourage accomplishment, belonging, and engagement are quite different, depending on cultural expectations. For example, many immigrant families, whether middle class or working/lower class, actively cultivate academic accomplishment. They use out-of-school time to be sure that children excel in school. However, they do not allow discussion or negotiation of rules and authority (Rong & Preissle, 1998) that Lareau describes for middle-class families.

Consider . . .

Encouraging concerted cultivation in the classroom and natural growth on the playground.

Given that children benefit from both concerted cultivation and natural growth, you can provide opportunities for both. Within the classroom engage students in the kind of discussion and idea exchange that typically occurs in middle-class families. Encourage children to form and advocate for their own opinions. While maintaining your authority as the most knowledgeable person in the classroom, give students a chance to make decisions or select among options (e.g., hold class meetings that they run, allow them to justify modifications to assignments, provide opportunities for community involvement projects that require them to discuss issues in their community). Allow natural growth to occur on the playground. Encourage students to engage in spontaneous play and to negotiate their own rules. Although playground activity needs to be supervised, provide guidance rather than intervention unless safety becomes an issue. Outside of recess time, teach students conflict-resolution strategies that they can use to resolve disputes during play. See Peace Games (http://www.peacegames.org) for suggestions on how to help children resolve conflict peacefully.

Friends and Peers

> *What makes me special is that I'm kind and nice and I'm a good friend. What makes me special is that I'm a good sport and I'm a good helper. I'm special because I help others when they need help. I am behaving a lot; I never got in trouble. I get really good grades and my parents are happy they have me.*
>
> —Fifth-grade boy

> *When I was in fourth grade, I was an outdoor girl. After school, every day I was outside either riding bikes, playing at our neighborhood fort, roller skating, playing around the world, jumping on the trampoline. I had a group of neighborhood friends (about eight or nine) with whom I hung out almost everyday. I was outside from the time I got home from school to suppertime in the evening. On the weekends I spent my time with the same group of neighborhood kids, and my mother took us ice skating every Sunday. In the summer the pool was always a great place to ride our bikes to and spend the whole day swimming. We also would often end the day in my front yard with a huge game of kickball until the day turned into night. Then we caught lightening bugs. Also during the summer we played in the creek, catching crawfish and minnows and always watching out for ourselves.*
>
> —Preservice teacher

I began this chapter focusing on the importance of the family in shaping children's lives outside of school. The importance of family is undeniable, but we too often underplay the importance of peers in this process. Judith Harris (1995, 2006) compiled an impressive body of research to argue that family does not exert as strong an influence on children's development as their peer group does. Although not without critics (Boocock & Scott, 2005), Harris convincingly argued that adults overlook the importance of peers in shaping children's development, too often devaluing or fearing children's friends and peers. For upper elementary children, peers are becoming a key influence on their sense of accomplishment, belonging, and engagement. Upper elementary children seek acceptance and approval from friends and use them as a valuable resource in working through problems and changes in their lives. One reason adults overlook and devalue peer influence is that much of information that passes between children does so in secret, through what social scientists call the *culture of childhood*.

> Mine eyes have seen the glory of the burning of the school.
>
> We have tortured all the teachers; we have broken all the rules.
>
> We plan to hang the principal tomorrow afternoon,
>
> Our troops are marching on!

> Glory, Glory, Hallelujah! Teacher hit me with a ruler.
>
> Met her at the door with a loaded forty-four,
>
> Our troops are marching on!
>
> —Children's version of "Battle Hymn of the Republic"

You probably remember singing this song or one much like it in the company of friends, thinking it was so funny, original, and clever. In fact, generations sang it before us and generations are singing it after us. Songs like this are expressions of one of the oldest cultures in the world, the culture of childhood (Boocock & Scott, 2005; Opie & Opie, 1987; Thorne, 1993). For generations and across the world, children share secrets, a language, and patterns of interaction. When groups of children are free to do as they please and talk freely, they often enter a world that adults dimly remember, but now feel quite alien from; it is the Never–Never-Land that Wendy grew out of and Peter Pan did not want to leave.

This is not only a world of jokes, rhymes, and risqué stories but also a context in which children develop a way or

> style of knowing—whether to admit ignorance or feign accomplishment, how to brag and when to boast, whom to name-call and when to do so. Thus it is a culture . . . which passes between generations of children in defiance of adult restrictions on what children "should" or "ought" to know. (James, Jenks, & Prout, 1998, p. 89)

Within the culture of childhood, information is exchanged with explicit instructions about retaining secrecy, especially in relation to adults. Much of the joy of membership derives from defying adult authority (e.g., watching prohibited television shows when parents are not home; telling babysitters that they are allowed to do forbidden things; blowing up things in the backyard; saying "bad" words); expressing subversive thoughts; and defining clear boundaries in which other children define accomplishment and belonging. It is also a culture that provides legitimate meaning and structure to the activities and interactions children engage in when adults are not controlling their time and energies (James, Jenks, & Prout). The knowledge at the center of the culture of childhood passes from older children to younger children. This often happens as younger children observe and listen to the interactions of older children, but it can also be more explicit teaching, such as when an older sibling, who identifies more as a teenager than a child, passes on important lessons and lore to younger siblings.

In terms of how children structure their peer interactions, groups form by age, gender, and similar interests (e.g., similar social class, culture, interests). Girls tend to form smaller and more emotionally intense groups than boys form and invest considerable time and energy into a best friend. Relations with best friends often resemble the emotional roller coaster of adolescent relationships with boys (Borland et al., 1998). Boys' friendship circles are important but less emotionally charged; they serve more as a vehicle for activity than for emotional support (Hartup, 1996). For both boys and girls, but especially for girls, popularity becomes very important in upper elementary years (Adler & Adler, 1998). Consider the following fifth-grade students' descriptions of how friends are part of what makes them special. The first student is a girl; the second, a boy:

> *I am a very nice person. People think that I am a nice, friendly person. When I came to this school, people did not know me. So I got to know Erin, Jamie, Maria, Caroline, Doris, Marsala, Nadia, and they were all my friends and they never argued about me, and sometimes I don't play with Erin or Jamie.*

> *What makes me special is soccer. When I first went to school, I played soccer with my cousin. I had a lot of friends at this school. Then I started playing soccer. Then a lot of people came to play. My dad put me in soccer, and I saw a lot of my friends. I started playing soccer with the middle school, and that's how I got more friends.*

Groups play a very important role in socializing their members to the group's norms, values, and actions. It is important that members of the group adhere to the expectations of the group and do not display any of the actions or beliefs of another group. For example, during the upper elementary years, gender groups are very important, and boys are chastised for "acting like a girl," and girls may be excluded from their peer group if they associate too much with boys or take on characteristics of boys. Many of us remember or see the consequences of violating taboos against associating or acting like members of other groups. I still remember being taunted in fifth grade for offering to help the boy who sat behind me in class with an assignment. My female peers teased me without mercy, extracting from this small indiscretion a desire to ultimately marry the boy.

By the upper elementary grades, cliques are quite evident, and children who are members or seek membership in the "popular" group are often hyperattuned to fitting in with this group. Children take cues from the dominant members of desired cliques in terms of what they wear, say, and do, often stifling their individuality. The whims of the group can change frequently, leaving a once popular child friendless, at least temporarily (Alder & Alder, 1998).

The behaviors and attitudes children exhibit while part of the group are often not seen when children are alone or with different children in another context. For example, when observed individually, differences between boys' and girls' behavior are minimal, but they become pronounced when enough children are together to break into gender-specific groups (Maccoby 1990). Given the increased involvement of upper elementary children in multiple contexts, they often have several peer groups, and their identity and behavior shifts according to the demands of the group. For example, a boy who may support his playground peer group's exclusion of any girls in their games may welcome girls as part of his church youth group. Any parent who drives upper elementary children to activities notices how their child's behavior changes when with friends from different groups; the bubbly extroverted child among school friends may exhibit a mean, aggressive edge among her soccer friends. Alder and Alder (1998) identified multiple friendship groups among upper elementary children: school friends, neighborhood friends, family friends, telephone friends, summer friends, activity friends. These groups may overlap, but each has slightly different behavioral expectations.

From infancy children respond to other children. Often one of the first words children learn is *baby*, which they gleefully say when they see another baby. Babies accept much rougher treatment from older children than they would from adults. They seem to recognize that they have more in common with children than they have with adults, and they typically favor playing with other children who are close to the same age (James, Jenks, & Prout). Age is an important source of status in cross-age groups. Older children typically make the rules, relegate less desirable jobs to younger children, and may even bully or intimidate younger children. Despite the potential abuse older children may inflict on younger ones, younger children are eager to learn from older children.

Consider . . .

Using peer affiliations to your advantage.

Your students' preoccupation with their peers may drive you crazy at times, but use it to your advantage. Too often we ignore how much children teach each other. I've already discussed this in relation to childhood lore, but it also works for academic content. Group work, peer tutoring, and having students demonstrate to the class different approaches to problems are effective teaching tools. Also allow your students to use their "big kid" status to their advantage. Arrange cross-age tutoring or reading buddies so that your students can bask in the glory of being the older child to younger children. Doing so increases their confidence in their academic ability. This is an activity reserved not only for the most capable students; struggling students benefit greatly from mentoring younger students.

Neighborhood and Community

I began this chapter with a contrast of different out-of-school environments. The idyllic context Rebecca describes contrasts sharply with the grittier contexts of the neighborhoods invoked by the America Promise Alliance figures and teacher quote. It is not hard to visualize the difference in neighborhoods and communities. Rebecca's middle-class community is probably largely residential. The houses are likely separated by well-kept lawns and lush landscaping. The streets are smooth and traffic moves slowly. Businesses are accessible by car. Few people are on the sidewalks or streets, although neighbors know each other and are friendly. The neighborhoods where the teachers work are quite different. Although in different corners of the country, they share many characteristics: dense living; predominance of apartments, small homes, or public housing; mixed residential and business/light industry; reliance on public transportation; constant traffic and noise; considerable adult interaction on the streets or in front of homes. One feature of many neighborhoods is that they are segregated, most often by economic level but also by race and ethnicity. Neighborhoods tend to reinforce people's inclination to affiliate with others who believe and act as they do, and they are comfortable, often feel safe, living around similar people (García Coll & Szalacha, 2004; Harris, 1995).

Geographical location, density, or affluence level does not guarantee that a neighborhood or community provides either a positive or negative environment. Middle-class, suburban children may be able to ride bikes in their neighborhood, swim in community pools, go to the library, and count on neighbors to look out for them. Urban children may experience the vibrancy of city life, walking to stores, parks, libraries, and other resources. Even the most impoverished urban neighborhoods can provide cultural cohesion and support (García Coll & Szalacha, 2004). Rural children may enjoy outdoor experiences, close ties to family and immediate neighbors, and deep connections in small-town communities.

Any of these neighborhoods or communities can also limit children, especially in the upper elementary years when children are gaining more independence and expanding their connections to a wider world. Lareau (2003) described the potential isolation of the overprogrammed upper middle-class children who do not have time or opportunity to get to know the people in their neighborhood. Working-class neighborhoods often lack recreation opportunities, and too many low-income neighborhoods are dangerous and lack healthy recreational options. Because of distance and limited community resources, rural children may have little sense of neighborhood or community and have few options for out-of-school learning.

Whether middle, working, or lower class, a neighborhood or community provides a context that influences children's sense of accomplishment, belonging, and engagement. Ideally, it provides "shared bonds, connections, and common values among community members" (Scales, Sesma, & Bolstrom, 2004, p. 49) that are consistent with family values and that provide a positive context for academic, social, and physical learning. In addition, supportive communities provide access to health, recreation, and human service resources so that children remain healthy and fit and have opportunities to give back to their community (America's Promise Alliance, 2006).

There was a shooting in one of our neighborhoods over the weekend. The kids treated it like no big deal. Some of our older kids were at the party where the shooting occurred. They are desensitized to these things. If a shooting happened in a neighborhood serving my daughter's school, they would have guidance counselors set up to deal with the stress.

—Third-grade teacher

One of the most important aspects of the neighborhood or community is that it provides a safe and nurturing place for children to live and play. Rebecca and Liz were able to roam freely and felt safe, day and night. Their parents undoubtedly warned them of potential dangers, but both the parents and children felt safe in the neighborhood. According to an America's Promise Alliance survey of young people's views on access to safe places, many children do not feel safe in their community and do not have access to nurturing and stimulating places to spend time. Table 5.1 summarizes data from this survey, illustrating that many 8- to 11-year-olds desire better places to spend time, are fearful in their neighborhoods (especially at night), and have real concerns about safety.

Not surprisingly, access to safe and nurturing neighborhoods is not equally distributed to all children. Poor children—most often African American, Hispanic, and recent immigrants—are much more apt to experience the harsh side effects of poverty, crime, drugs, violence, and prostitution

Table 5.1 Children's Perceptions of Safety in Their Neighborhood

Statements about safety in neighborhoods	*Percent of children ages 8 to 11 who strongly or somewhat agreed*
I feel safe walking around alone in my neighborhood during the day	72%
I wish there were more places I could hang out where I could feel safe and have fun	70%
I feel safe walking around alone in my neighborhood at night	34%
People my age aren't really safe anywhere they go because something bad could always happen	57%
In my town, people my age need to watch out for bullies	57%
In my community, too many people my age have guns, knives, or other weapons	20%

SOURCE: America's Promise Alliance. (2006). *Every child every promise: Turning failure into action.*

in their communities and are less likely to have access to health, recreation, and social service resources than more affluent children are (America's Promise Alliance, 2006; Boocock & Scott, 2005; García Coll & Szalacha, 2004; Lareau, 2003). For children living in dangerous neighborhoods, family becomes increasingly important, often vigilantly protecting their children from neighborhood influences. This becomes increasingly difficult as children get older and their neighborhood boundaries expand (Scales, Sesma & Bolstrom, 2004).

Consider . . .

Incorporating community service projects in your classroom or school.

Community service projects provide opportunities for students to feel connected and productive. Building on upper elementary children's desire to be responsible and part of a larger community, these projects work on many levels. If you do not live in the community in which you teach, community service projects provide a good way for you to get to know your children's community better. There are several steps to involving students actively in their community.

- Begin thinking about projects by asking children what they wish they had in their community or about domestic or international issues they would like to address.
- Work through your PTA, parent/community advisory group, or local nonprofit groups to identify potential projects and to obtain necessary funding and support.
- Scale the project so that upper elementary aged students can be successful. For example, they are unlikely to stop drug sales on a neighborhood corner, but they can volunteer at a senior citizen home. They may not be able to raise the money to build a neighborhood swimming pool, but they can initiate a petition drive at the school and in the neighborhood to demonstrate support for increased recreation offerings in the neighborhood.
- Be sure that you include your principal in your planning to be sure that the project is feasible and does not raise liability concerns.

A lot of 8- to 12-year-olds have done amazing things in their communities and the world. For example, Free the Children was established in 1995 by a 12-year-old boy who was moved to advocate for the elimination of child labor. Today it is run primarily by children and supports multiple projects around the world. See http://www.freethechildren.com/index.php for more information.

Other Important Contexts

> *In the third grade, I went to day care. My mom and dad both worked. My mom had to be to work by 7 a.m., so my sister (a year younger) and I were at day care early in the morning. We went to a church. They gave us breakfast, and we watched cartoons in the morning. "Bobby's World" with Howie Mandel was my favorite. Around 8-ish, the church van took us to school. After school, the church van picked us up. We pulled out homework after we arrived. The counselors would check over homework. I also remember eating snacks (animal crackers and juice). We would go outside on the playground, play board games, watch TV, play inside, etc. One time we played hide-and-seek upstairs in the church classrooms. I also remember a piano, and I learned "Mary had a Little Lamb" from a friend. My mom picked my sister and me usually last, around 6 p.m.*
>
> —Melissa, preservice teacher

Clearly day care was a formative experience for Melissa. She spent many hours at day care making friends with children outside of school and interacting with nonfamily adults; it provided her another place in which to belong. She undoubtedly established caring relationships with people who worked at the day care and with other children; she had opportunities for accomplishment and engagement that might not have been available otherwise. Other preservice teachers describe many hours spent in Girl or Boy Scout meetings and events, practicing and competing with sports teams, and at dance and gymnastic studios. Upper elementary children also spend a significant amount of time involved in religious services, instruction, organizations, and—during the summer— day and residential camps.

Increasing numbers of upper elementary children spend several hours each day in some kind of organized, adult-supervised afterschool care. Between 1991 and 1997, the number of children in such care increased from 1.7 million to 6.7 million. Federal funding became available in 1998 for beforeschool and afterschool care for low-income children, increasing the number of students attending afterschool programs (Mahoney, Lord, & Carryl, 2005). Afterschool care provides structure and supervision for children who would otherwise go home to empty houses. It also provides access to academic, athletic, and artistic resources and an opportunity for children to interact socially outside of their regular classroom. Afterschool programs appear to have limited impact on academic performance for middle-class children, but they positively affect low-income children (in terms of academics and motivation) if the programs are engaging, that is, ones that challenge and interest children (Mahoney, Lord, & Carryl, 2005). The difference in impact may reflect differences in access to academic resources and engaging activities for middle-class and low-income students. Too often children who are not in well-designed afterschool programs spend too much time in passive activities such as watching television and hanging out. High-quality afterschool programs provide multiple experiences that encourage accomplishment, belonging, and engagement.

Religious institutions play a major role in many children's lives. In addition to attending religious services, upper elementary children may participate in religious instruction and youth groups. Many Christian families spend the better part of Sunday and at least one night a week at church. By the time children are in fourth or fifth grade, they may be starting catechism or confirmation classes and attending choir practice or youth group meetings. Jewish children often attend Saturday school to learn Hebrew and prepare for bar or bat mitzvahs. Muslim children are also active in their mosque, attending services, Sunday school, and special classes focused on the Qur'an.

During the upper elementary grades, many children become actively involved in service or community organizations. For example, millions of children participate in Boy or Girl Scouts. Both organizations provide children an opportunity to serve their community, gain leadership skills, and participate in activities, such as hiking and camping. Upper elementary boys are moving through Cub Scout levels, working on their Arrow of Light Award to become a Boy Scout, usually by the end of fifth grade (Boy Scouts of America, 2007), and 8- to 11-year-old girls are Junior Girl Scouts (Girl Scouts, 2007).

Many children are actively involved in organized athletics, such as soccer teams, Little League, community sponsored youth league teams, and community swim teams. Additionally, children are part of dance troupes, gymnastic and cheerleading groups, and music and theater groups. These organized activities bring children into contact with other children outside of their school, engage them with nonfamily and nonschool adults, and offer opportunities for accomplishment, both team and individual. Coaches, teachers, other children's parents, and older athletes add another dimension to upper elementary children's lives. In the heat of competition, children may see the best and worst of adult behavior.

Summer activities also provide different opportunities for accomplishment, belonging, and engagement if parents are able to find constructive activities for their children (Duffett & Johnson, 2004). Children who have the opportunity to attend day and residential camps widen their interactions with peers and form strong bonds with counselors and coaches. Residential camps explicitly build connections to the camp community through shared stories, songs, rituals, and activities; a deep sense of belonging forms for campers. For some families summer camps are part of family tradition, with generations going to the same camp. For many children going to camp is the first exposure to people outside family and community and to activities that are unavailable in the children's community.

HOW CHILDREN SPEND TIME OUTSIDE OF SCHOOL

> *Fifth grade was quite a few years ago, but I can still remember how I spent my school days, weekends, and summers. Afterschool was taken up by one of two activities: gymnastics or Girl Scouts. My younger sister and I both attended gymnastics twice a week for about two hours each night. Another night was spent attending a meeting for the Girl Scout troop I was a member of. My sister was also in Girl Scouts. Her meetings were on another day of the week, and I would have to attend because my mom was her troop leader. Friday night was the only night that we didn't have an activity. We never minded the busy schedule because we had friends in gymnastics and Girl Scouts. The weekends were often spent at a Girl Scout event or gymnastics meet. Both of my parents were very involved in what we were doing, so these events turned into family time. The whole family would attend the events and meets, sometimes traveling to other parts of the state for gymnastics. Those weekends that weren't spent at meets and events were spent as a family. The summer was different. We had a relatively not-so-busy summer. We would spend a month with my grandparents and the rest of the summer was spent at home together.*
>
> —Jane, preservice teacher

As the preceding section and Jane's reflection illustrate, upper elementary children learn and interact in many different contexts outside of school. These contexts broaden their world, put them in contact with nonfamily and nonschool adults and children, and give them an opportunity to expand their sense of self to accommodate different contexts and demands. Exposure to different people and contexts challenges children's beliefs and values and provides them opportunities to modify their social interactions and to learn different skills and acquire new knowledge. However, just *being* in different contexts or around different people is less important than what children actually *do* in these contexts.

From Jane's essay she had little time, outside of summer, that was not purposeful and organized or supervised by adults. Through Girl Scouts and gymnastics, she learned many skills and developed close friendships, all under the supervision of adults. Rebecca and Liz, described earlier, spent most of their time organizing their own activities and finding purpose and gaining knowledge on their own. As Figure 5.1 illustrates, children's out-of-school time falls on a continuum from being shaped by adults (in terms of purpose, organization, and knowledge) to being shaped by children. Family time and, in many cases, afterschool programs fall in between the two ends of the continuum. In both cases adults are present and influence activity, but there is room for child-initiated activity. Upper elementary children need a healthy blend of activities that fall along this continuum. Too many adult-driven activities leave children with little time for spontaneous play and raise concerns about children being over-programmed, whereas too little adult attention and supervision leaves children with too much responsibility to use their time well and too few resources to build and develop skills and knowledge. Through involvement in a mix of adult-supervised activities and unsupervised child-initiated activities, children develop social interaction patterns; self-regulation and autonomy; time management; and specific academic, artistic, and athletic skills. They become increasingly knowledgeable members of the culture of childhood.

Figure 5.1 Continuum of Child Activities Within Different Contexts

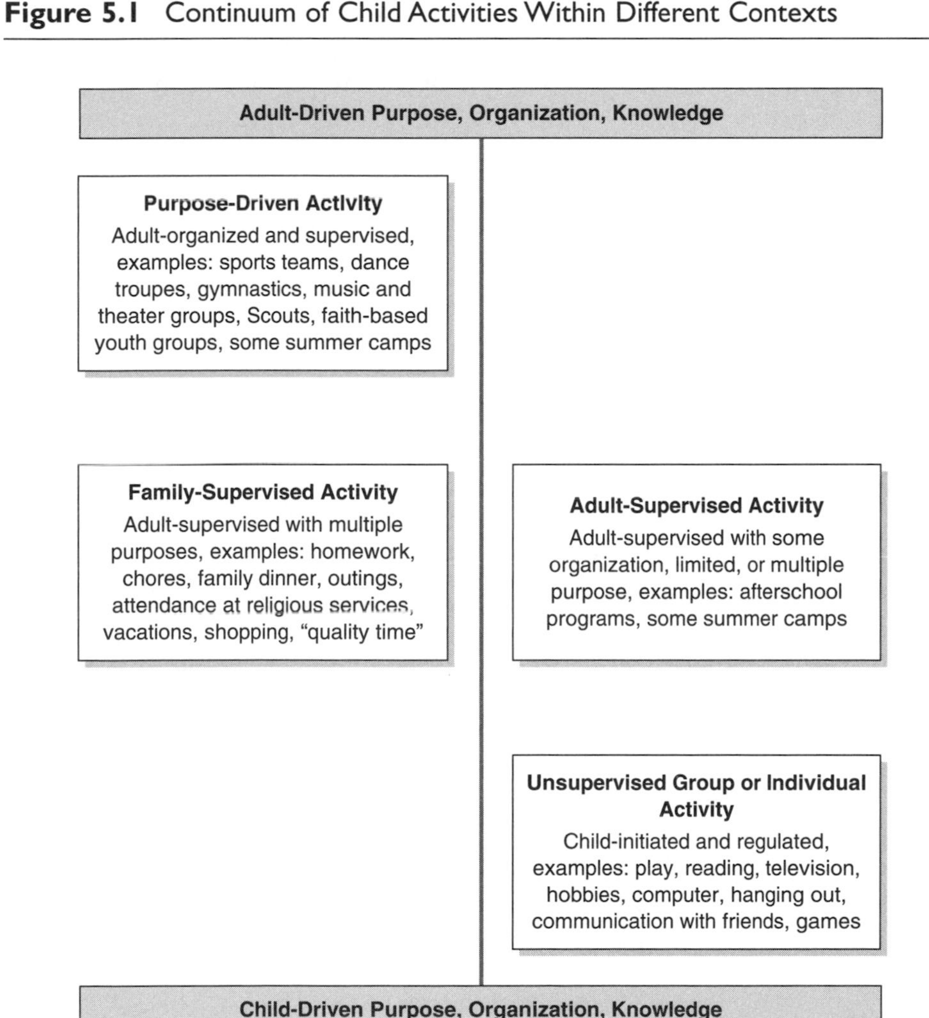

Adult-Organized, Sponsored, or Supervised Activities

Purpose-Driven Activities

Some contexts are organized and structured by adults to ensure that children learn specific skills and have well-defined experiences. For example, Jane's Girl Scout troop and gymnastics team had clear expectations and very well-defined purposes. In Girl Scouts she learned social and leadership skills as well as specific skills determined by her troop but consistent with Girl Scouts of America. In gymnastics she learned the skills necessary to use her body as a gymnast. Sports teams, faith-based youth groups, dance troupes, and musical and theater groups have clear ideas of what children will do in their activities and the specific knowledge and skills they will gain. All of these activities are closely supervised and organized by adults. In addition to doing specified activities and learning specific skills, children involved in these types of activities gain opportunities to work as members of teams, excel (or not) in nonschool settings, and gain a glimpse of other worlds than school and family. Within this structure, and in addition to acquiring skills and knowledge, children also develop relationships with other children that may become the driving force in their participation in these activities. Depending on the orientation of the leaders or coaches and the child's ability or interest, these experiences can build or quash children's sense of accomplishment, belonging, or engagement.

Adult-Supervised Activities

Afterschool programs are organized and supervised by adults but rarely driven by a single purpose. These programs provide adult-organized activities but also allow time and space for children to organize their own activities within the boundaries of the program and under adult supervision. As Melissa described regarding her day care experience, she had to finish homework, and adults were there to help her. Adult-organized activities were available for her, but most of the time she had the freedom to choose her own activities. Many afterschool programs resemble an extended family. Children know that adults are available and are aware of their activities. They understand basic expectations that they all need to meet (e.g., when and where to complete homework, clean-up responsibilities, and expected behavioral expectations). Academic, athletic, and artistic resources are available, although not always to children in low-income homes (Mahoney, Lord, & Carryl, 2005). And children are given considerable latitude to choose how they spend most or part of their time.

Family-Supervised Activities

Children's activities, when under adult supervision at home, vary greatly and reflect the family's values. Members of a family value family time, whether it happens through shared dinners, weekend outings, shopping trips, vacations, or informal evenings watching favorite television shows. Upper elementary children and parents are comfortable spending time together; in fact, children report that they would like to spend more time with their parents (Borland et al., 1995). Families develop comfortable routines doing things together that they value. For example, families that value discussion and sharing ideas set aside time, often family dinners, for discussions; families that value their faith ensure that all family members are active in faith-based activities; and families that value athletics and team sports place such activities ahead of others.

The amount of parental supervision and organization of activities varies within a family (i.e., by the expectations and demands of each individual child, in relation to the developmental levels of children) and across families (i.e., by the amount of time parents have at home, by parental beliefs about proper involvement in children's lives, by competing demands on parents' time). Some parents supervise homework every night, whereas others assume it is the child's responsibility. Some parents insist on a strict bedtime, whereas others vary bedtimes in relation to their child's behavior. Some parents are actively involved in organizing and coaching teams and clubs, whereas others struggle to get their children to the activity or intentionally separate themselves from their children's afterschool activities.

The upper elementary years can be challenging for parents and children as activities that were adult supervised or organized when they were younger (e.g., completion of homework and chores, arranging play dates) become the children's responsibility. This is especially evident in relation to homework, chores, selection of friends, and boundary setting. Parents know that their upper elementary children need and are often capable of greater independence and autonomy than they had as young children. They know that their children need to learn to take responsibility for actions, but parents often have trouble letting go of support they are accustomed to giving their children. Highly ambitious parents fear that allowing their children to suffer the consequences of incomplete homework or poorly executed projects will hurt their children in the long term. Parents may fail to realize that by fourth or fifth grade, their involvement in monitoring and helping in children's decision making is no longer seen by the children as support but as a suggestion of incompetence (Pomerantz & Eaton, 2000). Upper elementary children are also conflicted about parental involvement. In one situation they seek independence but swing back to heavy reliance on parents in another. They want responsibility and autonomy but do not consistently act on this desire (Borland et al., 1998; Krappmann, 1989; Lareau, 2003; Scales, Sesma, & Bolstrom, 2004).

Child-Driven Activities

Although many middle-class children have their out-of-school time filled with adult-driven activities (Lareau, 2003), most upper elementary children spend considerable time with other children or alone away from the watchful eyes of adults. This is not a bad thing, nor is it a modern phenomena resulting from dual income families. Children, especially those seeking to develop autonomy and peer acceptance, want to spend some time away from adults.

Children's Self-Structured Play

In self-structured, child-directed play, children enter the culture of childhood and create worlds in which they set the boundaries, make the rules, and flex their creative energies. Early childhood experts have long recognized the value of play in child development (Bredekamp & Copple, 1997), but it is equally important for upper elementary children. Pediatricians encourage parents and teachers to make more time for self-structured play because it makes children stronger, happier, and smarter (Ginsburg, 2007). The worlds that Rebecca and Liz created in their backyards extended their understanding of the books they read and provided opportunity to use their creativity and imagination. The pickup games that take place in vacant lots and suburban cul-de-sacs provide an opportunity to set rules, negotiate disagreements, and display prowess that may not be evident in school. Children use play to play with adult rules and roles (Finnan, 1982; Thorne, 1993) and to pass on knowledge that they are uncomfortable seeking from adults (James, Jenks, & Prout, 1998).

Upper elementary children's self-structured play differs from that of younger children's because it may involve more rules and a better articulated structure; the children can roam further from home (especially boys), and choice of play is more gender segregated (Finnan, 1982; Thorne, 1993). Although gender segregation in play begins early, it is pronounced in the upper elementary grades. Boys tend to gather for team games or set off on adventures that take them away from their immediate neighborhood. Girls tend to play with fewer friends and engage in more role playing and relationship-focused play. Whether they are organizing a team or a garage theater troupe, upper elementary children's play has a purpose, structure, and organization.

Media-Driven Activities

Children spend a lot of time in media-driven pursuits (e.g., television, movies, recorded music, videos, video games, the Internet). In fact, 8- to 13-year-olds are the most avid media consumers among the 0-to-18-year-old population. And the lower a family's socioeconomic status, the more television their children watch (García Coll & Szalacha, 2004). The media sends powerful messages to children, often ones that parents and teachers find inappropriate for upper elementary children. The emphasis on sexuality and violence in much of the media is evident in many upper elementary children's conversations and actions. Excessive exposure to television limits children's verbal skills, and certain programs (especially cartoons and action shows) increase impulsivity and limit analytic thinking (García Coll & Szalacha). Whether watching television alone or in a group, it is a relatively passive activity that is linked to overeating and obesity. The media, however, can open worlds to children who would otherwise live very isolated lives; it helps children develop technological expertise, and with careful monitoring for content, it can model appropriate social skills. Many children enter the world of electronic social networking in the upper elementary years, keeping up My Space and Facebook pages.

Other Child-Initiated Activities

Children also spend considerable time in less contested activities. Many spend hours, especially during the summer and weekends, reading, doing art or craft projects, and making music. Children this age devour books, especially those in series. Other children develop deep interest in collections, acquiring sports cards, shells, rocks, dolls, and other collectables.

Upper elementary children are also avid consumers. They like to go shopping, and their purchasing power has increased in recent years. They are bombarded with advertising targeted to them in all media. In fact, the term was created when market analysts recognized the buying power of this age group. In *The Great Tween Buying Machine: Marketing to Today's Tweens* (Siegel, Coffey, & Livingston, 2001), the authors explain why marketers should focus on 8- to 12-year-olds:

> The tween segment is the heart of the kids market. Its starting age occurs when kids begin social reading in earnest—meaning that they are beginning to tune in to kids' magazines. It is about the time in which the left hemisphere of children's brains are in the midst of rapid development—giving the power of reason and the mental capacity to understand marketing communication. It is the time in which peer pressure becomes a factor in a person's life and when the urge to grow and become independent and become "not a kid" takes hold. (p. 28)

They add that it is important for businesses to target this market because the tween years are when brand loyalty begins, and that brand allegiance is shaped by peers. Marketers recognize that children this age want to fit in, and they market to children's use of must-have brands to mark popularity. Siegel, Coffey, and Livingston conclude that the most important reason to market to tweens is that "they probably have the most significant influence on household and family purchases" (p. 29). It is not surprising that media consumption and material consumption are closely linked in the upper elementary years.

SUMMARY

Every afternoon when children leave school, they enter different worlds. They reenter the world of families, peer groups, and neighborhoods. Many children also interact in varied other contexts and with a wide variety of adults and children. Children's identities are shaped by each of these contexts and their actions differ according to the expectations and demands of the context. What children do in each of these contexts has a profound affect on their sense of accomplishment, belonging, and engagement.

Some children have little time to themselves as they move from one activity to another. Others spend hours alone, turning to video games, television, social networking Internet sites for stimulation. Between these extremes most children have varied experiences interacting with family and friends, and participating in a variety of organized activities. They move between adult driven or supervised activities to the child driven activities that exist outside of adult intervention. In whatever ways children spend time out of school, their experiences and activities frame how they process new knowledge in the classroom and provide them with other avenues to develop their sense of accomplishment, belonging, and engagement.

Given the importance of out-of-school time to upper elementary children, it is essential for teachers to develop a deep understanding of their students' lives. Consider the following questions.

- To what extent do you know about your students' lives outside of school, including family, friends, activities, interests?
- What can you do to help all of your students have experiences inside and outside of school that will provide them opportunities for accomplishment, belonging, and engagement?
- How can you work with students and families to find the best balance between adult-driven and child-driven activities?
- How can your school work with other community agencies to provide safe and enriching out-of-school activities?

6

The School Environment

Supporting Accomplishment, Belonging, and Engagement

I like to go to school because I so love to learn, not like others. I think people hate school because it takes so long. I love the school because I get to see my friends and play outside, also play sports I don't have at home. School is the best thing in my life, even my parents. This school is the best thing because I get an education. The best thing is that I get homework.

I like to go to school because I can learn stuff I have not now. School is fun, and we can do P.E. That is my favorite subject. I like school because I can read fun books and do projects. I like to go to school because I have friends. I love school because I like a lot of math.

I like to go to school because I have great friends. Also I'm going to try to get a good education. I also have great teachers.

These fourth-grade students express many reasons for liking school. They like to learn, especially certain subjects; they enjoy being with friends and enjoy activities outside of the classroom, and they have teachers they like and respect. These children are lucky because they attend a school that fosters positive interactions in all parts of the school (e.g., classrooms, cafeteria, common areas, playing fields). They like to come to school because they are part of a community that keeps them safe, values them as individuals, and challenges them to do their best academically, socially, morally, and physically. Their teachers like to come to school too because they can count on the school to mirror the environments they create in their classrooms and to support the values they bring to school. Yes, it takes more work to contribute to such a school environment, but to most teachers it is well worth the effort.

School is the most important institution in shaping children's sense of accomplishment. In school children find acceptance and belonging, and engage academically, socially, and physically. For young children school provides an introduction to organized life outside of home. They learn that people other than family can nurture, support, and engage them; they learn to interact with many other children, both those they like and those they do not like; they learn the rhythms, schedules, and procedures of school. These experiences are novel, exciting, and occasionally scary for young children, but typically they enjoy the experience and are confident in their role in the school.

Upper elementary students are familiar with school as an institution, but their relationship with it is more complex. They are beginning to look at themselves and their environments more critically. Some lose their unconditional love of school because of prior experience. A teacher profiled in Ladson-Billings' *Dreamkeepers* (1994) commented, "You want to see intelligence walking around on two legs? Just go into a kindergarten class. They come to school with fresh faces, full of wonder. But by third grade you can see how badly school has beaten them down. You can really see it in the boys. I sometimes ask myself just what is it we're doing to these children" (p. 89). This teacher places the blame for student disengagement solely in the hands of educators, but prior school experiences are not the only thing that influences upper elementary children's attitudes toward school. Developmentally, they are very different from kindergartens, and schools designed to serve kindergarten through fifth or sixth grade need to recognize that older children will question and critique their relationship to school as an institution (Scales, Sesma, & Bolstrom, 2004).

Elementary school structures, practices, and policies have to accommodate a wide range of cognitive, social, and physical developmental levels. By third grade, children seek increased responsibility, autonomy, connection, and meaning. They are more apt to question and doubt. They still seek accomplishment and affirmation, but they begin to perceive that some accomplishments are out of their reach (McDevitt & Ormrod, 2002). They want to belong and be accepted by both adults and peers as they seek more autonomy and independence. Finally, they want a balance of academic, social, and physical engagement (Scales, Sesma, &

Bolstrom, 2004). They approach school radically differently than they did in kindergarten.

Upper elementary children have rather basic desires: accomplishment and affirmation; belonging and connection; academic, social, and physical engagement. But schools' abilities to meet these desires for all upper elementary children are complicated by developmental contradictions; by adults' expectations of what students can and should be able to do; by school organizational structures and procedures; and by national, state, and district policies. For upper elementary children to develop maximally as learners, members of society, and as physical beings, schools need to provide a supportive, nurturing, challenging, and enriched environment that helps them meet these desires. Teachers, as key actors in schools, help to make this happen.

Consider . . .

Working in a school that shares your values, beliefs, and assumptions about students and learning.

When we get our first teaching job, we are so excited about the prospect of setting up a classroom and teaching our first class of students that we don't think too seriously about the importance of the broader school culture and how it intersects with our personal philosophy of education. It is true that as a member of a school faculty we can influence the values, beliefs, and assumptions that underlie the collective actions of the school, but this is a challenge for new teachers who still have a lot to learn.

If you are a new teacher, pay close attention to what people say about the students, community, and expectations about teaching and learning in your interviews. If possible, visit prospective schools before accepting a job. Listen to how adults talk to each other and to students. Do the students appear to be enjoying their experience? Do you feel welcome? What are the main concerns at the school? Do you feel as though people will support you as you start your professional career? You can pick up subtle cues about a school that are important to your teaching success.

If you are an experienced teacher, speak up for what you value. Work with your administrators to look at how you can support the school's efforts in establishing and maintaining an environment that engages everyone. Volunteer to mentor new teachers and help them retain their idealism and hope. Keep the students first, and help establish systems, programs, and opportunities to keep them engaged and connected.

SCHOOL ROLE IN DEVELOPING A SENSE OF ACCOMPLISHMENT

Defining and Measuring Accomplishment

What makes me special is my effort. I try to do my best at everything possible, for example, my chores, homework, and many other things. When I was little, I only had effort in drawing because it was one of my biggest strengths. But as time passed my parents showed that effort wasn't only in my strength but in everything. When I got older, I understood that if I used effort in everything, I would become smarter and, of course, a little more talent. I tried the hardest I could in math, spelling, homework, home reading, and drawing.

I started advancing and I saw my mom and dad and how proud they were. I was exited in seeing my report card. When it came, I ran to my mom and told her to open it. I saw that she too was exited. When my mom opened it and said, "Mija, great! You're going to third grade with an A+." That day I think I got on everybody's nerve because I kept bragging, Well, what can I say? I was happy. And from then on I try my best and the results have been great!

—Fifth-grade girl

As this fifth-grade girl describes, family is very important in encouraging accomplishments, but the school also sets the tone for what adults and students see as an accomplishment. Schools that create a positive learning environment define accomplishment more broadly than just scores on standardized tests; they include multiple avenues to show academic accomplishment, as well as social accomplishments (e.g., tutoring younger children, mediating disputes, taking leadership roles, controlling negative impulses) and physical accomplishments (e.g., excelling in sports or dance, meeting personal goals for physical activity, demonstrating fine motor skills in art or other projects). In these schools students' diverse accomplishments are affirmed.

For accomplishments to be significant to upper elementary children and adults, the school needs to support multiple measures of growth that reflect both individual gain and gains judged in relation to a standard. For example, academic accomplishments are measured in relation to students' prior accomplishments and against the school's expectations of real or authentic learning (Newmann, Bryk, & Nagaoka, 2001; Newmann, et al., 1996) and in relation to state and district expectations as described in standards and shared curriculum expectations. Measures of students' social accomplishments describe movement toward individual goals and school, community, and societal norms for appropriate actions. Physical accomplishments, likewise, are measured by students' personal gains and in relation to other children's performance and normed expectations.

Adult Expectations for Accomplishment

Schools bring together many adults who have expectations for what individual students, groups of students, or all students can or should accomplish. Schools that create positive environments see all students in the school as having unlimited potential as learners, as members of society, and as athletes, artists, or musicians. In these schools all children are expected to make considerable gains and accomplish great things. Adults in these schools do not hold the same expectations for accomplishment for all students, knowing that, as individuals, they differ academically, socially and physically; rather, they help students meet individually appropriate accomplishments. These schools recognize the strengths that come from diversity and use diversity to seek multiple kinds of avenues toward accomplishment. They expect all students to learn, even if they come to school without experiences and resources that facilitate learning. They provide opportunities for them to demonstrate their self-control and responsibility, dealing individually with students who do not meet the school's expectations (Ferguson, 2000; Hale, 1994; National Economic & Social Rights Initiative, 2007).

Student Expectations for Accomplishment

Schools also encourage children to hold certain assumptions about their own and each other's potential for accomplishment. Where schools celebrate all children's accomplishments, children see themselves and others as social, emotional, and academic resources and as positive influences on each other (Noddings, 2005; Pace-Marshall & Price, 2007; Stanton-Salazar, 1997). This is more apt to happen in schools that discourage competition and encourage open access or enjoyment of activities to all students. Although some students will excel and others struggle, the school will not perpetuate the belief that only some children's accomplishments are worthy (Scales, Sesma, & Bolstrom, 2004; Wang & Yang, 2003; Weinstein, 2002).

SCHOOL ROLE IN DEVELOPING A SENSE OF BELONGING

We do so much to make them feel connected. We have schoolwide celebrations, morning meeting of the whole school, cross-grade-level buddies. We have a lot of collaboration in this school, and there is good communication across grade levels. Our shared practices, such as Positive Behavior Intervention System and learning centers in all classrooms, give students consistency.

—Teacher-coach

Inviting Spaces and Warm Adult Relations

Upper elementary students appreciate consistency and life within the boundaries adults create in a school. They may grumble about rules and long to "do nothing" in the comfort of their home, but if the school's structures, routines, and procedures are reasonable and equitably enforced, the school makes children feel safe, nurtured, and connected; their sense of belonging increases. Upper elementary students who attend schools that care and value relationships have higher levels of school satisfaction, better nonverbal communication, better frustration tolerance and on-task ability, improved reading and math scores, and better behavior (Scales, Sesma, & Bolstrom, 2004). Schools make this possible through the way they use space and the kinds of relationships adults have with children.

When I was a superintendent, we built a new building and planned for the cafeteria to closely resemble a restaurant with round tables of six students, individual chairs, tablecloths, and flowers in the center. The change in student behavior between the old school's institutional layout and the new school was stunning. Students sat, visited quietly, and appeared much more relaxed.

—Former school superintendent

In schools where upper elementary children develop a sense of belonging, they know they are welcome all over the campus: in the office, media center, gymnasium, cafeteria, auditorium, playing fields, and halls. Even the spaces where large numbers of students interact at a time (e.g., cafeterias, auditoriums, and gymnasiums) are welcoming and inviting to students, as the former school superintendent's quote indicates. These schools recognize that students need to interact with each other inside and outside of the classroom, and they work with students to develop the social skills needed to converse in and move through crowded settings. Compare this to the lunchroom at this predominantly African American and Hispanic elementary school described by Lewis (2003):

> During lunch the room was a cacophony of sound, with children flowing in and out steadily from 11:20 until 12:15. Each age level had fifteen to twenty minutes to eat lunch before they were shooed into the yard for recess. There was no seating chart, and most students sat with friends from their class. These friendship clusters were almost entirely self-segregated by both gender and race. The

> student advisors and occasionally a classroom aide or teacher circulated through the room keeping students to the business of eating. When the noise level got too high, Mr. Jordan, one of the student advisors, would yell, capture attention by loudly dropping folding metal chairs from the raised stage, or otherwise engage in dramatic means to silence the crowd. On particularly rowdy days, the third-, fourth-, and fifth-graders sometimes spent their entire lunch-period recess "learning how to sit quietly." (p. 42)

Needless to say, this school does not foster a sense of belonging in its cafeteria.

> *As part of our schoolwide behavior system, we identify kids who need an adult to check in with. One boy checks with the secretary three times a day. This has calmed his behavior tremendously.*
>
> —Teacher-coach

Possibly the most important thing school personnel can do for upper elementary children is demonstrate that they care about each child (Noddings, 1992; 2005). They recognize that upper elementary children seek connections with adults, and they provide multiple opportunities for them to do so. By the upper elementary grades, children should have comfortable relationships with adults in the school office, with the principal, and with other support staff, especially school psychologists and counselors. These relationships offer stability and continuity for children. Children change teachers each year, but the office staff, cafeteria workers, bus drivers, and custodians may be constants throughout their years at a school. These nonteaching staff members can play very important roles for students. For example, as the teacher-coach's quote describes, some students, especially those with chronic behavior problems, respond remarkably well to consistent contact with some adult outside of the classroom. A few minutes a day for a quick chat or possibly just a high five can give the child the assurance that he is cared for and provides an opportunity for him to reciprocate care for the adult.

For most children caring relationships with administrators and support staff provide sufficient assurance that they belong at the school. However, some children need additional support from professionals (e.g., psychologists, counselors, social workers, nurses) to make strong bonds with adults and other children. Schools vary in their ability to provide these resources, but those that do recognize that many students lead complicated lives and have unmet psychological, social, and health needs that influence their ability to learn and interact with others. Other children have identified disabilities that may affect their sense of belonging. By law, schools have to provide services to students with exceptionalities, but schools differ in their efforts to include exceptional children as important members of the school community, providing as much interaction with students, teachers, and staff as possible.

Belonging Within the Peer Network

> *I like to go to school because I have great friends. Also, I'm going to try to get a good education. I also have great teachers.*
>
> —Fourth-grade boy

Adults often overlook the fact that children interact in a world within the school that has little connection to adult actions and interventions. Within this world children form connections, exchange forbidden information, establish an ever-changing social hierarchy, and engage in behaviors that often are not permitted within the adult sphere of influence (Boocock & Scott, 2005; James, Jenks, & Prout, 1998). Establishing a peer network is possibly one of the most important functions of school in children's minds. Because of the importance of peer interactions, children's sense of belonging at school typically begins as soon as they leave the house. In some cases they walk, ride the bus, or carpool with friends; in other cases they travel to school alone fearing taunts and rejection. Whatever the case, this sets the tone for their day.

> *Bob was at the top, number one, and Max was number two. They were pretty much the most popular people. Then there was a jump between them and the rest of the group. Nobody was at three, but Marcus was a three and a half, and so were three other guys. A few people were at three and three-quarters, then Josh was a four, and John was a four. Everyone else moved between three and a half and four, including me. It could shift a lot.*
>
> —Fifth-grade boy (Adler & Adler, 1998, p. 78)

> *Chad was the outsider in my fourth-grade class. It was said he picked his nose and ate his boogers. One day a group of students filled the back of his chair (there was a pouch that held books) with tissues. He was teased relentlessly. I felt bad about the way he was treated. However, I sometimes joined in. Chad remained to himself and never really talked to anyone. I don't remember if the teacher did anything. I never got in trouble so I don't think she told my parents.*
>
> —Preservice teacher

The social hierarchy described by the fifth-grade boy is familiar to most of us. The rejected child, unfortunately, is all too familiar as well. Children fall into well-defined categories and can be ruthless in maintaining their roles in the hierarchy (Adler & Adler, 1998). Away from adult control, children use time on the playground, in the cafeteria, and before and after school to work through their social dynamics. Although shifts in the social hierarchy are inevitable, a certain amount of social negotiation occurs between children without adult intervention, and adult-designed nonbullying interventions typically fail (Rigby & Johnson, 2006–07). Schools can blunt exclusion and bullying by promoting a sense of teamwork and belonging and by encouraging students to take responsibility to stop inappropriate behavior that they witness.

Schools that bring together students of different races need to be careful to not allow race to become the overriding influence on all social dynamics in the schools. In *Bad Boys* Ann Ferguson (2000) described how race shapes the role of African American boys in the upper elementary grades in one school, whether they are "troublemakers" or "school boys." School personnel and other students shared and perpetuated a belief that many of the African American boys will end up in prison. Amanda Lewis, in *Race in the Schoolyard* (2003), examined three different elementary schools and found that across schools with different racial make ups and efforts to confront racism, race continued to figure heavily in how adults interact with children and how children interact with each other.

Extending the Sense of Belonging to Family

It is 7:45 in the morning and the cars are snaking through the carpool line. As each car reaches the front of the elementary school, the principal opens the doors on the passengers' side and greets each child by name; before the car pulls away, he leans in and greets the parent, wishing him or her a good day. Meanwhile, other parents are walking their children through the front door. Teachers greet them and many short conversations occur. Some parents are clearly prepared to stay for a while to help in classrooms, the media center, or the front office. For parents who cannot come into the school during the school day, a Web site is actively maintained, describing daily events, providing parenting tips, homework help, and learning extension ideas.

If children are going to develop a sense of belonging in school, their families must feel similarly connected. Family members develop impressions of the school and gauge their involvement in it from their children's experience in the school, their own experience when they were students, the reputation of the school in the community, and the treatment they receive when they interact with school personnel. Families quickly sense if they, and their children, are welcome and valued. The school described in the previous paragraph invites parents as partners in children's learning. Another school described earlier in this book extends a sense of belonging to families by welcoming them to daily morning meetings of the whole school. Even though many parents or grandparents at this school speak little English, they enjoy being part of their children's school and sense that the staff members care about every child. Other schools are not so inviting.

For example, we moved across country when my daughters were going into second and sixth grades. I was in classrooms constantly in their former school and felt valued and welcome. That was not the case in their new school. The carpool system demanded that parents stay in their cars, and classroom doors were closed to all but official staff. Parents came only for organized events or to participate on a parent council that was devoted primarily to fund-raising.

Schools extend a sense of belonging to families by welcoming and reaching out to all families. Family members who had bad experiences in their own schooling, who lack trust in any public institution, who speak little English, or who come from cultures where family involvement is not an expectation respond to family involvement efforts hesitantly and with some trepidation (Lareau, 2003; Weis, Dearing, Mayer, Kreider, & McCartney, 2005). Parents living in poverty often assume that they are being judged, even when school officials have the best intentions (Swadener & Lubeck, 1995). Cultural differences are hard to cross when opportunities to interact are limited and when the cultural divide is wide.

Schools also encourage belonging by recognizing that the nature and extent of family involvement varies. Some families are happy to limit their involvement to making sure their children arrive at school with a backpack and lunch (Thorne, 2005); others enjoy fund-raising and are active participants on committees; others will be seen tutoring and helping in classrooms and in the office. Differences in family involvement sometimes reflect personal choice or circumstances (i.e., working parents' opportunities to be at school during the day are limited), but they also reflect class and cultural differences. Annette Lareau's (2003) comparison of the lives of middle-class and working/lower-class children contrasts the hyperinvolvement of some middle-class parents as they advocate for every advantage for their children against the more passive acceptance of children's fate in school taken by working-class and lower-class parents. Immigrant parents may hesitate to be involved in school in part because of language differences, but also because parents are not involved in schools in their country either because this is not common practice or because educators are viewed as experts (García Coll, Szalacha, & Palacios, 2005).

Extending Belonging to the Community

Schools that create a sense of belonging for students extend this to the wider community. Children see the school as an extension of their neighborhood and are comfortable moving between the two because the worlds of school, neighborhood, and home are fluid. These schools have open doors, bringing in community resources and agencies to work collaboratively, rather than competitively, to provide for children and their families. Because of neighborhood violence, family transience, social isolation, or vast cultural differences between schools and the community, many children do not experience positive connections between their lives outside of school and in the school. Too often they do not feel safe or connected in either the community or school; in some cases they do not even feel safe at home (America's Promise Alliance, 2006; García Coll & Szalacha, 2005).

Where schools assume that the community belongs in the school, they also assume that students belong in the community. They help coordinate opportunities for upper elementary children to give back to the community through engaging in community service activities, such as planting gardens, visiting the elderly, conducting food and clothing drives (America's Promise Alliance, 2006). This involvement not only provides assistance to the community but makes the children feel needed and connected.

SCHOOL ROLE IN ENGAGING STUDENTS ACADEMICALLY, SOCIALLY, AND PHYSICALLY

> *I love P.E. because P.E. is the time I can play hard and let my feelings out. Like when I play dodgeball I throw the ball really hard and dodge other balls being thrown at me.*
>
> —Fifth-grade boy

Academic Engagement

Academic engagement occurs primarily within the classroom, but the school sets the tone for what and how children learn. Schools that seek to engage students academically ensure that all students are involved in what they learn, see the relevance of the learning, and are challenged to think conceptually, to analyze, synthesize, and wonder (Anderson & Krathwohl et al., 2001; Hopfenberg, Levin, & Associates, 1993; Jacob, 2004; Newmann, Bryk, & Nagaoka, 2001). These schools provide opportunities for schoolwide projects, community service activities, and fluid movement between classes and grades. They encourage all teachers to engage students intellectually, not just actively (Kennedy, 2005).

Despite what some school leaders believe, active engagement in learning is the best way to improve performance on standardized tests (Newmann, Bryk, & Nagaoka, 2001). Standardizing and "teacher proofing" curriculum, instruction, and assessment, and focusing on knowledge and skills acquisition rather than conceptual knowledge may appear to better prepare students for tests, but if students are not academically engaged, these efforts typically backfire (Kozol, 2005; Pogrow, 2000), alienating teachers along the way (Education Alliance at Brown, 2004).

Social Engagement

Schools that establish clear, fair, and developmentally appropriate expectations for behavior encourage social engagement as students interact with each other and with adults within these boundaries. These schools are both orderly and joyous; students know how to behave while still having fun and being children. Children have opportunities to develop leadership skills and to guide, mentor, and support younger children before, during, and after school. These schools understand that upper elementary students, given the opportunity and skills, can monitor and mediate disputes outside the classroom, such as on the bus, the playground, and in the cafeteria (see Peace Games, 2007). The use of control and coercion to limit students' social interactions (Ferguson, 2000; Kozol, 1991; Lewis, 2003) is a missed opportunity to build on upper elementary students' growing sense of responsibility. If individual problems are addressed as individual problems and children learn that social norms appropriate to the neighborhood are inappropriate at school, there is no need to make upper elementary students walk silently in single-file lines with their eyes forward, limit recess time, and impose mandatory *silent-lunch* orders (Ferguson, 2000; Lewis, 2003; Sussman, 2006).

Physical Engagement

Schools also establish the value of physical engagement, recognizing that physical activities encourage social and academic engagement as well as overall development. They provide opportunities before and after school for student physical activity and value the importance of recess and physical education. Unstructured play is encouraged at recess and organized physical activity offered in physical education. Accomplishment in play and sports makes school rewarding for many children.

For most children the playground is their favorite place in school because of the liberating experience of recess, a few moments every day to do what they want to do in the company of those they want to play with. Recess offers a chance for spontaneous play, which has been found to support cognitive, social, and physical development as well as emotional well-being (Ginsburg, 2007; Pellegrini & Bohn, 2005; Thorne, 1993). Playing chase games, kickball or soccer, jump rope, or four square; practicing dance steps; or just talking and giggling with friends is often the highlight of children's day and leads to more academic engagement in the classroom.

Too often this time is limited to no more that ten to twenty minutes a day; sometimes no opportunities for physical engagement are offered children. A great controversy today involves reduction or total elimination of recess (Ginsburg, 2007; Pellegrini & Bohn, 2005). Some schools eliminate or drastically reduce recess time because they feel the time is better used for classroom learning, especially as testing nears. Some teachers withdraw recess from individual students or the whole class as punishment. They often later regret doing so because negative behaviors often escalate if children do not have this free time.

SCHOOL CULTURE, ORGANIZATIONAL STRUCTURES, POLICIES, AND PROCEDURES

Schools differ greatly in how they support student accomplishment, belonging, and engagement. In some, students are almost guaranteed to feel connected and to receive acclimation for accomplishments that derive from active engagement in multiple forms of learning. In others the opposite is the case. Many students feel alienated and disengaged, and they accomplish little that the school rewards. These differences arise because schools have very different cultures and organizational structures, policies, procedures, and resources. School cultures set a tone for the school, shaping expectations, assumptions, and beliefs of members of the school community; they determine what is considered normal and possible. Schools' organization, policies and procedures, and resources provide the structure for the school, shaping and directing actions. The school culture and the structural and procedural features of schools combine to create the diverse experiences upper elementary children have in school.

School Culture

I parked my car in the faculty parking lot and must have looked a little lost as I looked for the office. A mother walking her children to school stopped and asked if I needed help. When I said that I was looking for the office, her daughter proudly pointed the way for me and welcomed me to her school. Once in the office, the secretary greeted me warmly. As she started directing me toward the principal's office, a child burst into the office with his hands cupped in front of him; two friends eagerly followed. "Look what I found on the way to school," he beamed. The secretary knelt down and peeked through his fingers at the butterfly inside. The principal came out and also admired it. Asking me to wait a minute, she helped the child find an appropriate container for the butterfly, asked several questions about butterflies, and sent the boys off to their classroom to share it before releasing it back to its environment. When we sat down in her office she sighed, "It's the little interactions with the children that make me love my job."

—Teacher

Throughout this school everyone acts on shared assumptions about children, learning, and community. They celebrate students' accomplishments; the school community includes children's families and their wider community, and everyone grabs opportunities to engage students in learning. The shared assumptions and resulting actions are a reflection of the school's culture. Each school has a recognizable culture that shapes the values, beliefs, and actions of those who work and learn within the school. The school culture sets the boundaries of what is acceptable (Schëin, 1992).

Simultaneously it adapts to the constant change that is part of a complex society; it exists in the present but is shaped by the past. The enduring aspect of culture provides legends, heroes, traditions, and a reputation (Peterson & Deal, 1998). The school culture simultaneously influences and is influenced by each member of the school community. It provides unity while also defining (sometimes restricting) what members see as possible (McQuillan, 1998).

The preceding overview of schools' roles in encouraging accomplishment, belonging, and engagement for upper elementary students illustrates how school cultures define the possible. Where variation exists between schools, it usually reflects school cultural differences. People rarely see that their school's culture limits accomplishment, belonging, and engagement for students. The school culture takes what its members know about students (both collectively and as members of groups) and establishes overarching expectations about what students in this school should accomplish academically, socially, and physically. In addition, it provides a connective web encouraging the same expectations across individual classrooms in the school.

Although considerable variation typically exists among classrooms in most schools, classroom cultures develop within the more general expectations, values, and collective actions of the school. It is difficult for teachers to remain in schools that do not support the kind of culture they want to maintain in their class. They can only close the door and ignore the outside world for so long. Classrooms and the school benefit from open sharing between classrooms, and students feel safer and more connected when expectations for their accomplishments, sense of belonging, and academic and social engagement are shared among the school and each of the classrooms they encounter.

School Organization, Policies, Procedures, and Resources

Meeting the Needs of Different Student Populations

The ability or willingness of schools to welcome and engage all upper elementary students rests in part on the characteristics of the students they serve. Most children attend neighborhood schools, and given that most neighborhoods are relatively homogeneous both socioeconomically and racially/ethnically, so are the schools that serve them. The achievement gaps between groups of students presented in Chapter 3 are reflected in school performance ratings and in the expectations people within and outside of the schools have for their students. Reporting requirements by subgroups (i.e., race/ethnicity, socioeconomic status, language, exceptionalities) bring to light different achievement levels and possible differences in expectations within more diverse schools. Whether the population is homogeneous or heterogeneous, schools need to ensure that children across all groups have multiple and diverse opportunities for accomplishment, belonging, and engagement.

The upper elementary grades are nested in a wide variety of school configurations, which impacts how students' needs are met. Variations include K–12, K–8, K–5 or 6, and the intermediary Grades 3–5 (Stevenson, 2006). The grade configurations change the school experience for upper elementary children dramatically. For example, intermediate schools can focus solely on the academic, social, and physical needs and developmental levels of upper elementary children; fine-tune their focus on appropriate upper elementary curriculum, instruction, and assessment; and narrow school and classroom environments to upper elementary students. However, intermediate schools have drawbacks. They necessitate more transitions that are linked to achievement loss (Renchler, 2000, in Stevenson, 2006); they eliminate opportunities for upper elementary children to serve as the "big kids" to younger children; they end contact with primary-grade teachers; and they complicate parents' efforts to remain active. K–8 schools require fewer transitions, but upper elementary students are easily overlooked as the needs and demands of young children and young adolescents are met.

Leadership

School leadership and organizational structures are typically of little interest to children, but children do recognize when school leaders shape a school that encourages accomplishment, belonging, and engagement. In some schools the only time children see the principal is when they have done something wrong. They may feel the teacher's tension when the principal looms in the back of the classroom, or they may flee to remote corners of the playground when the principal comes outside. In other schools the principal greets the children by name, is a warm figure who serves as a sounding board for problems, and is a frequent, welcome, and active participant in the classroom.

Leaders who facilitate effective schools keep the moral purpose of schooling at the forefront of all school decisions (Fullan, 2007; Sergiovanni, 2006). They think first about what is best for children and the larger society; they focus more on values and ideas than on processes; and they ensure that all voices are heard. They make few executive decisions and resist merely enacting policies and directives from the central office. Their first instinct when making decisions is what is best and right for children. Then they concern themselves with creating an environment in which those decisions can be enacted. Given the pressures on schools today and directives from the federal, state, and district levels to improve test scores above all else, this is not an easy task.

Schools that encourage accomplishment, belonging, and engagement have stable leadership and shared, collaborative decision making. Described as *distributive leadership* (Spillane & Diamond, 2007), the workings of the school are transparent, and roles and responsibilities are distributed across all school community members. The roles of principals, other administrators, teachers, and staff are clear, and when possible and desirable, responsibilities are shared. By distributing leadership across the school community, everyone, including students, develops ownership in the workings, reputation, and climate of the school. Typically, structures are in place for shared decision making, inquiry into issues, and implementation of innovations (Finnan & Meza, 2003).

Working collaboratively to include faculty, staff, family members, and community members in your school.

What systems do you have in place at your school to examine what happens in your school and to take action in areas that need improvement? Schools vary greatly in their governance structures and willingness and ability to examine existing practices and take action to improve them. The school leadership has a lot to do with this, but as a teacher you can do your part to press to know more about how your school extends a sense of belonging to everyone and to take action to make your school more inviting. The first step is to become an active participant in the existing governance structure. If a structure exists that includes all faculty, staff, and parents, become an active participant in the committees, teams, or cadres at your school. If the structure is limited to a smaller group (e.g., a school council, leadership team, steering committee), try to become a member of this committee, or communicate regularly with members of the committee.

Maintaining a Safe and Orderly School

Ensuring that the school is safe and orderly is essential to engaging students and creating a climate for belonging. Schools need to find the right balance in establishing behavior and safety systems so that they are neither oppressively strict nor excessively lenient. Effective schoolwide behavior systems reward positive social interactions and have many of the following features:

- common language to describe behavioral expectations;
- attention to children's ideas and concerns;
- engaging classroom instruction across the school;

- clear expectations for student behavior that reflect students' desires and input;
- adult modeling of appropriate interactions;
- agreement on clear and consistent procedures for rewarding positive behavior and discouraging negative behavior; and
- use of data to understand individual behavior and provide additional support targeted to those students who need it. (Adapted from National Technical Assistance Center on Positive Behavior Interventions and Supports, 2007, and from Fenning & Rose, 2007)

Schools help students create community by providing them skills, such as peer mediation strategies, that they can use to help peers or younger children talk through disputes (see Peace Games, 2007, as an example). Others provide social and emotional skills training to all students either during school (Barrett & Salovey, 2002) or after school as a primary focus of afterschool programs (see Wings for Kids, 2007 as an example). In safe and orderly schools, everyone understands that it is better to identify the few students with serious behavior issues and address these individually than to establish punitive rules for the whole school.

Organizing Learning Experiences

Depending on the district, schools do have some discretion in determining how to meet state content standards and how to use human and material resources. For example, schools decide if upper elementary students are best served by one teacher teaching all subjects or several teachers focusing on one or two content areas, with either children or teachers changing classrooms. Many teachers like the latter approach because they can focus on their areas of strength and interest; they see departmentalization as a preview of how most middle schools are structured. Others prefer to work with one group of students so that they have more flexibility, can more easily integrate curriculum, and have more opportunity to develop close bonds within the classroom.

Decisions about grouping students for instruction have a profound impact on student engagement and sense of accomplishment. Addressing student academic diversity in the upper elementary grades is a challenge for most elementary schools. Decisions to group students by ability for all or part of the school day have been the subject of heated debate for years (Oakes 1985; Oakes, Wells, & Datnow, 1997). Some argue that ability-grouping across classes and even grades allows teachers the opportunity to fine-tune curriculum and instruction to children's needs and set realistic goals for accomplishment. However, this is true only when groups are flexible and allow all children access to engaging, conceptually challenging work. Most research shows that ability-grouping relegates groups of students, most often poor minority students, to a steady diet of basic skills work (usually through worksheets and drill) and widens the achievement gap between low and higher ability students (Oakes, 1985; Oakes, Wells, & Datnow, 1997).

Student engagement is most problematic for struggling students. Most schools try to provide additional support for struggling or failing students through tutoring, summer programs, or afterschool assistance, but they also frequently resort to grade retention in the hope that a second year will help struggling students. Thousands of students are retained each year in the upper elementary grades (Bali, Anagnostopoulos, & Roberts, 2005; Center for Mental Health in Schools, 2006; Nagaoka, & Roderick, 2004); given retention's link to disengagement and eventually dropping out of high school (Center for Mental Health in Schools, 2006; Roderick, 1993), it should be a decision of last resort.

Schools have some discretion in how they encourage engagement and build a sense of accomplishment and belonging for exceptional learners. Criteria used to identify children for these services are developed beyond the school, and states and districts have policies on how to provide services. But schools typically set schedules for how personnel are used, when and to what extent pullout programs are used, and how and when exceptional students are integrated into the rest of the school. Full inclusion of special education students is much more widely practiced today, and it provides the opportunity for regular and special educators to work collaboratively. Many schools begin offering special services for children identified as gifted or talented in the upper elementary grades (National Association for Gifted Children, 2005). These services help set a higher bar for gifted students' accomplishments, but they add a level of complexity to teachers' schedules and call attention to students' academic differences.

Linking to Social and Community Services

Many elementary schools extend the sense of belonging to the community through active partnerships designed to provide additional support for students and their families and to involve students in helping their community. Nonprofit organizations (e.g., Communities in Schools, faith-based groups, Boys and Girls Club, YMCA/YWCA), business partners, and social and health service organizations come to or are linked to the school to provide services for students. A growing number of schools, particularly those serving children in poverty, provide access to health care and other social services at the school site. These services are often available to the whole family and address health, housing, and other social needs that hinder children's ability to learn. These full-service schools develop healthy relationships with other social and health service providers and exchange nonconfidential information about children and families.

Upper elementary students are more apt to enjoy a sense of accomplishment and belonging if they are given a chance to contribute to the community. Schools can arrange for children to become involved in community service, such as planting gardens, visiting the elderly, and conducting food and clothing drives (America's Promise Alliance, 2006). They also combine community service with inquiry projects, involving children in finding or testing solutions to real community problems (e.g., charting traffic patterns, determining the effect of new developments or roads on existing neighborhoods, determining the effect of pollution on wildlife). Such involvement not only assists the community but makes the children feel needed and connected and promotes active engagement in learning.

Involving Families

As described earlier, students' sense of belonging is tied to their family's sense of belonging. Schools have structures to involve families through organizations such as the PTA/PTO or through school site councils, steering committees, and advisory boards. These organizations or governance units are important avenues for family involvement, but schools need to recognize that people active in them do not represent all families. If processes are not in place to assure equitable distribution of personnel and services, more assertive parents may try to manipulate school processes to ensure that their children have the best teachers and receive services or opportunities that may be limited, such as enrollment in gifted programs or roles in school plays (Lareau, 2003). Schools that encourage belonging convey the message to parents that all students are valued, including their children, and that decisions are made fairly and systematically.

Resources

The library of an inner-city elementary school is down a dark staircase in the basement of the old brick structure. It is open whenever possible, but the school does not have a full-time librarian or media specialist, so most of the time it is closed. The room is the size of a small elementary school classroom; books fill about three-fourths of the stacks that line the walls of the windowless room. Scanning the book selection, it is difficult to find books published after 1990. Many in the school's collection date to the 1960s. A single computer stands in the corner of the room. It is unclear if it works or not.

Located on a barrier island off the East Coast, the elementary school's media center has a panoramic view of the Atlantic Ocean; the room is spacious, with child-sized desks in the center and individual reading areas tucked away in corners of the room. Stacks of books are kept up to date by the full-time media specialist, and each classroom has a designated time to work with her on special projects and topics of interest. Although the district library budget is limited, parents happily donate books in recognition of their children's birthdays, and the active PTA is able to raise thousands of dollars to keep the books and computers in the media center up to date. After school, children eagerly visit the media center to pick out books and visit with the media specialist.

The media centers described here are a graphic illustration of the resource disparity between schools in the United States. The schools differ greatly in the resources available for facilities, personnel, and educational materials and supplies; that the first school serves primarily poor, minority, and immigrant children and the second school exclusively affluent White children is probably no surprise. Across the country schools serving poor, minority, or immigrant children often have less money to spend per pupil and greater need for special services, such as counseling, translators, special education, and family outreach; all of these services are costly. Since *Brown v. Board of Education* called attention to educational inequity in the United States, awareness of resource disparity between schools has risen, but the disparities continue (Ladd & Hansen, 1999).

Unlike that in most other countries, education in the United States is funded primarily through state and local, rather than national, funds. Considerable disparity between states exists in school funding. For example, in 2004 New Jersey spent $12,981 per pupil for public elementary and secondary schools, whereas Utah spent $5,008. This same year state governments provided 47.1 percent, local sources, 43.9 percent, and the federal government, 8.9 percent of the cost of public K–12 education (U.S. Census Bureau, 2006). Disparities exist within states because most often the cost of funding schools is split fairly evenly between state and local resources (Ladd & Hansen, 1999). For example, although suburban schools typically have more money to spend per pupil than urban and rural schools have, a comparison of disparities between two suburban schools in Illinois found that an elementary school in an affluent Chicago suburb spent $22,508 per student, whereas an elementary school in a less affluent suburb spent $8,675 per student (Rich School, 2004). Needless to say, the first district was able to offer many enrichment activities to students (e.g., a forensics lab, new musical instruments, field trips) that the other school would never dream of offering. Federal funding, much of which is targeted to schools serving low-income children, still does little to address the resource inequities; in fact, many federal mandates, No Child Left Behind as a prime example, cost more money for schools to implement than federal funds cover (National Education Association, 2006).

The inequities do not mean that underfunded schools cannot encourage student accomplishment, belonging, and engagement. The first school, despite its old building and inadequate media center is also the school that welcomes children and families with a daily morning meeting, that engages students in active learning in its classrooms, and that links students needing extra adult attention with nonteaching mentors. The building is clean and well cared for; children follow simple routines to ensure that everyone is safe, and each classroom is flooded with natural light from large windows. Yes, the building is old, but people take pride in the school and how it is maintained.

The greatest, and most expensive, resources in schools are its people. Children need highly effective professional and classified staff both inside and outside of the classroom. If you are lucky enough to have professionals such as psychologists, counselors, social workers, and nurses, make good use of their services; they can make a huge difference for students with pressing social and emotional needs.

Consider . . .

How you work with other adults across your school.

Every school has professional and support staff who can greatly assist you in the classroom. You are missing a great resource if you do not involve these people actively in your classroom. The school counselor, psychologist, and social worker are able to work one-on-one with students to gain a deeper insight into issues they may face. The special area teachers (e.g., physical education, art, music, media center, foreign language) see talents and social interaction patterns you may not see in the regular classroom. Special education and ESOL teachers become invaluable resources in your classroom. Noninstructional staff members (e.g., office support, bus drivers, custodians, cafeteria workers) also see another side to your children. Often they live in the community and know the children in other contexts. Finally, the principal and assistant principal are there to support you. They are the instructional leaders in the school and have a profound impact on its culture. In addition to shaping the school culture, they serve as a bridge to the district office, are responsible for the smooth operation of the building, and spend considerable time with families and community members. Despite these many responsibilities, they are advocates for you and your students. They can more easily advocate for you if they know you and your students well.

Teachers with more experience, advanced degrees, and National Board certification cost more than inexperienced, entry-level teachers and tend to concentrate in more affluent schools. For example, 81 percent of the National Board-certified teachers teach in schools in the top two-thirds of their state's accountability ranking (Humphrey, Koppich, & Hough, 2005, in Berry, Raspberry, & Byrd, 2007). These exceptional teachers are not only concentrated in the schools that need them least but cost states and districts more to employ, further exacerbating funding inequities.

Ideally, all schools would employ a range of experienced and novice teachers, have sufficient teachers to support low student-teacher ratios, have necessary support professionals (counselors, psychologists, parent coordinators, social workers, nurses), and enjoy flexible staffing so that mentor teachers have the time to work closely with new teachers and all teachers can participate in ongoing professional development. However, school budgets are usually very tight, and one funding decision, whether made at the school, district, or state level, usually has implications for other funding decision. Whether class-size reductions (often limited to the primary grades), teaching assistants in selected classes, teacher-coaches, or resource teachers, personnel decisions have huge impacts on how schools provide the support children need.

SUMMARY

School serves as the most important institution in children's lives, and it shapes their development as learners, members of society, and healthy, growing individuals. Its influence is positive when it provides multiple opportunities for accomplishment, a safe and caring place to belong, and opportunities for academic, social, and physical engagement. Upper elementary students have a more complex relationship to school than younger children have. Their prior schooling experiences, a developmental inclination toward more self-criticism, and pressure to meet increasingly high standards can lead to disengagement if the school does not provide a supportive environment. With school cultures shaping expectations and assumptions, and school structures and processes shaping actions, schools find the balance between seeing upper elementary children as a collective and as individuals while recognizing, accommodating, and, when necessary, combating, social and cultural assumptions that work for or against groups of students.

Here are key questions to ask about your school.

- How does my school define accomplishment and does it ensure that all children have the opportunity to achieve authentic accomplishments?
- Are certain groups of students more or less likely to have their accomplishments acknowledged? What reasons are usually given to explain these differences?

- Do all students and their families feel like they belong in my school? Do they feel welcome, safe, and connected in all of the public spaces (e.g., office, halls, cafeteria, playground)?
- Are social and behavioral expectations clear and resources available to students who struggle to meet these expectations?
- How does my school define academic engagement? How do accountability pressures influence this definition?
- What opportunities do all students have for social and physical engagement? How are they balanced in relation to academic achievement?

7

The Classroom Environment

Supporting Accomplishment, Belonging, and Engagement

When I was a principal, I met with the fourth- and fifth-grade teachers as a group to talk about how we would meet the social and emotional needs of these kids. We didn't talk about curriculum and instruction; we focused on making sure they felt connected and valued. This is something that comes naturally in the primary grades, but it's much harder in fourth and fifth, given all of the pressures on teachers. I did this because I know that children this age really need connections with each other and with adults. We determined that every day children in these grades needed some time to work in small groups and to have some one-on-one interaction with adults. That is hard with thirty students in a room. We worked together on this so that teachers were able to step out of their roles and think creatively about how we could use school resources to make this happen on a regular basis. That was about five years ago. When I work with schools now, all I hear is, "This skill, that skill, RIT bands, MAP (Measuring Academic Progress) tests." There is no thought to finding time in the day to support children other than to address math and reading weaknesses. I am saddened to think about what we are doing to children.

—Former elementary principal

Schools are important institutions in children's lives, but primarily because they house the classrooms where children have their most significant learning experiences. Most upper elementary children are comfortable in their school and familiar with its routines, rules, and organization. They are also familiar with life in a classroom, with its rhythms, routines, and procedures. Unlike school, which stays relatively stable, upper elementary students know that each classroom is different due to a different configuration of classmates, different grade level expectations, and, most important, because each teacher sets a different tone and interacts with students in his own way. By the time they reach third grade, students have probably had three teachers, each with a different style, personality, and focus. A student may have thrived in one classroom and struggled in another; he may have enjoyed the company of his classmates and his teacher more in one class than another; he may have felt more or less successful in different classes.

By third or fourth grade, students may feel like they know what to expect in a classroom, but many children are shocked at the change in climate and expectations between primary grades and upper elementary grades. As the former principal stated, life in upper elementary classrooms is often very different from that in primary grades. Differences include

- a shift in focus toward teaching content away from nurturing children;
- larger class sizes;
- teacher expectations for increased responsibility for homework and assignments;
- more rigid demarcations between content areas;
- increased emphasis on standardized testing; and
- puberty for self and peers.

The move from primary to upper elementary grades does not have to be a hard transition if teachers shape their classrooms to foster the same set of attributes that characterize effective schools: accomplishment, belonging, and engagement. By third grade, and especially in fourth, fifth, and sixth grades, expectations for accomplishment change. In relation to academic accomplishments, students are expected to use basic skills developed in the primary grades to learn more complex material. Their performance is monitored through paper-and-pencil tests and their yearly progress through standardized testing. They are increasingly aware of how they compare to classmates and to a general performance expectation. Expectations for social and physical accomplishments also become more demanding, and children are aware of their performance in relation to that of others.

Fostering a sense of belonging in the upper elementary classroom is also more complicated than it is in primary grades. Students want desperately to belong and to fit in, but they are also becoming more aware of their differences and judge themselves and others more critically. Peer relations become more complex, as do relations with adults; teachers quickly learn that these students don't unconditionally love them, but they want their teacher's approval and support.

Finally, although upper elementary students retain interest in learning, it is more difficult to engage them academically and more complicated to engage them socially and physically. Teachers in these grades are under pressure to ensure that all students meet content standards at the same time that some students are losing confidence and potentially disengaging. As Mary Kennedy (2005) wrote, "Upper elementary teachers . . . struggle with the competing ideals of nurturing students who are still young and emotionally immature, of managing students who are nevertheless old enough to be more brazen and boisterous, and of helping them learn important academic content" (p. 25). Social engagement also becomes more complex as children enact the social hierarchy described in previous chapters and as cultural and socioeconomic differences become more evident to them. Whereas most young children enjoy physical activity, many upper elementary children become less physically active than when they were younger, often because they do not live up to high expectations demanded of organized sports or because they spend more time with video games, television, and the computer. This contributes to a vicious cycle because lack of engagement in sports and physical play leads to less social engagement (Causgrove Dunn, Dunn, & Bayduza, 2007).

As this chapter illustrates, the classroom is a significant environment for teachers and students, but we need to recognize that expectations of what constitutes accomplishment, belonging, and engagement differ for each member of the classroom, especially between the teacher and her students. Children seek a safe haven where they will learn, accomplish goals, have fun, interact with friends, and be appreciated. The teacher's aspirations for herself and her students are not just her own; they also reflect the expectations of the state, district, profession, and parents to teach multiple subjects, prepare all students to perform well on standardized tests, meet the needs of twenty to thirty diverse learners, maintain a smoothly running classroom, complete required paperwork, and calmly address myriad other challenges (Kennedy, 2005). These differences in intention become more pronounced when students bring suspicion, anger, and resentment into the classroom. In these situations otherwise highly effective teachers struggle to create positive learning environments until they learn to take the time to show their students that they care and believe in them (Sussman, 2006). This chapter explores how teachers create and maintain classroom environments that shape students' sense of accomplishment, belonging, and engagement, focusing on how the classroom culture and classroom organization, routines, and procedures facilitate or hinder this development.

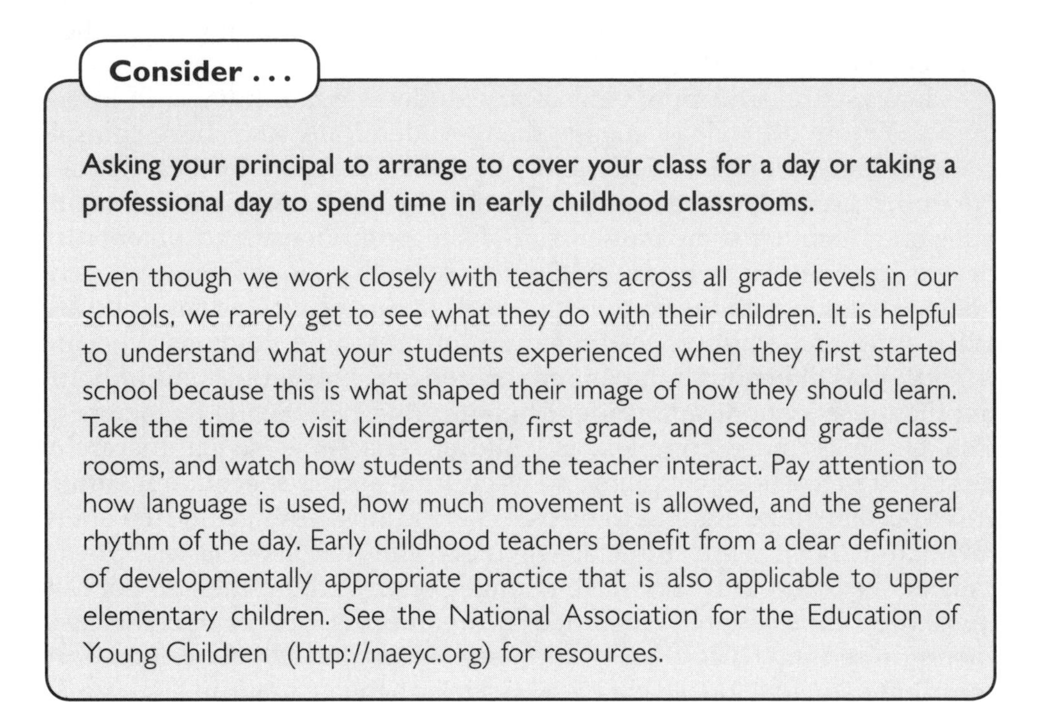

Consider . . .

Asking your principal to arrange to cover your class for a day or taking a professional day to spend time in early childhood classrooms.

Even though we work closely with teachers across all grade levels in our schools, we rarely get to see what they do with their children. It is helpful to understand what your students experienced when they first started school because this is what shaped their image of how they should learn. Take the time to visit kindergarten, first grade, and second grade classrooms, and watch how students and the teacher interact. Pay attention to how language is used, how much movement is allowed, and the general rhythm of the day. Early childhood teachers benefit from a clear definition of developmentally appropriate practice that is also applicable to upper elementary children. See the National Association for the Education of Young Children (http://naeyc.org) for resources.

CLASSROOM ROLE IN DEVELOPING A SENSE OF ACCOMPLISHMENT

> *I am special because I am musically talented. I am a beautiful, smart, healthy, young lady. I am also special because there is no one else just like me.*
>
> —Fifth-grade girl

Academic Accomplishment

> *These teachers hold high expectations for all students and communicate their belief that all students will participate and learn, including students for whom English is a new language and students with exceptional needs.*
>
> —Middle Childhood/Generalist, National Board for Professional Teaching Standards, 2001, p. 23

It is hard to argue with calls to assume that all children can learn or to hold high expectations for all students, but this is definitely one of those exhortations that is easier said than done. One complication is that, as described in Chapters 3 and 4, upper elementary teachers accommodate very diverse students in their classrooms; individual and group differences are wide, and the reasons for these differences are complex. Diversity does not mean that each of these individuals cannot learn; it means that each may begin at a different place, learn differently, have different interests, or require a different relationship with the teacher. Another complication is that we assume that we agree on what "high expectations" means; but, in fact, we do not. For some people high expectations are tied completely to meeting content standards and doing well on standardized tests. For others high expectations also function within the framework of content standards but tie in expectations to more authentic measures of achievement (Newmann, Bryk, & Nagaoka, 2001; Newmann, et al., 1996).

To foster a sense of academic accomplishment, teachers identify the place where each child is challenged and guide the children as they "reach at least a rung or two higher than they themselves can climb" (Wasley, Hampel, & Clark, 1997, p. 76). Because the child reaches higher than he expects, this learning is a personal, meaningful accomplishment. Where he stands in relation to standards is still important, but more important is the accomplishment of greater learning than the child expected. With a focus on academic accomplishment, teachers recognize and build on individual talents, interests, cultural and social background, and favored ways of learning while addressing challenges.

With between twenty and thirty diverse individuals in each class, creating an environment that fosters academic accomplishment for all is difficult. Teachers have to orchestrate competing demands. They must plan carefully and think quickly on their feet. They need to balance challenging and nurturing students. They must maintain lesson momentum and encourage student interests and ideas. And they must follow routines and act spontaneously (Kennedy, 2005). During most lessons teachers make many small decisions that influence the nature and degree of student learning. For example, a student asks a question that indicates a level of interest or knowledge beyond that of most of the class. Does the teacher encourage the precocious child and risk losing the rest of the class, or ignore the child and continue with the lesson? Does the teacher praise children for trying even when their answers are wrong or indicate shallow thought, or does she push them to think more deeply or carefully, risking discouraging future attempts to answer questions? These small decisions influence the nature and degree of academic accomplishment, especially for children who have a history of poor academic performance (Delpit, 1995; Dweck, 2006; Kennedy, 2005; Ladson-Billings, 1994).

Consider . . .

Developing strategies for returning to students who need more help.

Maintaining lesson momentum in the face of student diversity is a challenge. Although our intentions to come back to students who have questions or comments are good, we often forget. Try keeping a set of "I Owe You an Answer" cards with you, and give them to students who have questions or comments that are best answered individually. Or ask students to write a note on the board that will remind both of you of a question that arose. This validates the student and encourages her to question and extend learning while keeping the lesson moving.

Children are more apt to develop a sense of academic accomplishment when they learn with peers who expect them to accomplish academically but who also recognize that each child's accomplishments will be different. They learn that diversity means difference, not deficit (Nieto, 2000). Since upper elementary children are beginning to judge themselves in relation to others and are looking to peers for acceptance and confirmation, they need to learn in an environment that encourages cooperation over competition, honors cultural or social differences (Weinstein, Curran, & Tomlinson-Clarke, 2003), and provides multiple opportunities to demonstrate learning (Tomlinson & McTighe, 2006). Upper elementary students read signals from their teachers and are quite accurate in placing themselves and peers in the academic achievement hierarchy. Depending on the climate in the classroom, this knowledge can be used to encourage all learners (e.g., celebrating individual accomplishments) or can divide the room into the achievers and the nonachievers (Weinstein, 2002).

Social Accomplishment

I'm special because I think that I'm nice and special to people. It makes me special because I'm Mexican and talk bilingual.

—Fourth-grade girl

It makes me special because I help people when they get hurt.

—Third-grade girl

Typically we limit our thinking about accomplishments to academics. We praise students for getting good grades and scoring well on tests, but upper elementary students are also capable of a wide range of social accomplishments. Social accomplishments include taking responsibility for themselves and others, completing work independently, getting along well with others, mediating disagreements, and assuming leadership roles. As described in Chapter 4, children differ in their maturity and ability to interact socially with each other and adults. For a child who struggles to complete homework, one week of on-time homework is an accomplishment worthy of acknowledgment; for another child, homework completion is not an accomplishment since she always completes homework, but initiating a community action project would be a major accomplishment.

When encouraging and celebrating social accomplishments, teachers need to recognize that upper elementary students are excited about assuming more independence and responsibility and try to be good friends, but that they are still developing social skills and are inconsistent in exhibiting social maturity (Jarolimek, Foster, & Kellough, 2005). Their path to social accomplishments is likely bumpy. Their teachers find a fine balance that allows students opportunities to be responsible and independent in an environment where it is safe to make mistakes, where they are given multiple chances to succeed, and where they are treated with dignity and respect (Noddings, 1992). Children are unlikely to feel capable of social accomplishments if they are not given the opportunity to take responsibility for their actions or are severely punished when they do not meet expectations.

Consider . . .

Spending more time than you think should be necessary to provide clear instructions for group work.

Most of us realize that children learn more when they work together in groups, but we become frustrated when they do not work together as we hoped. Remember that they are learning to act responsibly and need guidance on how to assume and share responsibility. If you find that your students are not good at group work, be sure that you give them clear instructions on what they are to do in the group, what roles they should assume, and what the final product should be. Be sure that there are roles for each group member (e.g., facilitator, recorder, illustrator, timekeeper, instruction reader, materials go-fer, etc.) and that roles rotate so that all children have a chance to develop skills. For more resources on effective group work, see your guidance counselor or see the Cooperative Learning Center at the University of Minnesota, http://www.co-operation.org/.

As described later in this chapter, children are more apt to enjoy social accomplishments in classrooms that establish a strong sense of community, where students expect and demand responsible behavior from each other. In this environment the teacher assumes the role of a coach, encouraging students to combine talents to work together for the advancement of the group (Ladson-Billings, 1994). These classrooms also foster kindness, leadership, and inclusiveness among children. Upper elementary children are capable of great kindness and cruelty, and their behaviors reflect their environment. In classrooms that function as communities, they are more apt to treat each other with respect, whereas in classrooms that foster competition or that limit opportunities for social interaction, fewer children will enjoy social accomplishments.

Physical Accomplishment

Most sports are designed to celebrate physical accomplishment, and many upper elementary children participate in at least one sport. Given that games have clear expectations for accomplishment, even losers can feel as though they have accomplished something if they play beyond their expectations and if game organizers downplay the importance of winning. Physical accomplishments, whether in organized sports and games or in spontaneous play, are extremely important for many children and may offset academic or social struggles (Causgrove Dunn, Dunn, & Bayduza, 2007; Ogbu & Simmons, 1998; Solomon, 1992). Given that most physical activities occur outside of the classroom, physical accomplishments may not be as evident to teachers. Also, with the single-minded emphasis on academics in many elementary schools, teachers may not want to divert attention from lessons by allowing students time for physical activity during recess or by praising athletic success.

Physical accomplishments are most evident on the playground, but they also occur in the classroom. For some children who struggle to remain in their seats or who learn best in motion, a physical accomplishment may be learning to control physical impulses or upholding their end of an agreement with the teacher about appropriate movement in the classroom. Physical accomplishments are not only tied inherently to gross motor activities but also reflected in students' gains in fine motor activities, such as handwriting, drawing and painting, crafts, and keyboarding. Again, with so much focus on academic accomplishments, these accomplishments may not receive much acclaim.

CLASSROOM ROLE IN DEVELOPING A SENSE OF BELONGING

Belonging in a Community

The first two weeks of school are spent building community. We get to know each other at this time. I have them prepare "me bags" that help them talk about themselves, their family, and what they like. We establish the rules together and talk about my expectations and theirs. We have a constitution that we all sign. We have a community circle that meets weekly unless we need an emergency meeting for some reason. I am clear about the expectations and let them know that next year, fourth grade, is challenging.

—Third-grade teacher

I create three learning zones in my class. I have a community circle area, a separate carpeted area in the front, and a desk area, pie-shaped desks that form table circles of eight students. The kids get to move around, and they have choices in where to work. We have a private library area where they can sit alone or with other kids. My expectations are high, and I don't allow for much craziness. I am strict at first so that they know what is expected, but I make a personal connection with each child. They know that they can talk to me. I'm strict and orderly, but we still have fun. The students seem to know what role I'm in, when to play and when to work. I repeat constantly why they do things. I also hold class meetings to allow students to express their views. I also make sure that they have access to what they need.

—Fourth-grade teacher

I want my classroom to be friendly and caring. I stand out of the door every morning and give each kid a hug. I go out in the hall with them when they need to cry. They can talk to me about their problems, tell me about what's happening at home. They can take academic risks; they aren't held to one norm. I set up a sense of community and don't talk to them like they are kids. We set the rules together so that we all buy into them; they have to have ownership or it's you throwing words at them. We do cool things like have a secret fifth-grade hand shake and a fifth-grade song. That makes it special.

—Fifth-grade teacher

These three teachers articulate clearly the importance of establishing a sense of community or belonging in upper elementary classrooms. They are highly successful teachers in large part because they recognize the importance of belonging, of feeling safe and cared for, of connecting with each other, of participating in democratic processes. These teachers recognize that without taking the time to create a community, students are unlikely to develop a sense of belonging. There are several key characteristics of community that provide a sense of belonging: They are happy places that stress cooperation over competition; they are democratic and equitable; they provide safe places for difficult discussions and disagreements; they encourage caring relationships to form; and they welcome people from outside the classroom.

Joy and Cooperation

What makes a teacher fun is when they make you laugh or when he lets you play a game in class. Also when we do fun science projects or when he rewards you for doing something that he asked perfectly fine and when you go on a field trip.

—Fourth-grade boy

A teacher is always fun when they're funny and happy. If teachers want to be fun, they should make things fun and at the same time teach. Then when the kids get older, they always remember what the teachers taught them.

—Fourth-grade girl

Classroom communities should be joyous places with serious intent. Children appreciate teachers who laugh with them and know when to be silly and when to be serious, who encourage children to be playful and imaginative while teaching them important content, concepts, and skills. Humor goes a long way in creating a community and in developing a sense of belonging for diverse students. Upper elementary teachers have to understand appropriate uses of humor. Teachers understand what upper elementary children find humorous, that humor has to be used carefully because it can unite and divide, and that some forms of humor, especially sarcasm, have to be used sparingly. Classrooms can be fun places to learn if routines and schedules are clear but flexible. Children count on classroom procedures and routines for stability and a sense of mastery, but they also welcome flexibility that allows their teacher to grab teachable moments or just to have some fun (National Board for Professional Teaching Standards, 2001).

In my classroom I stress cooperation, not competition. Competition tears a class apart. I award table points that they can use to get a prize, or they can contribute their table points to a larger pool for a class party. The students are all working toward having a party.

—Fifth-grade teacher

My teacher is fun because she gives us a little bit less worksheets, is not strict, and that's good for the class. My teacher is cool and fun because she always gives us a reward or a hand of applause or a thumbs up. Also if your table team gets ten points, you can turn it into a prize or bank points. Bank points are used to get parties once the whole class reaches to fifty points; it's PARTY TIME, depending on what time your class or teacher wants it. My teacher has lots of fun games that are cool if we have the time, that is. These are all the things I or the class needs for a fun, exciting, stupendous, awesome teacher!

—Fifth-grade girl

American society is very competitive, and many children enjoy competition. Teachers often use competition within their classroom to motivate and engage students. Competition becomes a problem when the stakes are high in children's minds. It creates winners and losers, with the losers outnumbering the winners. Although competition may encourage some high-ability students, the overall effect on students' sense of self-worth is negative (Wang & Yang, 2003); students, even when they win, do not necessarily feel better about themselves following a competition. For children raised in more collectivist cultures, (i.e., cultures that reward group rather than individual accomplishment) competition is unsettling and counterproductive (Greenfield, 1994; Trumbull, Greenfield, & Quiroz, 2003) and often favors children from more individualist cultures (Tyler, Boykin, & Walton, 2006). As the teacher and one of her students describe in the previous paragraph, an achievement drive can be channeled toward collective reward, which enhances the sense of community she has created in her classroom.

Democracy and Equity

In the press for academic rigor and accountability, we often forget that one of the primary purposes of education in the United States is to prepare children to actively participate in a democracy (Dewey, 1900/1990; Finn & Ratvich, 2007; Jarolimek, Foster, & Kellough, 2005; NBPTS, 2001). A classroom community allows children the opportunity to practice democratic actions, such as accepting responsibility, playing fair, and respecting others' rights, opinions, and possessions. It also provides a safe place to learn that prejudices they bring from home are unacceptable in the classroom, and that differences can be resolved through open discussion (NBPTS, 2001). By encouraging open discussion of difficult topics (e.g., prejudice, inequity, homophobia) in the classroom, children have a rare opportunity to discuss and disagree with peers. There are no big kids or older siblings to make fun of their ideas and opinions (Harris, 1995).

Even in the most democratic classroom communities, teachers acknowledge that they have more power than the children (Noblit, 1993). They are responsible and accountable for student learning and safety, and children look to them for recognition and confirmation. Although upper elementary children may not love their teacher unconditionally as they did in the primary grades, they look to teachers for confirmation and reassurance; for some children the teacher may be the only source of confirmation in their lives. How teachers use, or even share, power greatly influences the development of community. When teachers are *authoritative*, they use their knowledge and experience to guide and shape a positive community; when they present themselves as the *authority*, they dominate and control, a far cry from a democracy (Darling-Hammond, 1997).

Care and Nurture

> *In schools, the emphasis on academic knowledge and skills has so overshadowed our concern for the qualities of relationships that we do not give much attention to relational issues in the selection of teachers, the evaluation of teaching, or teacher preparation. The high priority placed on outcome accountability tends to silence concern with the interpersonal processes and classroom cultures that produce the objectively measurable outcomes.*
>
> —Smith & Paul, 2000, p. 8

> *I feel happy when I step in the classroom. I feel safe here. I know my teacher will protect us, that nothing will happen.*
>
> —Fifth-grade girl

> *I like to go to school because people don't treat me like I'm not there. I have a lot of friends that want to play with me and enjoy it, and that's why I like coming to school.*
>
> —Fifth-grade boy

It is amazing how important the little things can be in helping children feel as though they belong in an upper elementary classroom. Remembering a child's pet's name, asking about family members, knowing a child's favorite ice cream flavor are small things that indicate to children that you care, that you have a relationship. The National Board for Professional Teaching Standards (2001) for middle childhood specialists encourages teachers to show both "interest in students' lives, ideas, and activities and dignify students' efforts, . . . [and] create an atmosphere where students feel welcomed, valued, and respected" (p. 23)—in other words, to create a caring environment.

Nel Noddings has spent most of her career championing the importance of care in the classroom, not as a virtue teachers bring to their work, but as a relationship that forms between the giver and receiver of care. As the Smith and Paul quote indicates, taking the time and having the skills and dispositions to build caring communities are not currently high priorities in our accountability-driven schools (Noddings, 1984, 1992). Care is not synonymous with being nice to children; it involves knowing the children and making the classroom a space where they can explore and wonder, where their growth as a whole human is encouraged, where they see care in action through teacher modeling, where dialogue that explores relationships is encouraged, and where all parties model caring and being cared for (Noddings, 1984, 1992). Children feel physically and emotionally safe in a caring environment.

Consider . . .

Arranging your day to make time for students.

How often do you arrive at school a little late, still needing to run off copies and touch base with a colleague? For some reason those are the days that your children seem to always come in the room needing your attention. Before leaving school each evening, try to have everything you need for the next morning so that you can devote your first interactions of the day to your students. Some teachers create morning rituals, such as shaking hands and exchanging greetings at the door. Requiring that students look at you and speak to you can tell you a lot about their state of mind coming into the classroom. Others bring in a comfortable chair and sit in it as children enter the room; they welcome children to spend a couple of minutes cuddling next to them or just exchanging greetings and news. See Strachota, 1996, or Tollefson & Osborn, 2008, for other good ideas on strategies to let children know you care.

Grace Sussman (2006), a veteran upper elementary teacher learned midcareer that creating a caring environment involves listening to and respecting students' lives. A highly successful teacher in suburban schools, her sense of effectiveness and professionalism was shattered when her usual procedures and routines had no effect on the anger and violence that followed students into her inner-city fourth-grade class. It was not until she systematically studied her students inside and outside the classroom and engaged them in conversations about issues of violence and social relations did her students open up to learning. She wrote:

> Without planning it, I noticed that a kind of free zone had sprung up around us. Assured of my care for them because of my more obvious interest in their lives, students let down their guard. They were also free from my constant grammatical corrections. I didn't even think to correct them as I began to delight in the richness of their language. I released myself from the pressure to teach and allowed myself to let them teach me about their values, needs, and beliefs. I saw them spring to life. (p. 2)

Extending Community to Others

> *Our low-income, minority parents often seem defensive, and I don't blame them. They get called to a meeting about their child, and there are seven school people there. I would feel ambushed and defensive. I always call them before a meeting and explain what will happen and why each person is there. I hope that I have a good enough relationship with them that the meeting will not be a surprise.*
>
> —Fifth-grade teacher

Possibly the most important adults in the classroom, aside from the teacher, are parents and other family members. Their involvement is so important in the upper elementary grades that the National Board for Professional Teaching Standards (2001, pp. 47–48) for middle childhood specialists devotes an entire standard to family involvement, encouraging teachers to view parents as peers and strong allies. These teachers build on parents' strengths, especially concerning their child and their culture and community. To truly create community, all families are welcome even if family members do not speak English, are reluctant to come to school, or are leery and combative. Because upper elementary students are expected to take more responsibility and often juggle multiple activities outside of school, teachers and parents need to work together to find the right balance of activities and to establish common expectations about homework and organization.

Classroom Role in Developing a Sense of Engagement

> These features of teaching must be accommodated by any reform theory: teaching requires a large number of students to occupy a small space; students are novice thinkers and are highly likely to veer off in unanticipated directions; and children are physically active, quickly bored, and frequently restless. These are the nonnegotiable circumstances of teaching that can thwart even the most zealous reformer. (Kennedy, 2005, p. 234)

As Kennedy indicated, teaching is a much more complex activity than many outside of the classroom realize. We can design many interventions and reforms to better engage students, but although these efforts look good in theory, they can be thwarted or diluted when they meet the reality of the classroom. Engaging twenty to thirty individual students is not easy. Teachers want all students to be engaged, but they also want to maintain lesson momentum, keep the classroom orderly, keep the students on task, complete lessons within the constraints of the school schedule, meet state and district expectations, and avoid distractions (Kennedy, 2005). That challenge is met every day by upper elementary teachers through small actions in the midst of an otherwise ordinary lesson and by carefully planning with engagement in mind.

Academic Engagement

Intellectual or Activity Engagement

The third-grade students are listening to a taped reading of a story from a basal reader while following along in their textbooks. The teacher frequently stops the tape to ask questions. Toward the end of the story the teacher asks, "What is Beanie doing while out with dad?" Many of the students respond, "Counting stars." The teacher responds that Beanie has tried to do this twice and can't keep doing it. She asks the class, "Do you think Beanie will be successful counting the stars?" Some students say yes, and others, no. The teacher pauses and says, "Wait; think about it. OK, third grade. Close your eyes and imagine the night sky. I want you to count the stars." All students' eyes close; their faces turn to the ceiling; smiles are on faces. As they "count stars" the teacher says, "Oops, I need to start over." A few seconds later she stops again and says, "Hum, have I already counted that one?" The students open their eyes, smile, and talk quietly with their neighbors. The teacher repeats her question, "Can you count stars?" This time all of the students reply emphatically, "No!" The teacher explains that even astronomers don't know how many stars there are.

When we say that students are engaged academically, we usually base our opinion on their behavior: Are they paying attention, answering questions, and getting along with each other? Seeing that children are having fun is icing on the cake. The children described in the previous paragraph are engaged in this lesson; they pay attention, answer the teacher's questions, treat each other respectfully, and enjoy the role play. The beauty of this lesson segment is that in a very short time (no more than three minutes) the teacher is able to capture their imagination and pique their curiosity; she engages them in a fun activity, but it has a conceptual, not an entertainment, purpose. She finds a simple way for them to ponder a difficult concept: that some things do not have answers and are best enjoyed for what they are. In the hands of a different teacher, students could have been actively engaged, (e.g., drawing pictures of starry skies, sticking star stickers on a worksheet). They would have spent much more time on the activity and ultimately missed the underlying concept; they would have engaged in "hands-on learning but not . . . minds-on learning" (Kennedy, 2005, p. 9).

Inside the fourth-grade classroom, desks are pulled together in clusters. Students are freely accessing their own materials while a productive buzz fills the air. Discussions in at least three different languages take place as students work in collaborative teams of four at desks, tables, and on the floor. While looking for the teacher, I ask a student what he is working on. With a smile on his face, he tells me all about the project. A county engineer from the department of transportation has taken the class up to a busy city corner nearby to collect data about traffic. The county is trying to decide if they need to widen the street. The students are involved in the process of collecting, digitizing, and analyzing the traffic data, with the assistance of the engineer. I asked why they are doing this, and the student says it is helping the city and they are getting to use what they learned about statistics in math. I smile to myself. Now, this is the type of classroom environment I would want for my own intermediate student!

—Service provider, Accelerated Schools plus

These two lesson segments engage students academically but do so very differently. The first segment is embedded in a typical reading lesson; the students listen to a story and answer teacher questions. The role-play segment provides a brief moment of deeper engagement. The second segment is part of a longer inquiry-based lesson that extends over several days and requires considerable planning and organization. As described in more detail in the next chapter, upper elementary students benefit from both kinds of academic engagement; they are likely to experience many typical lessons like the first one, but these lessons become more engaging when teachers find opportunities to dig a little deeper.

Upper elementary students learn best through problem- or inquiry-based lessons. In these kinds of lessons, teachers "use many strategies to promote conceptual understanding and to encourage innovation, creativity, independent inquiry, and student engagement, making it a point to provide consistent recognition for a wide variety of student accomplishments and positive behaviors" (NBPTS, 2001, p. 23). Lessons like the second one do not occur every day in part because many teachers worry that their students will not master required standards. They are also rare because these complex inquiry- or problem-based lessons are difficult to organize and facilitate; teachers are often drained by the end of them, and students may not fully grasp their intent (Kennedy 2005; Tyack & Cuban, 1995). In addition, the current accountability climate and lack of faith in teachers has led many schools and districts, especially those serving low-income students, to adopt scripted curriculum or follow strict curriculum and assessment pacing guides that focus on skills and factual recall rather than inquiry, problem solving, and conceptual learning.

Language and Academic Engagement

As the second lesson illustrates, academic engagement typically shifts talk away from the teacher to the students. This changes the dynamic of teaching so that "teaching is mostly listening and learning is mostly telling" (Meier, 1995, p. xi). Teachers like the one in the second example recognize that learning is more apt to occur when children are presented with interesting and stimulating situations or questions and are encouraged to talk through their thinking and draw their own conclusions rather than engage in a one-way transmission of knowledge from the teacher to the students (Jennings, 1998; Kennedy, 2005). They are comfortable with some ambiguity and are willing and able to field varied questions and move the lesson toward their goals and students' interests.

Too often, though, with the press for time and concern over losing lesson momentum, communication in classrooms is tightly controlled by the teacher, and lessons move only toward the teacher's goals. In most classrooms discussion occurs primarily through ubiquitous question-and-answer routines in which the teacher poses questions that have one correct answer; students bid for the opportunity to respond, and the teacher evaluates the response (Cazden, 1988; Florio-Ruane, 1989, 1994; Kennedy, 2005; Mehan, 1979). The segment from the third-grade reading lesson represents typical classroom discourse. The teacher is definitely in control of the questioning; she is looking for specific answers and evaluates student responses. The vignette illustrates how the typical question-answer-evaluation sequence can be modified for deeper understanding. She has a decision to make when student responses to her question about counting stars vary. Rather than engage in the role play, she could just tell the class the right answer, that we cannot count stars because we do not know how many there are. Or she could repeat the question in a way that indicates her support for students who said "no," allowing peer pressure to bring the class to agreement.

Consider . . .

What kind of questions you ask your students and what you hope to gain when you ask them questions.

Richard Paul, founder of the Foundation for Critical Thinking (see http://www.criticalthinking.org), suggests that by answering questions with questions you develop children's critical thinking. Rather than accepting or rejecting students' answers to your questions, press them to explain why they answered as they did, what point of view their answer represents, or what assumptions underlie their answers. By probing deeper they learn to express their ideas, and you and the students understand their thought processes.

Social Engagement

I like to go to school because I see my friends.

—Fourth-grade boy

What makes a teacher fun? When a teacher makes math fun. She is so cool. She lets the whole class make projects two times each week. She likes

> *to play a lot with kids, and she likes kids. And she lets us paint with watercolors. She even takes us to field trips three times in a month. She chooses four people that work hard and she puts them as student-leaders. The student-leaders get to go to the bathroom without owing time to the teacher, and if they didn't finish their homework, they don't have to go to detention to do his or her homework. I already had two teachers that were fun. This teacher I have is my second fun teacher.*
>
> —Fifth-grade girl

Social engagement is closely related to belonging. As described earlier, upper elementary students are more apt to feel as though they belong if they are able to engage socially with the teacher and each other in the classroom. I have emphasized throughout this book that upper elementary children are social and that they learn best when they can learn together. This involves learning in a safe and orderly environment, being able to converse with classmates, and knowing that they are valued as individuals and as members of the classroom community.

Social engagement does not mean that children are playing and interacting with each other without an academic purpose or without boundaries. Upper elementary children enjoy social interaction, but they also gain a sense of accomplishment and belonging when they learn within fair and equitable rules and boundaries. I would guess that the student-leaders described by the fifth-grade girl rarely abuse their opportunity to use the bathroom freely and do not flirt with the possibility of serving detention for not completing their homework. These students are socially engaged and want to be part of the classroom community.

Teachers also recognize that for students to be socially engaged, they need to be able to talk with each other in a language that is comfortable for them. Teachers rightfully discourage off-task talk, but there are times within the rhythm of the classroom when students need to be able to speak freely with each other. Issues and interests from outside the classroom surround students and, as Grace Sussman (2006) said about her inner-city fourth graders, students will open up to academic learning when they know that their teacher values the richness, cadence, and rhythm of their home languages. Home languages and standard, or as Jesse Jackson said, "cash English" can coexist when teachers respect language diversity while preparing students to work in a world of standard English.

Upper elementary students will likely be socially engaged if they feel as though they are valued as individuals and members of the community. Although it is important that clear and fair rules and procedures guide the interactions within the classroom, all students, even those who struggle to behave within expectations, are recognized for their individual strengths and as contributing members of the community. Back to the fifth-grade girl's description of student-leaders: Notice that these leaders are selected for their hard work; behaving within expectations could be considered hard work for some students, and they are likely to relish the opportunity to be considered a leader.

Physical Engagement

Children in a sixth-grade classroom are working independently on a math assignment. A boy at the back of the room stretches his legs out under the desk in front of him, rearing back in his seat with his arms over his head. He looks over to his neighbor, smiles, and looks down at his paper but does not write anything. A few minutes later he starts beating a rhythm on his desk with his pencil. His teacher cuts him a look indicating that she is not amused. He stops and completes one problem. A little more time passes, and he is out of his seat, slowly walking over to the pencil sharpener. After sharpening his pencil he takes the long route back to his desk, greeting classmates on the way. He stands at his seat, arms on the table, shifting from one leg to another as he finally completes the assignment.

We have all been in classrooms with children who cannot sit for long periods, so this boy's behavior is familiar. As Mary Kennedy (2005) said in the opening quote, upper elementary children are "physically active, quickly bored, and frequently restless" (p. 234). This does not mean that they cannot be physically engaged in class; in fact, it is all the more reason why we need to consider children's physicality as part of our efforts to engage them. It is certainly harder to engage students physically in most classrooms than it is outside, and it is harder to allow for physical activity in upper elementary grades than primary because children are bigger, and there are usually more of them in classrooms that are no larger.

Within classrooms teachers, preferably in consultation with students, determine the nature, timing, and extent of allowable movement. Where teachers rely heavily on whole-group instruction and individual seat work, movement is generally restricted, whereas teachers who rely more on group work, performances, demonstrations, and individual projects have more fluid rooms. In the vignette pictured earlier, the teacher allows the boy a certain amount of movement; in fact, she knows that if he can stand while completing work, he is likely to complete it. Forcing students to sit for long periods at tables or desks diminishes not only physical engagement but also academic engagement; they become restless and inattentive.

Although upper elementary teachers often feel pressed for time, they usually regret decisions to eliminate or reduce recess time. After a few minutes of physical activity, children concentrate better on academic tasks (Ginsburg, 2007; Pellegrini & Bohn, 2005). Many teachers take away recess for behavioral infractions, but this often backfires on them because behavior worsens. Better disciplinary measures are to have students walk or run the perimeter of the playground or engage in a physical activity that the teacher, rather than the student, selects. Restricting activity at recess exacerbates bad behavior and eliminates a valuable opportunity for physical engagement.

SUMMARY

From the start of the school year, teachers involve their students in setting clear expectations for classroom behavior, and they uphold these expectations consistently. Through democratic processes, they develop and discuss classroom rules, consequences, routines, and behaviors for effective learning. In so doing, these teachers create a climate for working together as a community of learners that embraces all students.

—National Board, 2001, p. 23

When I set up my room, it is important that they know the expectations. By October the room flows. They know the basic school rules (safe, respectful, and responsible). I fit other rules into that frame. They work them out as a class in the beginning of the year. They know the consequences of not following the rules. First is a warning. Second is the "think tank," where they have to write a fifty-word paragraph about what happened and what they could have done. Their parents have to sign it. They hate this, so I rarely have to move to numbers three and four: lose recess for a week and go to a behavior-support room.

—Fifth-grade teacher

Creating classroom environments that foster accomplishment, belonging, and engagement involves facilitating a supportive culture and having routines and procedures in place. The culture provides a web of shared understanding and expectations; classroom routines and procedures provide tangible support and boundaries. Classrooms vary greatly; some encourage the development of children's sense of accomplishment, belonging, and engagement, whereas others leave children demoralized, isolated, or disengaged. This variation is partially attributable to the expectations and assumptions conveyed as part of the classroom culture and partially either to the lack of consistent routines and procedures or to ones that stifle and limit children. The culture shapes the climate, feeling, tone, or ethos of the classroom, providing the meaning and connection behind the actions that occur in classrooms. All classrooms have a structure, routines, procedures, curriculum, materials, furniture, and technology, but it is the culture that determines how all of these actions and resources come together, whether students feel as though they belong, believe that they can accomplish, and want to engage. Students' influence on the classroom culture is in the context of an environment heavily controlled by the teacher; she sets the classroom structure, routines, and procedures, as well as the general tone of the class.

This chapter's focus on accomplishment, belonging, and engagement emphasizes teachers' and students' expectations that are revealed in the classroom culture and supported by routines and procedures. In relation to accomplishments, the culture sets and reflects expectations for what can be accomplished and who is likely to accomplish what. These expectations about accomplishment grow from teachers' and students' prior experiences and from outside influences in the school, community, and society. Routines and procedures allow all students to know what is expected of them and how to demonstrate their accomplishments.

Similarly, the classroom culture frames expectations of who should belong in the classroom and what it means to be a member of the community. Everyone enters the classroom with different expectations for belonging and varied prior experiences of acceptance and rejection, but these differences come together within a classroom culture. The boundaries created through thoughtful routines help children feel enveloped in the classroom environment. Finally, the classroom culture shapes and reflects expectations about academic, social, and physical engagement. The classroom culture provides a definition of engagement and provides the rationale and purpose for organization, routines, and procedures that support engagement.

Here are key questions to ask about your classroom.

- Are routines and procedures designed to encourage accomplishment, belonging, and engagement? Or are they mainly to maintain order?
- How do I define accomplishment? And does it ensure that all children have the opportunity to achieve authentic accomplishments?
- Are certain groups of students more or less likely to have their accomplishments acknowledged? What reasons are usually given to explain these differences?
- Do all students and their families feel as though they belong in my classroom? Do they feel welcome, safe, and connected when they enter my classroom?
- How can I better juggle the need for academic engagement with the pressures associated with accountability and testing?
- How can I maintain instructional momentum while still allowing for social and physical engagement?

8

Teaching and Learning

The third-grade teacher welcomes half of another teacher's class to join her class in an exploration. The thirty-five students eagerly watch the teacher go to her desk and return with a bag. She missed the previous two days of school because of an out-of-town conference, and the students are excited because she said she brought them each something. As she walks around the room placing a small shell in front of each child, she talks to them about the conference and the lure of the nearby beach. She tells them to write down all of the words that come to mind about their shell. Students eagerly begin to examine their shells. They hold and rub them, smell them, hold them to their ears. One boy asks, "Can I taste it?" The teacher says, "Sure, if you want to; I assume that you are old enough not to eat them." The students laugh.

As she circles the room, she encourages them to focus on their particular shell because everyone's is different. She says that she wants them to make both qualitative and quantitative observations. She reminds them that qualitative observations involve what the shell looks like and feels like. It can be a comparison to something else they have experienced. Quantitative observations involve measuring and weighing. One student asks, "Can I go to the back and weigh my shell?" The teacher responds, "Great idea." Another student asks if he can use a microscope. She praises him for thinking of it. She passes microscopes around the room. She also hands out rulers and suggests that they measure their shells with the metric rule. Students busily write down their observations. They start experimenting beyond touch and sight; some blow into them (the shells are very small, about three-quarters of an inch) and, despite their size, some still get a little whistle from them. Children patiently wait their turns to use the scale and microscopes. At most tables children consult with each other, but some work alone by choice.

After about ten minutes, the teacher mentions that there are other things they can write about. She asks, "Where did I find these shells?" The students name the beach community. The teacher asks, "Is that a town or a state?" The students reply in unison, "A town!" The teacher presses further, "Where is it; if I found these at the beach, what region is it in?" The students respond eagerly, "Coastal plain." The teacher continues to ask geography questions until it is time to wrap up the lesson. She gives the students one final assignment. She says, "In the last six minutes, I want you to write three persuasive sentences that will convince me to let you keep this shell." She reminds them of a persuasive paragraph they wrote earlier. Students begin to write; many are smiling and sharing ideas with each other. In the last couple of minutes, she has students read their statements aloud. Several say they should keep it because they already have shell collections. Others talk about what a wonderful teacher she is, and that's why they should get to keep it. One student offers to trade a sand dollar for the shell. The teacher asks, "What's it called when you exchange things without money?" The students reply, "Barter!" She states that they all persuaded her to let them keep the shells.

If the goal for upper elementary teaching is to promote accomplishment, belonging, and engagement for all students while providing opportunities for them to acquire academic knowledge, this teacher meets the goal. This vignette illustrates that teachers meet this goal not only through the environment they establish but also in the day-to-day lessons they teach. In this lesson the teacher gives the children a sense of accomplishment by allowing them to discover what they think is important about their shells and by praising them for going deeper into the exploration than she requires. She envelops them in an inclusive community not only by seamlessly welcoming children from another classroom but also by encouraging students to interact with each other in ways they find comfortable. The students are engaged academically, socially, and physically. They discover aspects of the shells they did not anticipate, and they use prior knowledge of shells, measurement, geography, and persuasive writing to better understand and describe their shells. They do so with considerable interaction with classmates, and their movements are purposeful and support their learning.

Determining what to teach and assess and providing instructional experiences to move students toward desired outcomes requires a fine balance between what the teacher does, teach (i.e., move students toward learning outcomes) and what students do, learn (i.e., use their prior knowledge, interests, and experiences to make sense of new content). To keep the balance even, teachers constantly adjust their teaching to accommodate their students (as a whole class, as members of groups, and individuals) and the content expectations. They adjust the balance by relating content expectations to compelling ideas and concepts that make the learning relevant to students; they adjust it through diagnostic and formative assessment to better gauge students' prior knowledge and knowledge acquisition; and they further adjust the balance through diverse and varied instructional activities. Providing too much weight on the student side of the balance may result in thin content and fun but shallow activities, whereas too much weight on the content side may alienate and bore students (Ackerman, 2003). Given current pressure on upper elementary teachers to meet standards and raise performance on high-stakes tests as well as accommodating increasing student diversity, it difficult for teachers to keep the scale balanced (Rothstein & Jacobsen, 2006).

Teachers have so much to balance that they resemble the circus performers twirling multiple plates on sticks. Each time they balance what looks like an impossible number of twirling plates, more are added. If one plate stops twirling, it falls, and others are likely to fall too. At this point the act is over. So goes teaching. As teachers find the balance between teaching students (individually and collectively) and teaching content, they also balance working within time constraints, meet obligations outside the classroom, and encounter multiple distractions that break instructional momentum. More plates spinning over their heads.

This chapter focuses on the teaching and learning process in upper elementary grades, exploring how teachers balance knowledge of their learners and knowledge of the learning expectations in determining what is taught, how assessments are selected and designed, and how instruction is planned and delivered into a coherent whole. The chapter also looks at the consequences of policies, such as accountability to uniform standards and mandatory high-stakes testing, and to the daily challenges that impact on the teaching and learning process.

IMPORTANT KNOWLEDGE

Addressing What Students Are Expected to Know

> When I first heard about the possibility of statewide standards, I was intrigued. I thought that it might be nice to have a clear idea of what students were expected to know and be able to do in each subject at each grade level. But when I saw the drafts of the standards I was appalled. There were so many. There were 85 standards in sixth grade English language arts (my specialty area); there were more than 100 in sixth-grade mathematics. And they were so vague. I remember one in particular. "Describe connections between historical and cultural influences and literacy

selections." What connections? What influences? What selections? And what do they mean by describe? I asked myself, "How can these things possibly help me teach better and my students learn better?" (Anderson, Krathwohl, et al., 2001, pp. 3–4)

Upper elementary students are expected to acquire a wide array of knowledge in disciplines such as reading and language arts, mathematics, science, social studies, health, art, music, physical education, computers, and, possibly, another language. Whether taught by one or several teachers, this is a lot of diverse knowledge for students to acquire. The standards movement has clarified the expectations of what should be taught at each grade level, but as the preceding quote illustrates, this clarity comes with another challenge. If we address each standard individually as something to check off of a list, meeting the standards is impossible; attention to content overwhelms attention to students. As the teacher quoted earlier describes, across the subject areas there are hundreds of standards and even more benchmarks or indicators (according to one study, 3,968 of them). To make a point of the impossibility of teaching all of the standards, Robert Marzano and John Kendall calculated that it would take approximately 15,465 hours, or about nine more years of school, to address the 3,968 benchmarks, allowing thirty minutes a benchmark (Marzano & Kendall, 1998, in Tomlinson & McTighe, 2006, pp. 24–25).

This is obviously impossible, but through careful planning and identification of big conceptual ideas, the myriad standards students are expected to meet can be blended and their key concepts addressed. These can be seen as *power standards*, or the standards that are absolutely essential for student understanding and success (Ainsworth & Viegut, 2006). The wording of the standards actually gives us considerable information about the kind of knowledge students are expected to gain; each set of state standards includes a mix of factual, conceptual, procedural, and metacognitive knowledge (Anderson, Krathwohl, et al., 2001). In other words, standards include factual knowledge organized by a frame of conceptual knowledge; processes or skills acquired through procedural knowledge; and perspective, or self-knowledge, gained through metacognitive knowledge.

Factual knowledge, or the bits of information that one learns about a subject or process, is the most specific knowledge students are expected to learn. It is the information that provides substance to the *conceptual knowledge*, which provides a structure, frame, or system to connect the factual knowledge into a sensible whole (Anderson, Krathwohl, et al., 2001). Without this structure factual knowledge often swims in children's minds without a schema to organize it. Given upper elementary children's interest in categorizing and serializing, they enjoy learning concepts that help them make order of what they learn. For example, larger concepts such as survival, community, conflict, or exploration provide a frame for the dreaded dates and names that turn students against studying history. Power standards most often describe conceptual knowledge.

Procedural knowledge and *metacognitive knowledge* both describe processes of learning rather than the products of learning characteristic of factual and conceptual knowledge (Anderson, Krathwohl, et al., 2001). Procedural knowledge involves knowing the steps, sequences, techniques, and methods to do something (e.g., multiplying fractions, conducting inquiry, editing a story). Metacognitive knowledge involves knowledge of how people, specifically one's self, think and learn. It is demonstrated in upper elementary students' ability to empathize, recognize different perspectives, and understand themselves as learners and in relation to others. The four types of knowledge work in tandem. Students do not need to know one before the other; they weave together to form a whole, making learning relevant and meaningful for students.

Consider . . .

Asking why your students should learn what you are teaching.

Sometimes we are hard pressed to explain why students should learn certain content. Answers like "Because you will need it next year" or "It will be on the test" are adequate to a point, but isn't it better to pose more conceptual and authentic questions? For example,

- In introducing equivalent fractions, ask your students to explain the difference between equal and the same. This will help them see that something can be equivalent without being identical.
- In teaching a science unit on the food chain, start with the proposal that we completely eradicate mosquitoes. After a discussion, students should see that we need these pesky creatures because of the interdependence of life.
- In teaching grammar, provide examples of poorly written work and well-written work, and ask students to write profiles of the people they imagine wrote the pieces. They should realize that we form impressions of people based on their use of grammar and see more value in learning these conventions.

Addressing Student Interest and Knowledge

Standards have made it clear what students are expected to know, but what is not clear is what students already know and are interested in. Students come to upper elementary grades with prior knowledge, misconceptions, interests, and experiences. These shape how they will process new learning, fitting it into schema they already use to organize their knowledge. Diagnostic assessment and awareness of standards from previous grades are important first steps in teaching but so is presenting content so that it is relevant to students. Overarching concepts, compelling big ideas, and evocative questions allow teachers not only to combine multiple standards within and across subject areas but also to help capture students' interest and curiosity (Ainsworth & Viegut, 2006; Tomlinson & McTighe, 2006; Wiggins & McTighe, 1998). Big ideas let the students know why it is important that they learn material or processes. These ideas should be relevant to students' lives, helping students who lack confidence tackle learning that they may otherwise believe is too hard or uninteresting.

The following is an example of the power of big ideas. In most states United States history is taught in fourth or fifth grades. Teachers struggle to make this subject interesting; textbooks are often dull, and time devoted to social studies is usually limited (McMurer, 2007; Rothstein & Jacobsen, 2006; West, 2007). However, history can come alive for upper elementary students if it is taught conceptually and through big ideas. Table 8.1 provides one example of how standards can be made more relevant to students by identifying concepts and big ideas. In this example a fourth-grade social studies standard, "The student will demonstrate an understanding of the exploration of the New World," and more detailed indicators are addressed as concepts, big ideas, and in regard to relevance to students. A unit on early exploration can seem very remote from upper elementary students' lives unless the teacher helps them see that concepts such as migration, exploration, mutual adaptation, and technological advances were as relevant then as they are now.

Using Knowledge to Meet Student Needs for Accomplishment, Belonging, and Engagement

Curriculum standards were developed to describe what experts in various disciplines believe educated people should know and be able to do. They were not developed with the intention of helping students experience accomplishment, belonging, and engagement. Absent the issues addressed earlier, teachers can move students toward content expectations and meet students' needs. If we pay attention to how students receive and process knowledge, we will go a long way to using rigorous content to build students' sense of accomplishment, belonging, and engagement.

As described earlier, students develop a sense of accomplishment when they master new skills and increase their knowledge in areas of

Table 8.1 Combining Big Ideas and Standards

Standard 4-1: The student will demonstrate an understanding of the exploration of the New World

Standard 4.1 indicators	*Big ideas*	*Concepts*	*Relevance to students' lives today*	*Type of knowledge*	*Cognitive process domains*
4.1.1 *Explain* the political, economic, and technological factors that led to the exploration of the New World by Spain, Portugal, and England, including the competition between nation-states, the expansion of international trade, and the technological advances in shipbuilding and navigation	• Why governments spend money exploring the unknown • Advances in technology make exploration possible	• Quest for power • The known and unknown • Limits and possibilities of technology	• Compare to space or ocean exploration • Analyze how people's lives have changed because of technology	Factual, conceptual	Explain
4.1.2 *Summarize* the motivation and accomplishments of the Vikings and the Portuguese, Spanish, English, and French explorers, including Leif Eriksson, Christopher Columbus, Hernando de Soto, Ferdinand Magellan, Henry Hudson, John Cabot, and Robert LaSalle	• Motivations to take risks vary • Many factors contribute to the nature and degree of accomplishment	• Risk and reward • Autonomy and connectedness • Power, fame, and wealth	• Compare to current immigration issues • Compare to students' experiences moving • Explain why some risks work out and others don't	Factual, conceptual, metacognitive	Summarize

(*Continued*)

Table 8.1 (Continued)

Standard 4-1: The student will demonstrate an understanding of the exploration of the New World

Standard 4.1 indicators	*Big ideas*	*Concepts*	*Relevance to students' lives today*	*Type of knowledge*	*Cognitive process domains*
4.1.3 *Use* a map to identify the routes of various sea and land expeditions to the New World and match these to the territories claimed by different nations—including the Spanish dominance in South America and the French, Dutch, and English exploration in North America—and summarize the discoveries associated with these expeditions	• Geography, technology, and oceanography influence accomplishments	• Survival • Conquest and power	• Compare to current modes of travel	Factual, conceptual, procedural	Use, match, summarize
4-1.4 *Explain* the exchange of plant life, animal life, and disease that resulted from exploration of the New World, including the introduction of wheat, rice, coffee, horses, pigs, cows, and chickens to the Americas; the introduction of corn, potatoes, peanuts, and squash to Europe; and the effects of such diseases as diphtheria, measles, smallpox, and malaria on American Indians.	• Encounters between people have anticipated and unanticipated consequences	• Survival • Change • Mutual adaptation • Unanticipated consequences	• Explain how different life in the United States would be without these changes • Hypothesize future changes and their impacts	Factual, conceptual, metacognitive	Explain

interest and in areas that were previously unknown. True accomplishment is the result of learning to do something or know something that previously seemed unattainable. Students develop a sense of accomplishment when they obtain procedural knowledge that they can apply appropriately in multiple contexts. For example, a fourth-grade student experiences a sense of accomplishments when he easily adds, subtracts, multiplies, and divides fractions while building a model. Students also feel real accomplishment when they gain a heightened level of expertise in new or familiar areas by obtaining conceptual and factual knowledge. For example, a student with little understanding of climate change experiences a sense of accomplishment when he can explain why environmental challenges exist and provide factual evidence to support his argument. Finally, students feel a sense of accomplishment when they develop metacognitive knowledge of themselves and others. For example, a fifth-grade girl feels accomplishment when she learns how to organize her time after school so that she can complete her homework.

The curriculum in upper elementary grades can be an extremely effective tool for creating a sense of belonging for students. Literature, discussions, and experiences promote a sense of belonging in society. Literature can contribute to a sense of belonging by helping all children develop pride in themselves, their families, and their culture. Discussions and experiences that relate topics back to students' lives promote connections to each other and to the community. By gaining metacognitive knowledge, students develop a better understanding of themselves and can appreciate multiple perspectives and view points. By using the curriculum to create a sense of belonging, teachers build students' pride in who they are and what they know while extending their sense of belonging to include those who are different from themselves.

It is not difficult to envision how content can promote student engagement. Most upper elementary students want to learn and are curious about their world. They are most likely to be engaged when teachers build on their interests and encourage them to develop new interests. By differentiating by interest, teachers easily promote engagement (Tomlinson, 2003). The vignette opening this chapter is a good example of engaging content. The teacher knows that most of her students are interested in the ocean and find shells fascinating. The students actively engage in the lesson in part because of how she teaches it but also because most of them are curious about the content. Engaging content provides the factual and conceptual knowledge that students can carry with them to make subsequent learning engaging. E. D. Hirsch (2007) is critical of the current emphasis in reading instruction on skills development because a skills focus does not build sufficient factual and conceptual knowledge to make future reading compelling. High-quality literature, thought-provoking discussion, and content discovered through exploration and inquiry all encourage intellectual engagement.

As described in Table 8.1, it is not difficult to relate the content students should learn to aspects of their lives that they value and find interesting. In this way the content belongs to them and engages them. All children, especially those living in poverty, need content that will expand their worlds, show them places they have not been, grapple with ideas that may not be discussed in their homes. However, they need to get to this place through what they do know. They may not relate initially to dolphins jumping in blue waters or wolves walking across snowy fields (Sussman, 2006), but by linking lessons to what they do know (e.g., by stressing relationships between human and animal social patterns or by comparing how humans and animals sustain life and their young), new worlds open to them.

SELECTING OR DESIGNING APPROPRIATE ASSESSMENTS

Assessing Acquisition of Desired Knowledge

Standards not only provide guidance on what students should know but also give an idea of what experts (i.e., standard writers) think students should do with the information. This shapes how teachers engage students in instructional activities, but it is especially important in designing assessments. Because we need to know if the goals of learning (set out in standards and objectives) are met, these goals should drive all assessments. Although counterintuitive, Wiggins and McTighe (1998) made a strong case that assessment should be planned before instruction, ensuring that we know from the beginning when and how students will demonstrate learning. In this way assessment becomes an essential part of the learning process, occurring frequently and in multiple forms throughout instruction.

Knowing how to assess becomes easier if we begin with the verbs used in standards (Anderson, Krathwohl, et al., 2001) as long as the verbs describe cognitive processes that can be assessed. For example, students' ability to *describe* can be assessed, but their ability to *understand* cannot unless more specific verbs are found. Let's return to Table 8.1 as an example. The verb in this standard is *demonstrate*, not a very helpful verb in focusing assessment because all assessments are an opportunity to demonstrate knowledge. However, the verbs in the indicators are more useful. These verbs call on students to *explain* (4.1.1, 4.1.4), *summarize* (4.1.2, 4.1.3), *match* (4.1.3), and *use* (4.1.3) the knowledge they gain about exploration of the New World. Because the standards call for students to be able to explain, summarize, match, and use the knowledge they gain, assessments should focus on these processes. Notice that the standards do not specify that students will remember or recall facts; the standard writers assume that students will use factual knowledge to support more demanding cognitive processes.

Obviously there are many other verbs that can be measured and that call for very different types of assessment. Anderson, Krathwohl, and colleagues (2001, pp. 67–68) revised Bloom's Taxonomy of Educational Objectives into six domains that describe how students can demonstrate learning. In revising the taxonomy, they separate knowledge from action. Unlike in the original taxonomy that categorized types of learning objectives, they distinguish between four types of knowledge—factual, conceptual, procedural, and metacognitive—and six cognitive processes:

- Remember: calls for students to recognize and recall relevant knowledge. Some assessments remain at this level, such as spelling tests, identification of state capitols, multiplication tables, whereas other assessments combine some remembering with other cognitive processes.
- Understand: includes many processes, such as to interpret, exemplify, classify, summarize, infer, compare, explain, and match. Assessments measuring students' understanding usually require spoken, written or graphic explanations. Carefully crafted multiple-choice questions may also call upon these cognitive processes.
- Apply: includes opportunities for students to carry our or use a procedure. Assessments testing students' ability to use mathematical procedures in different ways or situations or to use their understanding of grammar to edit a classmate's essay are examples of applying procedural knowledge.
- Analyze: involves differentiating, organizing, and attributing. In doing so students break material into parts and find relationships, structure, or purpose. When students analyze in an assessment, they determine what is relevant and irrelevant (e.g., they find important elements in a story plot), they organize information into like categories (e.g., they conduct an opinion survey and organize responses), or they determine a point of view, bias, or intent (e.g., they take on the role of a revolutionary war figure and write a letter to the editor from his or her perspective).
- Evaluate: involves making judgments based on criteria or standards. Assessments calling for evaluation may ask students to judge the conclusions drawn about a scientific experiment, or they may critique different arguments posed by authors.
- Create: involves putting elements together to form a coherent whole or reorganizing them into a different pattern or structure. These assessments call upon students to hypothesize explanations, plan a project or activity, or invent something.

Under this frame assessments of our fourth-grade social studies students should allow them to demonstrate *understanding* by explaining, matching, and summarizing the knowledge they gain about exploration to the New *World*. Additional assessments should allow them to *apply* their map skills by using them to track explorers' routes. Explaining, matching, and summarizing require that students take factual knowledge and place it in a conceptual framework. Applying, in this case, requires students to use procedural knowledge.

Assessing Students' Prior Knowledge and Knowledge Assimilation

Through assessments we gain insight into changes in students' knowledge. We know that students come to any lesson with prior knowledge, experiences, interests, and misconceptions. As students learn new knowledge, they assimilate it with what they already knew, and, it is hoped, reframe misconceptions and build a solid knowledge base for future learning. Given that children have at least two years of schooling by third grade, we are aware of what some of their prior knowledge should be. In addition, they are expected to have acquired basic reading, writing, and mathematical skills by this time, so we can use a wider range of assessments than are appropriate in primary grades.

No matter how students are assessed, they should have multiple opportunities and means to demonstrate their knowledge and understanding. Assessment is a process, not a one time act. As Tomlinson and McTighe (2006) stated, assessment should be a "photo album," not a "snapshot" (p. 60). As in photo albums, lives or knowledge are captured over time and in multiple activities. From a psychometric, or testing, perspective, multiple measures are always best because they provide a more valid assessment of students' knowledge or understanding. From what we know of the range of learner diversity, multiple forms of assessment offer students the opportunity to demonstrate their learning in ways that are better aligned to their strengths (Tomlinson & McTighe, 2006). Additionally, multiple assessments can call upon different cognitive processes, allowing teachers to assess different types of knowledge (Anderson, Krathwohl, et al., 2001).

When assessment occurs throughout the instructional process, it serves multiple purposes. Diagnostic assessments allow teachers to determine what students already know, where their misperceptions lie, and what their interests are. Diagnostic assessments—such as pretests, KWL charts, interest surveys, and informal questioning—are ungraded assessments that help the teacher design and differentiate instruction. In our example of the fourth-grade unit on exploration of the New World, the teacher needs to assess students' knowledge, interest in, and misconceptions of the major concepts that guide the unit; what do students already know about motivations for exploration, about differences between the Old and New Worlds, and about unanticipated impacts of exploration? In addition, she needs to determine students' knowledge of and ability to use maps. This diagnostic assessment helps her shape subsequent instruction and to provide tailored learning opportunities for students with different knowledge, interests, and strengths.

Formative assessment occurs throughout the instructional process. Teachers use formative assessments (e.g., graded and ungraded quizzes, observations, questions, review of drafts) to make sure students are acquiring the desired knowledge and skills and to adjust their teaching to the needs of students. These formative assessments provide students an opportunity to use the cognitive processes described in the standards (Ainsworth & Viegut, 2006). The fourth-grade teacher uses formative assessment to check on acquisition of knowledge of New World exploration and to provide opportunities to use the designated cognitive processes (explaining, matching, summarizing, and applying). She uses formative assessment to dispel misconceptions, to keep on track, and to encourage students' specific interests.

Summative assessment provides students an opportunity to demonstrate what they have learned at the end of a unit or at key transition times within the unit. This type of assessment (e.g., tests, final exams, projects, reports, presentations, portfolios) receives the most attention from students and parents because they are usually graded (Tomlinson & McTighe, 2006, p. 71). Our fourth-grade teacher has to determine the best ways to allow students to demonstrate that they can use factual, conceptual, and procedural knowledge to explain, match, summarize, and use what they have learned about exploration of the New World.

Because there is such diversity among upper elementary students, it is important to provide as many assessment choices as possible. It is easy to fall back on assessments that are provided with curriculum or are easy to grade, but these assessments may not truly offer students an opportunity to demonstrate their knowledge. We all know students who appear to understand material when discussed in class but do poorly on tests. Their reading ability may prevent them from doing well; they may become anxious when tested; or the test may not tap into their preferred mode of expressing their knowledge or understanding.

If we are assessing reading or writing, it is important to focus on these skills, but often we are assessing other kinds of knowledge that can be demonstrated in many ways that do not require reading or writing. Let's return to our unit on exploration of the New World; this topic provides fourth-grade teachers many opportunities, in addition to tests, to assess students' knowledge. For example, students can explain the factors leading up to exploration through oral presentations, charts, power points, or other graphic representations; they can summarize the motivations and accomplishments of various explorers by creating a class display of the major explorers; they can explain the effect of the introduction of disease through pictures, diaries, or role playing. The key to offering diverse opportunities to demonstrate learning is to use the same primary assessment criteria across different products (Tomlinson & McTighe, 2006). For example, if one group of students chooses to draw a mural of the effect of disease on American Indians, they need to show, either through the mural or in an oral explanation of it, that they acquired the same level of factual and conceptual knowledge another group of students might demonstrate through diary entries or essays.

Consider . . .

Developing common formative assessments.

Larry Ainsworth and Donald Viegut (2006) provided a clear process and rationale for working collaboratively to develop formative assessments. By jointly identifying power standards and big ideas and developing common formative assessments, including scoring rubrics, you will have data to compare student progress in relation to a larger sample of students. This information provides you with credible data on student achievement as well as feedback on your teaching. The process of creating common formative assessments builds faculty unity and focuses the entire school or grade level on student outcomes.

Assessment without feedback does not help students learn. Most upper elementary students desire more than smiley faces, "good job" stickers, and checkmarks at the top of papers. Grades are inevitable for most upper elementary students, but grades rarely provide guidance to students on how to improve. Good feedback is timely; remember your frustration when your college professor assigned second papers before returning the first paper? It is also specific (e.g., points out where the work is good and provides specific suggestions for improvement) and understandable (e.g., language used in rubrics is written so that children understand what it means). It also allows for adjustment (e.g., revisions, opportunities to retest) (Tomlinson & McTighe, 2006, pp. 77–78). Student self-assessment is another form of feedback that gives teachers insight into how students see their accomplishments, and it develops students' metacognitive knowledge. Upper elementary students have the cognitive ability to learn to reflect on their work and distinguish what they do well and where they need to grow. Because they are comparing themselves to others and to standards set by the teacher, they are ready to learn processes of goal setting and reflection.

Using Assessment to Meet Diverse Students' Needs for Accomplishment, Belonging, and Engagement

Given that assessments provide validation of the degree to which students have learned, all forms of assessment are capable of encouraging a sense of accomplishment. Assessments make learning public (even if only between the teacher and the student), and they provide an incentive and vehicle to organize learning. If assessments occur frequently and in multiple forms, and if teachers provide targeted feedback on students' progress (emphasizing both strengths and weaknesses), even struggling students can develop a sense of accomplishment. David Ackerman (2003) distinguished between "absolute excellence," what standards call for, and "personal excellence," a true accomplishment given where students begin. He gave the example of golfers; Tiger Woods may demonstrate absolute excellence, but a weekend hacker can achieve personal excellence through practice and determination (p. 3).

There are many opportunities in the classroom to encourage personal excellence or accomplishment. A fourth-grade student who struggles with reading may choose to pictorially or graphically demonstrate his knowledge of the exchange of crops between the Old and New Worlds. If his teacher conferences with him throughout the project, prodding him to delve deeper into the subject and holding him to the same high standards used to assess written assessments, his sense of accomplishment grows along with his knowledge and skills. Well-designed assessments provide a sense of accomplishment for any upper elementary student if students are allowed to use cognitive processes that go beyond remembering and recalling. In the preceding case, the boy may have classified and compared, and depending on how he presents his findings, he may have planned or produced a creative project; he can use factual knowledge to support his findings.

We typically do not think of assessment as contributing to students' sense of belonging, but it can when assessments are differentiated and when teachers demonstrate their care by providing timely, specific, and frequent formative assessment to students, especially to those who struggle. When teachers wait until the end of a unit to assess students, assign grades, and then move on without providing additional help to struggling students, the students take from this that the teacher does not care about them. Students, especially higher achievers, appreciate constructive criticism from teachers and feel that those who do not give them such feedback do not care (Phelan, Davidson, & Cao, 1992). In addition, where students are provided different ways to demonstrate their knowledge, many people in the school have the opportunity to see students' strengths and to see the advantages to multiple approaches to addressing problems or representing learning.

Assessments can definitely engage students. Think about how excited students become when they work together on a performance or when they create a model representing the solar system or when they compose a song based on a story they have read. These actions are all demonstrations of learning, and they can be assessed against rigorous criteria. Many demonstrations of knowledge allow students to be engaged academically, socially, and physically, which enhances their chance of retaining and transferring the knowledge. Students also become more engaged when the assessment pushes them beyond what they thought was possible.

DELIVERING INSTRUCTION

Instruction is essentially a process of providing students multiple opportunities to link their knowledge, skills, experiences, and interests with learning expectations delineated in standards and objectives. As described earlier effective teachers constantly adjust their instruction to accommodate their students' needs and interests while meeting content expectations. They know that the experiences they provide students and the pacing of lessons require another balance between boring some students and confusing others. They also know that they need to find yet another balance between providing opportunities for students to perform as expected by standards and other opportunities that provide different experiences; let's hope they can keep all of these plates spinning most of the time. All of this is done within severe time constraints, in a context of multiple distractions, and with a group of students whose social and physical development must also be accounted for.

Teaching the Content

As teachers we want students to enjoy learning, and we also have the responsibility to expand their factual, conceptual, procedural, and metacognitive knowledge. Sometimes students have to be persuaded that they want to learn what we believe they should learn. Active, engaging instruction is the best way to persuade them. Let's analyze the lesson at the beginning of this chapter to see if it finds this balance. This third-grade teacher surprises her class by bringing them each a shell she collected while at a conference at a beach community. They proceed to write down all of the characteristics of the shell that they observe. As they work she asks them a wide range of questions, both scientific and geographic. She concludes the lesson with a request to write a persuasive essay.

This lesson is clearly fun and engaging, but is it a purposeful activity designed to help them meet state standards? A quick look at the state third-grade standards indicates that they are clearly aligned with the state's science standard 3–1: "The student will demonstrate an understanding of scientific inquiry, including the processes, skills, and mathematical thinking necessary to conduct a simple scientific investigation"

(South Carolina Department of Education, 2005, p. 25). In addition, the teacher weaves other subjects into this lesson by asking about the geographic region where the shells were found (Social Studies Standard 3–1: "The student will demonstrate an understanding of places and regions and the role of human systems in South Carolina") and ending the lesson with a request for a short persuasive essay (Writing Standard E3–5.4: "Create persuasive writings such as editorials, essays, speeches, or reports that address a specific audience and use logical arguments supported by facts or expert opinions").

Teaching is much more efficient if students use the cognitive processes and gain the types of knowledge outlined in the standards in their instructional activities. Much like designing or selecting assessments, we need to focus on the verbs used in the standards to shape what students should do. The science standard's indicators provide a good idea of what students can do to "demonstrate an understanding." They can classify, generate questions, use tools, predict, infer, and explain (South Carolina Department of Education, 2006). It is easy to see from the vignette that students are using many of these cognitive processes in the lesson. Paying attention to the verbs in standards and objectives helps teachers avoid three instructional pitfalls: activity engagement, content-free instruction, and textbook-driven instruction (Ackerman, 2003; Kennedy, 2005; Wiggins & McTighe, 1998).

Activity engagement, possibly more of an issue for primary grades, provides more fun than substance. Teachers put a great deal of time into cute activities or fun experiences, but there is little intellectual engagement. Returning to our fourth-grade unit on exploration of the New World: A teacher who organized an "exploration" of the playground in hopes of simulating the experience of risk taking and adventure would probably waste considerable time because students would gain no factual knowledge, and they might develop misconceptions about the larger concepts. As David Ackerman (2003) wrote, "'Active learning' is understood as *mentally* active and not something necessarily requiring hopping around the classroom" (p. 4).

Content-free instruction does not favor students or content; it is merely a waste of instructional time. For example, students may spend more time organizing notebooks, building structures, or setting up papers in specific ways that have little to do with the content to be learned. For example, when my oldest daughter was in fifth grade, a major social studies project involved building a colonial village. She spent hours carefully cutting out patterns of houses and other buildings from templates provided by the teacher; we searched art and hobby stores for materials to represent trees and other natural objects. When I asked her what she was learning about colonial times, she could tell me very little; she did know how to transform flat sheets of paper into cubes. Our fourth-grade teachers could easily do something similar in the exploration of the New World unit.

Textbook-driven instruction, and other forms of didactic instruction, may be thick in content, but they ignore hooking the students. Without accommodating students' prior knowledge and interests and actively engaging them in higher level conceptual activity, students become bored by such instruction. In addition, they may not be able to put their content knowledge to use in the ways standards specify, and they may miss the concepts linking the factual knowledge presented in the textbooks. Although textbooks introduce and are organized by concepts, these concepts are derived by experts in the discipline and can be unintelligible to novice learners, especially ones as young as upper elementary students. When textbooks drive the instruction, teachers often feel compelled to take a forced march through the chapters, perpetuating the criticism of American education as a "mile wide and inch deep" and limiting the amount of time students can create their own explanations, comparisons, and analyses. If the exploration of the New World unit were taught primarily through the textbook, students would be likely to be *presented* with the content, but they would unlikely be able to explain, match, summarize, or use it even though that is what the standards require.

Teaching the Students

How do they like to learn? Cooperative learning is big; they want to be with friends. They like hands-on, even though as they get older, we expect them to get the content without hands-on, but they love it. They love technology; they like to go on the Internet to find information or watch streaming videos, anything with a computer.

—Fifth-grade teacher

If instruction is a process of linking expected learning with students' prior knowledge, experiences, and interests, teachers have to account for where students' knowledge starts, how they progress in acquiring new knowledge or refining existing knowledge, and how to ensure that while teaching a group of students, each individual learns. In general, students this age are concrete thinkers. They learn best when they can relate new knowledge to prior knowledge, when they can find relevance, and when they can work together discussing and explaining what they are learning. They are conceptual thinkers; they like to categorize, sort, serialize, and classify. They have prior knowledge and experiences to draw upon. Teachers' knowledge of these general characteristics shapes how they plan for instruction.

If all students came to instruction with the same interests, prior knowledge, experiences, and abilities, the balance between meeting students' needs and content expectations would be much easier. Teachers could assume that if the class understands and is interested in the content, they could move forward as a whole. However, teachers have to engage the diverse group of students that comprise an upper elementary classroom toward common outcomes without boring students at one end of the interest-ability-prior-knowledge scale and confusing students at the other end of the scale. Bored students and confused students usually end up acting the same; they disengage or they disrupt.

With a focus on teaching students, teachers plan with their students in mind and refine their plans following diagnostic assessments. With this knowledge teachers know where the class and individuals in the class are in relation to their prior knowledge, interests, misconceptions, and relevant experiences. This knowledge helps teachers know how to hook students (Wiggins & McTighe, 1998), or pique their interest in the unit. As described earlier general concepts and big ideas help students see the relevance of what they are learning. To introduce a lesson on why explorers left their homes, a teacher might begin with provocative questions aimed at getting students to identify with the explorers. For example, he could ask, "Would you be willing to leave home for a million dollars?" As the students respond, he can keep asking questions relevant to the conditions in Europe at the time of exploration (e.g., What if you would probably never see your family again? What do you think the person giving you the million dollars will want from you? What if you had to go somewhere no one has ever been before?). Taking time to ask provocative questions pays off by helping students see the relevance of what they are learning and by giving teachers insights into students' thinking.

Upper elementary students remain interested in learning if they are provided a variety of learning activities; if they have the opportunity to work in different groupings (i.e., as a whole, in groups, and individually); if they are encouraged to discuss, question, and express ideas; and if a range of materials and resources are available to them. Even if standards make clear the cognitive processes students will be expected to use, students still need varied and multiple instructional experiences and rich resources and materials to make appropriate links between new knowledge and their prior knowledge. They may benefit from exploring Web sites, watching videos, working in teams, role playing, playing games, reading primary or secondary sources; the range of activities is dependent on the subject to be learned and the preferences of students and the teacher. In our unit on exploration of the New World, any of these activities would help students explain, summarize, and use their newly gained information. An added bonus is that such activities, if designed to encourage intellectual engagement, are more effective than more didactic instructional processes are (e.g., rote memorization, direct instruction, drill) in raising students' scores on standardized tests (Newmann, Bryk, & Nagaoka, 2001).

I have repeated throughout this book that upper elementary students are social and that it is important to encourage them to talk about what they are learning. If our goal is for students to retain and transfer learning, they need to process it through language. If size of vocabulary separates children living in poverty from their more affluent peers, they need multiple opportunities to use new words, express ideas, and explain their thinking. Discussions, open-ended questions with multiple correct answers, and probing for their thought processes provide opportunities for students to develop conceptual knowledge, support arguments with factual knowledge, and, by doing so, learn more about themselves as learners (metacognitive knowledge). Such discussions should occur in small groups, as a whole class, and, as often as possible, one-on-one between the teacher and each student.

Consider . . .

Using learning centers.

One of the hallmarks of early childhood teaching is a heavy reliance on learning centers. Learning centers can be set up permanently or temporarily (e.g., the teacher can make one student's desk a center for the duration of the lesson). In well-run centers, children move in groups to each center for a specific activity, and all students have the opportunity to experience each center. For example, for a third-grade lesson on sources of heat, students move in teams of three to six centers with the task of determining if the activity they engaged in generated heat—for example, rubbing their hands together, turning on a lamp, turning on a hair dryer, sanding wood, bending wires, or lighting a candle (with teacher supervision). They fill out a data sheet at each station. At the end of the lesson, they compare data sheets and reach a class conclusion on heat sources.

Centers provide opportunities to explore a topic from multiple directions; they allow children an opportunity to work together without direct teacher oversight; they engage students of diverse interest and ability levels; and they give the teacher a chance to work with children in small groups. Centers require

- careful planning so that each station has a meaningful purpose;
- gathering and organizing all materials at each station before the start of rotations;
- clear directions to students on the procedures before moving to stations;
- clear expectations for behavior while at stations;
- an easy system to keep track of time, such as setting a timer; and
- a well thought-out introduction to the lesson and debriefing following the lesson.

Using Instruction to Meet Diverse Students' Needs for Accomplishment, Belonging, and Engagement

It should be easy to see how instruction can encourage accomplishment, belonging, and engagement. When the instructional tasks push students to do more than they think is possible or help them use and share knowledge about people, places, or things that were previously unknown, their sense of accomplishment grows. Providing varied and multiple instructional activities allows students to build on their strengths to develop skills and knowledge in areas that may previously had been weak. For example, let's assume that at least one of the third-grade students described at the beginning of this chapter is good at math and interested in science but a poor writer. His success and interest in the inquiry lesson could give him confidence to write a more persuasive essay than he might have written in another context.

All good teachers use instruction to cement the sense of belonging in their community. They allow students to work in groups and help them develop skills needed to work collaboratively. They have clearly established routines and procedures so that instruction proceeds smoothly and students can trust each other to stay on track and take responsibility for their work. By working toward shared goals and recognizing students' varied strengths, instructional time helps students feel connected.

Instructional time should be intellectually engaging. Having fun is good as long as fun involves learning something worthwhile. Teachers need to establish the expectation that learning can be both engaging and challenging and that to struggle through difficult work or ideas is more rewarding than coasting through something students already know. For upper elementary students, intellectual engagement is supported by social and physical engagement. Lessons that allow students to work collaboratively and to use and refine gross and fine motor skills increase their academic engagement. Intellectually engaging instruction strikes the balance between instructing to the learner and instructing to the subject; when students know that their teacher builds lessons around what they bring to the class and gives them the opportunity to acquire knowledge they did not previously have, they become intellectually engaged.

IMPORTANCE OF ALIGNING CONTENT, INSTRUCTION, AND ASSESSMENT

Putting the Pieces Together

Although this chapter is broken into separate discussions of content, assessment, and instruction, in the classroom these aspects of teaching and learning come together as one process. Separations between what is taught and learned, and how learning is assessed and facilitated should not exist.

In good upper elementary classrooms, content, assessment, and instruction mutually support each other and are designed to support the growth of all students. The process begins where student knowledge starts and moves them toward clearly defined outcomes. This seems self-evident, but too often there is a lack of alignment between content, assessment, or instruction. For example, students may be assessed on material they were not taught, or lessons do not provide opportunities to develop the knowledge or use the cognitive processes set out in the standards. When this happens, students become confused, discouraged, disengaged, or bored. Alignment occurs through thoughtful planning, maintenance of instructional focus, and organization that is both flexible and predictable. In schools where high-stakes standardized testing drives all classroom practice, it may also necessitate some advocacy and courage to do what we know is right.

Thoughtful planning is at the heart of effective teaching. As described throughout this chapter, planning provides an opportunity to balance content expectations and students' prior knowledge, interests, and experiences. Planning that balances the end (i.e., what we expect students to know and be able to do) and the beginning (i.e., what the students already know, enjoy, have experienced, misunderstand) both clarifies the experiences students need to gain knowledge and shapes the assessments that will inform the teachers and the students of their growth. By planning for instruction and assessment at the same time, it is easier to stay on track, meet content standard expectations, and anticipate needed materials and resources (Wiggins & McTighe, 1998).

Maintenance of content focus is also extremely important. Standards provide guidance on the types of knowledge students are expected to acquire and the cognitive processes they will use to demonstrate their knowledge. Activities and assessments throughout the instructional process need to support the content focus while taking into account what students bring to learning in terms of prior knowledge, interest, and experiences. Maintaining content focus does not mean that students have to march lockstep toward the outcomes laid out in the standards; the route to meeting the standards should provide multiple opportunities to use different cognitive processes and acquire different types of knowledge. For example, if students are expected to *explain* why animal habitats differ, they may engage in instructional activities that call upon them to use other cognitive processes (e.g., *comparing*, *hypothesizing*, or *constructing*) to gain knowledge that they can then use to explain. In addition, they may relate animal habitats to geography, botany, and human architecture. Teachers choose instructional activities based on students' prior knowledge and interests, time, materials, and feedback from diagnostic and formative assessments. One area where focus often breaks down is in aligning summative assessments with the content objectives and instructional activities. Too often assessments focus heavily on recalling factual knowledge when students have actually been prepared to demonstrate their ability to understand conceptual knowledge. This problem has been exacerbated by the focus on preparation for high-stakes standardized tests (Jehlen, 2007).

Teachers have to organize their instruction to allow for both flexibility and predictability to assure that all students acquire desired knowledge. Flexibility and predictability seem contradictory, but, in fact, they support good teaching. Flexibility allows teachers to accommodate students' interests, needs, and questions, whereas predictability gives students and teachers a structure that they can count on. Teachers need to be flexible in accommodating students' diverse interests and learning needs, anticipating and responding to distractions, and navigating lessons to maintain lesson integrity and student engagement. Students appreciate predictability because they like to know when they will be learning certain content, what they will be expected to do to demonstrate their knowledge, where materials needed for their work can be found, when they are able to get up and move around, and other aspects of a supportive routine. Both flexibility and predictability help teachers maintain lesson momentum, stay within the daily school schedule, and pace lessons so that students have the opportunity to gain expected knowledge.

Issues Surrounding Teaching and Learning

Last year I was a little anxious to get started with academics, which there is so much of. We get the scope and sequence and on Day 1: This is what you are supposed to do. But in the long run, it made it harder to spend time on community building because I still had to constantly go back to the procedures and routines, and if I had taken the extra time at the beginning of the year it would have made a big difference . . . a very big difference.

—Fifth-grade teacher

Our district has told us to focus on reading, writing, and mathematics. Therefore, science and social studies, unless I can teach them in a reading, writing, or mathematics format, then they don't get taught. I don't teach science and social studies nearly as often and not purely as science or social studies. In the past I had hatched out baby chicks in the classroom as part of a science unit. I don't have time to do that. I have dissected body parts, and I don't have time to do that. I have waited until now to start my economics unit for minisociety because it takes so much time. I can do it now because [the state test] is over. We don't take as many field trips. We don't do community outreach like we used to, like visiting the nursing home or cleaning up the park because we had adopted a park and that was our job to keep it clean. Well, we don't have time for that anymore.

—Taylor, Shepard, Kinner, & Rosenthal, 2002, p. 30

At the beginning of this chapter, I identified some consequences of policies and classroom dynamics that affect the teaching and learning process. The most influential policies result from state and federal legislation mandating standards and accountability. The consequences of these policies heavily impact teaching and learning in upper elementary classrooms, but there is little concerted outcry about their effect on upper elementary children. It is difficult to *keep the joy* in the classroom when policies pressure us to teach differently than we know is right.

The standards-and-accountability movement, as enacted before No Child Left Behind, received mixed reviews from educators. It originated at the state level in response to concern that it was unclear what students should be learning across their public school years and that gaps existed in the curriculum. Although each state developed or adopted its own standards, they are similar across the country because they reflect standards developed by national subject-area organizations. Standards are criticized because they represent optimal knowledge in each subject and have not been adjusted in number or focus to accommodate the reality of upper elementary teaching. Additionally, they often vary from being either too specific or not specific enough (Anderson, Krathwohl, et al., 2001; Marzano & Kendall, 1998).

Despite initial criticisms, standards are widely accepted, and they guide most teachers' instruction (Taylor, et al., 2002). Standards appear to have contributed to an improvement in students' performance on achievement tests during the 1990s. One reason for this improvement is likely the efforts made to align standardized tests to the standards, increased opportunities to demonstrate conceptual knowledge on some of the tests, and opportunities to use cognitive processes beyond recall (Jehlen, 2007).

Since high-stakes standardized testing has been coupled with accountability, the effect on upper elementary teaching and learning has been less positive. Student achievement gains while annual testing was mandated in third through sixth grade have been contested, with some studies showing no gains in NAEP scores (which are seen as the most accurate test of student knowledge) and other studies showing modest gains on state tests since mandatory testing was put into place (Center on Educational Policy, 2007; Jehlen, 2007). However, research clearly points to a narrowing of the content focus to reading and mathematics and to basic skills over conceptual knowledge (Au, 2007; Jehlen; McMurrer, 2007; Rothstein & Jacobsen, 2006). In addition to reducing or eliminating time for social studies and science, many students have less time for the arts, physical education, and recess, and teachers spend less time building community and encouraging democratic processes (Finn & Ravitch, 2007). All of this increases stress on students, teachers, and the whole system (Center on Educational Policy, 2006; Landry, 2006; National School Board Association, 2003; Toch, 2007).

Many people are unhappy about the status of teaching and learning in upper elementary classrooms today; they want to enjoy the children and create joyful learning environments. However, the content has narrowed; there is less time for in-depth exploration and discovery; drill and practice characterizes the learning experience for many students; students and teachers report levels of stress that should not characterize these years. One might ask why so little is being done to remedy this situation. This issue is dealt with in more depth in the next chapter, but I suggest two reasons: no clear conceptualization of developmentally appropriate practice for upper elementary grades, and no professional organizations or advocacy groups devoted to these grades.

These issues are added to the inherent difficulty of teaching twenty to thirty diverse 8- to 12-year-olds. Teaching any grade span certainly has its challenges, but upper elementary teaching has a unique set of challenges. Subject-area curricula become increasingly complex and demanding, which is especially challenging when students lack basic math and reading knowledge and skills or English-language proficiency. Class size is often considerably larger than it is in primary grades, and the range of student diversity is great. Disruptions of many kinds occur frequently, including pulling students out of class for special services. Whether seen as an advantage or not, these grades are frequently targeted for classroom reform efforts (Kennedy, 2005).

Aligning Content, Assessment, and Instruction to Promote Accomplishment, Belonging, and Engagement

Aligning content, assessment, and instruction provides consistency and predictability that upper elementary students need to accomplish academic goals.

For upper elementary students, academic accomplishment is extremely important, and they know when they are not being challenged and resent missing opportunities to grow. Although they may complain about difficult work, they want to experience success. They are more likely to be successful if their teachers account for their prior knowledge, interests, and experiences in planning for assessments and instruction and then remain consistent and predictable in moving toward the content goals. For some students this requires that teachers present material in multiple ways until they understand; for others it requires that teachers provide extension or enrichment opportunities to further challenge these more advanced students. No matter how academically gifted or intrinsically motivated the students, they want to be successful in learning content that they previously did not know; they want to engage in activities that make them think; and they want to have appropriate opportunities to demonstrate what they have learned.

By accounting for what students bring to the learning process, being clear about expectations, and balancing flexibility and predictability, teachers use the teaching and learning process to assure all students that they belong to and are important members of the learning community. Teachers build community by ensuring that students understand how content is relevant to their lives, using it to demonstrate commonalities and differences, and building on students' varied strengths and interests. They use instructional activities to encourage students to work together productively and equitably. Through discussion and by asking probing questions, students acquire the language needed to interact effectively with each other inside and outside of the classroom. Assessment encourages a sense of belonging in classrooms where cooperation is stressed over competition and where multiple opportunities to demonstrate learning are offered.

Aligning content, assessment, and instruction gives direction to efforts to engage students. Rather than equating fun with engagement, teachers find the balance between the learners and what needs to be learned. They couple students' interests, experiences, and knowledge with compelling ideas and interesting questions drawn from the curriculum to engage students in intellectually challenging activities. They provide students different ways to demonstrate their knowledge and, when possible, allow individual students or groups of students to go deeper into areas they find interesting. They use multiple materials and resources to engage students and stimulate them to seek more knowledge.

Through careful planning, a focus on important knowledge, and flexibility and predictability, teachers are able to align content, assessment, and instruction. They do this within a school and classroom environment that supports and encourages students' accomplishment, belonging, and engagement. In the following chapter, I turn to three questions that I posed in the preface to this book. The first question calls for a synthesis of this chapter and Chapter 7 and calls for a definition or framework for developmentally appropriate practice. The second question focuses on teachers: What does it mean to be a professional upper elementary teacher? The third question focuses on the future for upper elementary grades: What should we advocate for?

Before turning to these questions, consider the following questions about your teaching practice:

- How do you keep the joy in your teaching?
- What do you do in your teaching to ensure that all students have opportunities for authentic academic accomplishment?
- How do you use the teaching and learning process to build a sense of belonging among the members of your classroom community?
- How do you work within the constraints of federal, state, and district policies to provide opportunities for student engagement?

- Are there policies or mandates that influence your teaching that you think could be changed through advocacy of a professional organization or advocacy group?
- How would a clear conceptualization of developmentally appropriate practice influence you as a teacher and the policies and mandates that influence your teaching?

9

Supporting Upper Elementary Students

Developmentally Appropriate Practice, Professionalism, and Advocacy

It takes a certain type of person, a certain mentality and responsibility to appeal to children in this demographic. My third-grade teacher, whom we called Mr. B., exemplified these qualities. Mr. B. enjoyed coming to school every day. He enjoyed teaching, had a thorough knowledge of content, and loved his students. Through fairness, slight deviation from conventional teaching methods, and compassion, Mr. B. ensured that this love was reciprocated. Mr. B. told stories, had fun, understood, and I learned more from him than any other teacher I have ever had. Above all, what Mr. B. had that made him so successful was that he never stopped learning from us. He was not set in any ways; he adapted all the time. In this sense he was as much a student as we were, and that is what makes a good teacher great.

—Preservice teacher

Three lessons can be drawn from the preceding chapters. First, we need to view upper elementary children as whole people; they are not just content learners; they are not the labels we put on them: "below basic," "English-language learner," "student at risk," "learning disabled." They are academically, socially, and physically active individuals who share some characteristics with the general pool of 8- to 12-year-olds but differ from each other as a result of group and individual characteristics. Anyone involved in education realizes that race and ethnicity, socioeconomic level, gender, language, and exceptionalities contribute to student differences, but even within these subgroups considerable variation exists. Each upper elementary student is a unique blend of social, emotional, physical, spiritual, moral, and intellectual traits. Their experiences at home, with friends, in the neighborhood, and in out-of-school activities influence who they are. We do upper elementary children a serious disservice if we treat them only as students who need to make adequate yearly progress.

The second lesson is that we can keep the joy in upper elementary classrooms if we provide students opportunities to experience accomplishment, belonging, and engagement. This needs to happen in all aspects of their lives; as educators we can assure that this occurs in schools and classrooms. This is especially true for students who lead lives with few opportunities for these experiences. Teachers can expect great things from them even if little is expected of them to accomplish out of school or their accomplishments are not recognized. In joyful classrooms some upper elementary children find a haven from feeling unwanted, disconnected, and alone. Even for those children with multiple opportunities to demonstrate accomplishment; who are surrounded by a loving, caring family and community; and who are engaged academically, socially, and physically out of school, school and classrooms remain the primary venues for these experiences and need to be designed to optimize their experiences.

The final lesson is that there are actions we can take to improve the lives of upper elementary children.

- Define and advocate for the use of developmentally appropriate practice.
- Encourage upper elementary teachers to develop a professional identity supported by a professional organization, conferences, Web sites, and journals.
- Advocate for compassionate policies and practices, a continuity of age-appropriate out-of-school services, and teachers trained and supported to teach students as whole children, not just as content learners.

This chapter is devoted to discussing these actions.

A FRAMEWORK OF UPPER ELEMENTARY DEVELOPMENTALLY APPROPRIATE PRACTICE

In Chapter 1 I introduced the skeleton of a framework for developmentally appropriate practice. It is based on actions of students and teachers in the context of learning environments and the teaching and learning process. The preceding chapters provide examples from research and classroom practice that illustrate either actions or context. The framework I present, like the NBPTS core propositions, can be applied to any good teaching and all effective learning environments. Whether teaching young children or adult learners, we know that certain characteristics of the teaching and learning process or the learning environment hold for all learners. The overall goals of education—encouraging accomplishment, belonging, and engagement—apply to learners of all ages. However, advocates for early childhood education and for the middle grades determined that general descriptions of good learning environments or good teaching are not sufficient. Learners do differ as they grow and mature, and as long as we continue to place children in classes by age, we need to consider these differences and provide the best possible learning experiences that account for both commonalities and differences among 8- to 12-year-olds.

Although focused on very different age groups, organizations dedicated to early childhood and middle grades are committed to educational practices that respect the child and are purposeful about learning. Their call for developmentally appropriate practice starts with knowing children who fall into the particular age span. This includes knowing about child development, social and cultural group influences, and individual variation. In addition, they define developmentally appropriate practice in terms of using knowledge of students in combination with knowledge of subject-area disciplines to guide teaching, engage students, and bring out their interests and voices.

Without an organization to develop a statement or definition of developmentally appropriate practice for upper elementary grades, I propose using a general framework of good teaching and focusing it on the special characteristics of upper elementary students and content expectations. The framework I have adapted derives from research several colleagues and I have conducted over the last decade (Finnan, Schepenel, & Anderson, 2003; Finnan & Swanson, 2000). We examined literature on best practice (Cohen, McLaughlin, & Talbert, 1993; Darling-Hammond, 1997; Knapp et al., 1995; Ladson-Billings, 1994; Newmann et al., 1996), analyzed the Middle Childhood Generalist criteria (NBPTS, 2001) for advanced certification, and spent considerable time observing in schools.

This framework is grounded in practice; is consistent with the focus on encouraging accomplishment, belonging, and engagement; and works with the reality of teaching upper elementary grades (i.e., it works through thoughtful planning, maintenance of instructional focus, and organizational flexibility and predictability). The framework combines elements of the classroom environment and teaching and learning process. Underlying the framework is the assumption that the school environment supports this kind of practice.

As introduced in Chapter 1, developmentally appropriate practice for upper elementary grades combines actions of students and teachers in the context of classroom environment and the teaching and learning process. Following are the components of developmentally appropriate practice; a short description; and an example from a third-, fourth-, or fifth-grade classroom. Through enacting these components, upper elementary students experience a*ccomplishment*, *belonging*, and *engagement* with challenging, rigorous material.

Actions of Students

Involved in learning: Students are actively involved in the process of learning rather than being merely passive recipients. Through involving themselves in learning, students take the opportunity to demonstrate *engagement* in their learning. It is not enough for teachers to present opportunities for engagement; students have to act on those opportunities.

Example: For the last week, students have collected trash on the playground and brought it back to the classroom. Groups of students are working together to categorize the kinds of trash and to determine the best way to present a plan to the school to eliminate litter at the school. Students eagerly suggest ideas about how they can encourage their peers to use trash cans and to recycle. (fourth grade)

Cooperate and collaborate: Students work collaboratively and productively with one another. Students play a major role in creating a sense of *belonging* in their classroom and school by working well together, valuing the contributions of classmates, and seeing and building on each other's strengths.

Example: Before starting a group project, the teacher puts students into groups of four and assigns each student a role. They move out into the halls equipped with yardsticks, rulers, paper, and pencils to measure the halls. The custodian asked them to figure out how much wood is needed to replace the baseboards in the hall. All groups work cooperatively, and each group approaches the task differently. One group agrees to add by yards, using a finger to hold the spot before moving the stick. Another group uses a scrap of paper to hold the spot. Another group uses a pencil to write on the floor to hold the spot. (fourth grade)

Successful and empowered: Students develop a sense of *accomplishment* by experiencing success and by being expected to take responsibility for their learning. Students work collaboratively with their teacher to set goals that are challenging but attainable.

Example: The students have been studying animal habitats and, as a final project, are working in groups to determine the best way to show what they know about the habitat they have been assigned. The teacher suggests some possible ways of demonstrating their knowledge (e.g., dioramas, murals, PowerPoint presentations, reports), but she lets the students decide what they want to do. She suggests starting the discussion by identifying things that each person in the group is good at—such as drawing, building, or using the computer—and to use these skills to their advantage. Students begin to talk about ideas and volunteer to take responsibility for specific tasks. Before leaving for lunch, they report their plans to the teacher. (third grade)

Actions of Teachers

Understand students: Teachers encourage a sense of *belonging* and *accomplishment* when they understand their students deeply. This understanding encompasses general knowledge of developmentally appropriate practice and specific knowledge of each student.

Example: The students are completing work on models of the respiratory system. Some of the tasks require that they manipulate straws, paper, and cotton balls in the small space inside a liter soda bottle. A large boy struggles to work inside the soda bottle because his hands are large. The teacher asks if he wants some help because he has "adult hands." He gladly accepts the help and proudly displays how the "lungs" fill with air once his model is finished. (fifth grade)

Learning leaders: Teachers are learning leaders in the classroom, encouraging *engagement* by transmitting passion for ongoing learning and explicitly modeling how to learn.

Example: The teacher has been gone for two days to attend a conference. The students were not perfectly behaved while she was gone, and she expresses concern, explaining that it is important for them to allow her to attend conferences so that she can learn new things. She explains that she learned several interesting ways to teach that she is excited to use with them. (fifth grade)

Characteristics of the Classroom Environment

Mutual respect: By displaying mutual respect, the students and teacher jointly create a climate of *belonging*. Discourse in the classroom is kind and interactions are considerate.

Example: The students are working in small groups to answer a series of questions based on the book *Out of the Dust*. The discussions are active and focused on the questions. Students listen to each other and suggest different ideas. Ideas are accepted as valid, but sometimes students ask for clarification if the idea does not make sense to them. The phone rings and a girl gets up and answers it saying, "Ms V's room, Maria speaking." She motions to the teacher that the phone is for her. One girl begins coughing and the teacher bends over her and says quietly, "I hope you are going to bed early tonight with that cough. Are you taking any medicine? The girl nods; the teacher rubs her shoulders and moves on to talk to another group. (fifth grade)

Diversity as strength: By treating diversity (i.e., cultural, economic, gender, exceptionality, learning style) as a strength to be built upon, rather than a problem to be solved, the sense of *belonging* in the classroom increases. In addition, providing varied opportunities to demonstrate learning extends a sense of *accomplishment* to diverse students.

Example: Students are creating a word problem in math and then solving it. The teacher goes to two Spanish-speaking students and talks to them in Spanish about their homework; she praises them for what they accomplished. She calls across the room to another student asking for the Spanish word for *tablecloth*. (fifth grade)

Responsible behavior: The teacher and students reach agreement on procedures to promote positive behavior. By doing so collectively, the procedures promote a sense of *belonging*. By making the procedures reasonable, students are more apt to follow them, increasing their sense of *accomplishment* and diminishing disruptions; in this way all students can be *engaged* in learning.

Example: The teacher begins the lesson saying, "Let's review the rules of working with partners. Who can remember the rules?" The students respond in unison, "Work together; work in a calm manner; stay on task; no personal comments about someone's family." The students then work quietly in pairs and threes on the vocabulary assignment. (fourth grade)

Characteristics of the Teaching and Learning Process

Authentic: Student *engagement* is enhanced when curriculum relates to the outside world and connects to what they know and have experienced.

Example: The students have set up a government as part of their social studies curriculum, and they are focused on the judicial system. They have a unique opportunity because the student teacher in their class has invited her mother-in-law, a municipal judge, to preside over a mock trial that will be held the following day. The case involves a student accused of stealing a money box from another student's desk. All students have roles (e.g., jury members, prosecution and defense lawyers, witnesses, bailiff, and court recorder) that they have researched. To be sure that they follow proper procedures on the day of the trial, they hold a practice session to go over the case. (third grade)

Integrated curriculum: Because most upper elementary students gain better understanding when knowledge is presented holistically, their level of *engagement* increases when the curriculum is interdisciplinary and thematic, emphasizing connections across subject areas.

Example: The science lesson focuses on scientific inquiry, but the teacher ties in geography and provides an opportunity to practice persuasive writing. As the students measure, weigh, and describe the physical characteristics of a sea shell the teacher brought back from the beach, she asks them geography questions about the beach and coastal area and about the difference between regions, cities, and states. At the end of the lesson, she asks them to write a persuasive essay about why she should let them keep their shells. (third grade)

Instruction as dialogue: Student learning and *engagement* are enhanced when they are encouraged to discuss their ideas and explain their thinking process. By encouraging dialogue, students' sense of *belonging* also increases.

Example: The students are reviewing the story "The Keeping Quilt," and the teacher asks what we would call something like a quilt. One girl offers that it is an heirloom. The teacher asks if anyone has other names for it. Another girl talks about how the quilt is like what you do for holidays. Based on further discussion, the teacher realizes that some students are confusing heirloom with tradition. She offers that an heirloom is a thing and that traditions apply to things we do. Before moving on, she asks if being named after someone is an heirloom or a tradition, and the students agree that it is a tradition. (third grade)

Inclusive instruction: Instruction is structured to *engage* all learners in varied activities that allow for different ways of demonstrating knowledge, and to provide different levels of challenge. By including all students in meaningful and challenging activities, their sense of *belonging* increases.

Example: The teaching assistant is working with one boy. She busily writes down his ideas. At one point she calls out to the class, "Do you know what Johnny said? He had such a good idea!" The other teacher praises Johnny, and he beams. The students turn to him and smile. I walk over to see what he is writing and comment on how much he has written. He says that he isn't writing it, that the teaching assistant is. She immediately adds, "But they were all your ideas." He smiles broadly and they return to their work. (fourth grade)

Active knowledge construction: Student *engagement* and sense of *accomplishment* increases when instruction provides opportunities for learners to construct knowledge through experimentation, exploration, and discovery.

Example: The students develop hypotheses about how the lungs fill with air when we breathe. They then build respiratory systems from soda bottles, straws, balloons, plastic bags, and cotton balls. When they have properly assembled their system, they see how the diaphragm functions to fill the lungs with air. Once they complete the system, they return to their original hypotheses and modify them if necessary. (fifth grade)

Meaningful learning: Learning is organized by big ideas or concepts. Student *engagement* increases when they are able to use the concepts to make sense of what they are learning. Providing conceptual frameworks to organize learning increases their sense of *accomplishment.*

Example: The teacher wants students to be aware of how statistics can be used to make different points. She has introduced three ways of determining averages: mean, median, and mode. She provides a data set of the cost of one fourth-grade classes' shoes ($5, $10, $10, $25, $27, $35, $35, $35, $35, $40, $40, $42, $45, $45, $45, $200). She then poses several questions: If you want to make the case to your mom that you should spend more money for shoes, would you tell her the mean, median, or mode? If you want to know what most kids spend for their shoes, which would you use? When the lesson is over, students write in their math journals about what they learned about statistics and averaging. (fourth grade)

Connectedness: Students' sense of *accomplishment* increases when they perceive knowledge within a subject holistically. They can make connections between prior knowledge and new knowledge.

Example: The class is beginning a unit of the Civil War. Half of the class is the North and the other half is the South. Within each of these groups, students are assigned a perspective to investigate; some are business owners, some farmers, some slaves or former slaves, some factory workers. They use the data they collect to write a persuasive essay on why the person they represent supports or opposes going to war. Once the students read their essays to the class, the teacher engages them in a discussion of how economics, politics, geography, and social and cultural differences influence any decision to go to war. They discuss current events and relevant global issues. (fourth grade)

These components of developmentally appropriate practice encourage students' experience of *accomplishment*, *belonging*, and *engagement*. They are the product of the interplay of actions of students and teachers and characteristics of the classroom environment and the teaching and learning process. In this framework developmentally appropriate practice is not something teachers do for or to students; it is an interaction, a negotiation, or a team effort. There are specific actions that students or teachers take. Students take responsibility for their success and empowerment, and they cooperate and collaborate; teachers take responsibility for understanding students and for being a learning leader. Students and teachers jointly create the learning environment and facilitate the teaching and learning process. Granted, teachers hold more authority in this creation and process, but students definitely influence the nature of their learning environment and how and what is taught and learned.

Consider . . .

Using the developmentally appropriate practice framework to guide changes in classroom practice.

Each school addresses professional development differently, and each teacher looks at improving classroom practice in an individual way. This framework can be used to guide either individual or group professional development. Below are some suggestions for using the framework for professional development.

- As an individual you can use the characteristics of a developmentally appropriate practice as a reflection tool. Take one of them each day, and keep it in mind as you teach. You may even want to write it on the board and let your students know that this is your focus for the day. For example, you may choose to focus on *responsible behavior.* Ask yourself what you are doing and what your students are doing throughout the day to encourage responsible behavior. Have you given them opportunities to take responsibility for their actions? Have they respected the agreements you made as a class? If you choose to involve your students in your self-examination, ask them to write about how they see the class in relation to the chosen component.
- Many schools have established either grade-level or cross-grade-level teams to encourage professional growth. Use the framework to guide discussion of professional practice. For example, you can use the aforementioned individual exercise, but do it across your team. By sharing your reflections with team members, you can gain additional insights. You can also agree as a team on a weekly focus. One week you may all focus on actions of students and share them with each other.
- If you are a mentor teacher or have a mentor teacher, use the framework to guide classroom observations. The mentor can script a lesson and go through the framework and highlight where she saw positive examples of components. It is unlikely the mentor will see all fifteen components in one lesson, but it helps to find patterns across observations.

PROFESSIONAL IDENTITY

Where do you find your sense of professional identity and resources to help you improve your practice? As an upper elementary teacher, you probably turn to P–12 teacher organizations, your union, district and state networks, and publications targeting all teachers. Unlike your primary or middle grades colleagues, you do not have an organization that helps set a more specific professional identity or provides targeted resources (see Table 1.1 for a comparison of resources available). The Middle Childhood Generalist certification offered by the National Board for Professional Teaching Standards is the lone source of professional identity for upper elementary teachers. Did your teacher preparation program focus on issues unique to the upper elementary grades? Given how certification levels are set and the lack of a definition of developmentally appropriate practice for upper elementary grades, my guess is that your answer is probably "No."

Becoming Upper Elementary Teachers

I want to teach third to fourth grade. I want to teach this grade span because I feel as though students are a lot more mature at this age. I feel like a teacher of students this age should be creative, patient, innovative, and caring. These characteristics not only will make teachers better but also will make their students better learners. I never really had a teacher who was an excellent role model at that time in my education, so it makes me want to be this type of teacher for future students. I want to be an elementary school teacher because I want to change the way students feel about school.

—Preservice teacher

Teacher preparation programs are shaped by the grades included in elementary certification or licensure. States offer a wide variety of certifications or licenses that cover the upper elementary grades; the most common certifications are K–6 and K–8. Most of the states offering these degrees also offer more targeted certification, licensure, or endorsements in early childhood education, typically ending at second grade, and many states require more extensive content knowledge of middle school teachers. Few offer certification, licensure, or endorsements specific to upper elementary grades.

Most professors teaching in elementary education programs turn to general teacher organizations such as Phi Delta Kappa, National Education Association, American Federation of Teachers, Association for Supervision and Curriculum Development, and the American Education Research Association for resources and support. People teaching subject area methods courses maintain active involvement in organizations such as the International Reading Association and National Council for Teachers of Mathematics. Unlike their colleagues in early childhood and middle grades, they do not have a professional organization that targets upper elementary education.

Future upper elementary teachers join student chapters of Kappa Delta Pi, Phi Delta Kappa, and the Future Teachers of America. These organizations are available to all future teachers. Students interested in early childhood, middle grades, and special education can turn to student chapters of NAEYC, NMSA, and Council for Exceptional Children.

Supporting Upper Elementary Teachers in the Profession

> *I really could benefit from a professional organization. When I read, some of the magazines focus on younger and others on older, and I ask, "Where do my kids fit in?" There is a little piece here and there. We get fifth graders reading at second- or third-grade level, and how do you incorporate that into fifth-grade stuff? You have to take everything and modify it. You ask, "How will I use this; how will I change it?" Sometimes it's nice to have someone give it to you.*
>
> —Fifth-grade teacher

> *Even when I'm at a teacher store or a conference, it's all for little kids. It's not for our kids.*
>
> —Fifth-grade teacher

The lack of support or professional identity that exists in teacher preparation extends to professional teachers. With the exception of the National Board Middle Childhood Generalist certification, targeted journals, conferences, and networks are unavailable. Early childhood teachers have several active professional organizations (e.g., NAEYC is dedicated to children 8 and younger and their teachers, and Association for Childhood Education International is heavily oriented toward young children) and at least eight journals devoted to sharing research and best practice in working with young children. Middle school teachers can turn to NMSA for conferences, journals, and professional networking, as well as to discipline-specific organizations (e.g., associations for math, science, English, or social studies teachers). Special education teachers are served by the Council for Exceptional Children (CEC, 2007) and have numerous journals, conferences, and network opportunities.

Upper elementary teachers, like their higher education colleagues, turn to more generic organizations and publications or to content-specific organizations (e.g., International Reading Association). National teacher organizations/unions National Education Association (NEA) and the American Federation of Teachers (AFT) advocate for all teachers' rights and serve as professional organizations. Phi Delta Kappa is an international organization for all teachers that advocates for public schools and teachers. These organizations sponsor excellent magazines and journals, such as *Kappan* (Phi Delta Kappa), *Journal of Research in Childhood Education, Childhood Education* (both published by ACEI), *NEA Today* (NEA), and *American Teacher* (AFT) that serve P–12 teachers. Only one academic journal, *The Elementary School Journal* (published by University of Chicago), exists, publishing articles ranging from prekindergarten through middle school. The National Association of Elementary School Principals' journal *Principal* is a good resource for elementary and middle school principals. *Educational Leadership*, published by the Association of Supervision and Curriculum Development, supports all district and school-based administrators. Valuable as these resources are, upper elementary teachers cannot assume that their specific needs and interests will be addressed by these organizations.

Consider . . .

Forming an upper elementary committee or task force within your local chapter of a professional organization.

For preservice teachers identify the professional organizations that have student chapters on your campus. Become active in the organization, and establish a task force or committee within the organization that focuses on upper elementary students and teaching. You can use this task force to make recommendations to improve your teacher preparation program and to meet needs of upper elementary students in your community.

For new teachers become active in organizations such as Phi Delta Kappa or your teacher's union, and press for an upper elementary committee or task force. Use this organization to examine policies and practices and to advocate for upper elementary students.

For experienced teachers, especially NBPTS-certified middle childhood generalists, take the lead in establishing networks at your school or in your district that allow upper elementary teachers to share ideas and concerns. Become a mentor or friend to new teachers to help them overcome some of the initial teaching hurdles. Serve as a model for keeping the joy in your classroom.

National Board Middle Childhood/Generalist Certification

I decided to go for National Board certification because some friends I really respect did it and encouraged me to also. I must admit the pay increase was motivation. Aside from the pay increase, I think it was worth it. It forces you to stop and reflect. When you write for other people, it's different. When you stop and think about it professionally and tell people about it professionally, it's different. We talk about our kids, but to put it down on paper for someone who doesn't know our children, who hasn't been in our class, really doesn't know us, is really different. It really helps you grow because you really have to look at yourself, especially the video. It's the little things, the little gestures, like I can't believe I fold my arms like that! From a psychological background, that's bad. Why did I turn my back then? To a child that's what it looks like. That was the hardest part.

—National Board-certified teacher,
Middle Childhood/Generalist

The National Board for Professional Teaching Standards was established in 1985 to develop a set of professional standards and an evaluation process driven primarily by teachers. By 2007, 55,000 teachers had received board certification; twice that number had attempted certification. The process is rigorous, requiring an estimated 100+ hours to complete the portfolio. Most states provide financial incentives, typically substantial pay increases that board-certified teachers enjoy for many years (NBPTS, 2007a). Board certification is designed to recognize exceptional teachers and improve teaching practice.

The National Board for Professional Teaching Standards grew out of the work of the Carnegie Task Force on Teaching as a Profession in the late 1980s. They wanted to develop standards of excellence for teachers and determined that they needed to recognize that teachers "teach something to someone" (D. Mandel, personal communication, September 21, 2007). For this reason they recognized the need for certification as subject experts but also as subject generalists who know a great deal about the students they teach. Recognizing that one certification as a generalist was too broad, they determined to focus on children and use groupings common among developmental psychologists: early childhood, middle childhood, early adolescent (S. Wilson, personal communication, October 5, 2007). The generalist certifications strike a balance between students and content, focusing on demonstrating content knowledge within the context of students' lives.

ADVOCATING FOR UPPER ELEMENTARY CHILDREN

What would I advocate for? Better training to help students in crisis; it might be divorce, death, or even the addition of another sibling. Students need help with the emotional stresses out of school. Our school has good counselors, but students need more help academically.

—Fourth-grade teacher

They need more science and social studies. We need to find a way to incorporate it because kids love science. The push for testing has something to do with the lack of emphasis on science and social studies even though we test science now.

—Third-grade teacher

My students are in transition. I used to think this happened in middle school, but the line has been pushed back academically and socially. Teachers would benefit from having a place to turn to. This may ultimately help with teen problems.

—Third-grade teacher

I wish people would advocate for class size. Why do we think they can handle thirty in third grade? Reading is also a big thing. It's much harder. The social aspects are also difficult. Particularly at fifth grade, they are going through so many changes. They need someone else other than the teacher. You are with that person all day, and you start tuning them out. We spend a lot of time on nonacademics; emotionally and physically they are changing. Those are things that we deal with that they aren't in first and second grade.

—Fifth-grade teachers

These teachers focus heavily on the need to address student needs when they think about advocating for upper elementary students. Unfortunately, they do not have an organization dedicated to student advocacy. This is not the case for other groups of students. Consider what happens when issues affecting young children arise. The National Association for the Education of Young Children's Web site has a link to its Action Center (NAEYC, 2007). Through this center people can contact governmental representatives, learn about policies and pending legislation, and view officials' public stands on key issues. The organization also posts many resources that inform members of policy issues. The National Middle School Association's Web site is similar, with a link to Advocacy (NMSA, 2007). At this link are position papers, and information members can easily access when advocating for young adolescents. Finally, the Council for Exceptional Children maintains links to Policy and Advocacy (CEC, 2007) that also provide important updates and information to members. These organizations have ready vehicles to mobilize members to take action through supporting or opposing legislation and policies, through grassroots activism, through discussion, and through research.

For upper elementary students and teachers, these resources are unavailable, but by identifying issues, we can begin to advocate more effectively. Following is the skeleton for advocacy that involves disseminating information about upper elementary children and examining policies and practices that may not be serving them well. In relation to disseminating information, we can coordinate and share existing research. We also need to examine the effects of policies and practices on students' lives to know the extent to which upper elementary students are being harmed by the current policy environment. Policies impacting students' lives in school, resources available to meet students' needs, and teacher quality need to be examined in light of these students and their need for accomplishment, belonging, and engagement. By disseminating information and examining policies and practices, we can structure school and classroom environments and teaching practices to address the whole child and to assure that all children learn in an environment that promotes accomplishment, belonging, and engagement.

Compiling and Encouraging Research on Upper Elementary Children and Teaching

There is a growing body of research on upper elementary child development, the context in which students live, and issues in upper elementary grades. Even though it is not currently coordinated into easily accessible sources, you can help colleagues and parents if you share any research you find about upper elementary students and encourage colleagues in higher education and district offices to compile and disseminate findings directly affecting upper elementary students. The following six areas have the potential to enlighten our understanding of issues surrounding upper elementary education and can be found in magazines, journals, books, and Web sites.

1. *Research on cognitive development:* Our knowledge of cognitive development has been enhanced by advances in neuroscience research (e.g., Jensen, 1998; Wolf & Brandt, 1998), and although the upper elementary years are typically presented as a relatively uneventful stage between the dramatic brain growth in infancy and early childhood and later developments in adolescence, we do know from this research that considerable pruning and strengthening of neural connections occurs during the upper elementary years. You can share this research with administrators, teachers, and parents to advocate for active, conceptual learning; to better understand problems that linger in reading and mathematics for some students; and to identify problems that begin to surface during these years, such as issues related to motivation.
2. *Research on social and cultural context of learning in upper elementary years:* You can discover great insights into the lives of upper elementary children by reading books and articles written by sociologists, anthropologists, and psychologists, such as Boocock and Scott (2005), García Coll and Szalacha (2004), James, Jenks, and Prout (1998), Lareau (2004), and Scales, Sesma, and Bolstrom (2004). Their work provides a rich understanding

of the social, cultural, and environmental influences on upper elementary children, as well as a larger framework you can use to better understand your students' actions and to inform decision makers of the complexity of students' lives.

3. *Research on effective teaching practices:* The preceding discussion of developmentally appropriate practice is grounded in research on effective teaching practices, especially studies targeting students in poverty (e.g., Cohen, McLaughlin & Talbert, 1993; Kennedy, 2005; Knapp, 1995; Newmann, et al., 1996). You can share research with your colleagues, administrators, and decision and policymakers to support practice that ensures that student needs are met as content is taught.
4. *Research on school and classroom environments:* Although research clearly shows that schools and classrooms are difficult to change (e.g., Finnan & Swanson, 2000; Kennedy, 2005; Sarason, 1996; Tyack & Cuban, 1995), it also indicates that teachers can create environments that encourage upper elementary students' sense of accomplishment, belonging, or engagement. You can add to this evidence by working with local college and university researchers to examine and disseminate best practices.
5. *Research on effective teachers of upper elementary students:* Upper elementary teachers are often the focus of studies of teacher effectiveness (Kennedy, 2005; Ladd, Sass, & Harris, 2007; Valli & Buese, 2007), but the results of these studies are not shared widely with upper elementary teachers or elementary teacher educators. Work with your local teacher preparation programs to coordinate and disseminate best practices. You can help focus attention of teacher-educators on the unique strengths and needs of upper elementary teachers.

Examining Policies and Practices

Policies and Practices Affecting Students' Lives in School

The teachers' quotes at the beginning of this section hint at some of the educational policies and practices are of concern to them. One of the most pressing is the effect of performance pressure that high-stakes standardized tests have on students. Accountability and testing in and of itself is unlikely to disappear, and some benchmarking of performance to a normed or criterion-referenced test is useful for teachers and parents. However, our current focus on THE TEST, whether coming from the state, district, school, or teacher, is not healthy for students or teachers. Evidence of test pressure is everywhere in elementary schools. For example, I was waiting outside a fourth-grade classroom three weeks after school started in the fall. On the wall a teacher posted essays students wrote to the prompt "I get the jitters when . . . ". The essays were about one page in length. Most of them mentioned how they "get the jitters" when they take their state test. These essays were written in early September; just think about how serious their jitters will be in May!

Another policy that upper elementary teachers would like to examine is the jump in class size many elementary students experience between primary and upper elementary grades. Early childhood advocates made a very compelling case for class-size reductions, and many states and districts limit class size to fewer than fifteen in the early grades; however, districts find it difficult to extend to these reductions to upper elementary grades because of the increased personnel and facilities costs. Considerable research exists on class size reduction (Wang & Finn, 2000), and the findings are mixed. Although exploration of extending class size reductions is useful, it is likely more productive to focus an examination on improving transitions between grades.

Another practice that affects upper elementary students' school experience is the prevalence of departmentalization in upper elementary grades. Teachers have mixed feelings about the practice. Some like it because they can specialize in one or two content areas; others do not like it because they do not develop deep relations with their students, and they lose flexibility and time to transitions. Given that decisions to departmentalize the upper grades are usually made at the school level, faculty need to weigh the advantages and disadvantages for students and seriously consider whether they are working from a student or content perspective when making these decisions.

Promotion and retention policies, although not focused only on upper elementary grades, need to be carefully applied in these grades. One can argue the advisability of separating students by age because each child's developmental trajectory is different (Creitz, 2007), but by the time students are in third grade, they are well aware that repeating a grade is an indicator of their failure. Given the correlation between grade retention and high school dropouts (Roderick, 1993) and the frustration students feel when they do not have the skills or knowledge expected in higher grades, we need to consider alternatives to both grade retention and "social promotion." Students who underperform are usually best served through individual attention to areas of weakness, instruction that reengages them, and social and emotional supports to address root causes of underachievement (e.g., loss of motivation, poor attendance, disruptive behavior, or inattentiveness).

Continuity of Supports In and Out of School

We call on communities—educators, parents, businesses, health and social service providers, arts professionals, recreation leaders, and policymakers at all levels—to forge a new compact with our young people to ensure their whole and healthy development. We ask communities to redefine learning to focus on the whole person. We ask schools and communities to lay aside perennial battles for resources and instead align those resources in support of the whole child. Policy, practice, and resources must be aligned to support not only academic learning for each child, but also the experiences that encourage development of a whole child—one who is knowledgeable, healthy, motivated, and engaged.

—Stephanie Pace Marshall and H. B. Price,
ASCD Commission on the Whole Child, 2007, p. 8

We have a long history of attempting to help our neediest students, but the results are usually disappointing. Too often we target the symptoms, not the cause, of problems, and we provide support in fits and starts. Agencies compete with each other for funds and influence, losing sight of the ultimate goal. Finally, we do not fully consider the impact of decisions on children, teachers, and families. Just at the point when interventions begin to take hold, funding ends, children pass beyond the age scope of the intervention, or organizations or schools are damned by their success and no longer eligible for funding. The examples are too numerous to list; reading assistance ends at the end of second grade because the grant does not extend to third grade; tutoring is available only to "bubble" children who might move one quartile to another with a boost; preventative health checkups are not available if families lose Medicare eligibility. Numerous organizations, such as America's Promise Alliance and the Association for Supervision and Curriculum Development (ASCD), have begun to advocate actively to pool resources to honor and support the whole child. America's Promise Alliance (2006) calls on us to keep five promises to every child: that they experience caring adults, safe places, a healthy start, effective education, and opportunities to help others. ASCD's Commission on the Whole Child, as noted by Marshall and Price, calls for agencies to work in partnership to address the academic, social, emotional, and physical needs of children. These organizations support children throughout their development, but their message is especially important for upper elementary students because no one is advocating exclusively for them. Ensuring that upper elementary children experience accomplishment, belonging, and engagement both in and out of school requires that we place children's interests first and work in partnership with families, communities, and other support organizations and agencies.

Highly Qualified Teachers

Anyone concerned about upper elementary children recognizes the importance of ensuring that every child experiences highly qualified teachers. No Child Left Behind raised recognition of the importance of high quality teachers to new heights by calling for all teachers to be "highly qualified" by 2005. However, NCLB's definition of highly qualified misses much of the complexity of teaching by ignoring the interplay between content knowledge, instructional practice, and knowledge of children (Emerick, Hirsch, & Berry, 2004). NCLB placed most of its focus on teachers' content knowledge, as demonstrated through college course work and performance on tests of content. As previous chapters indicate, content knowledge is critical for upper elementary teachers, but it is not the only knowledge that is important. Teachers need to build on their professional knowledge and experience and advocate for a better balance between knowledge of students and that of content to ensure that children experience high quality teachers.

High-quality teachers bring some innate dispositions to the job, but they also become better teachers through their preparation programs and ongoing professional development. If we want the best for upper elementary children, we need to ensure that teachers receive strong preservice training that balances knowledge of students, curriculum, instruction, and assessment with considerable experience working in upper elementary classrooms. Formal teacher preparation programs are under attack (Levine, 2006), and increasing numbers of teachers are entering the field through alternative routes that provide little or no formal training. Federal policies have accelerated the trend toward alternative certification by considering teachers who pass content exams "highly qualified" (Emerick, Hirsch, & Berry, 2004).

This book has focused on the characteristics that make upper elementary teachers effective with their students, but additional tasks and roles are being added to their jobs that may not ultimately make them better teachers. For example, with accountability pressures, teachers, especially those in tested grades (i.e., third to eighth grades) spend more and more time filling out reports, analyzing data, and coordinating with administrators and other teachers to group and move student in an effort to address skill deficits. This work is typically not what attracted teachers to the job (Valli & Buese, 2007). In addition, although the importance of high-quality professional development is clear, funds and time for professional development are limited, and teachers often struggle to implement new curriculum, instructional strategies, or assessment tools because of inadequate professional development and follow up. When advocating for the best possible teachers for upper elementary children, we need to think about the qualities and skills that are truly important, provide high quality preparation and professional development to build these qualities and skills, and free teachers to focus on what is best for their students.

WHAT CAN YOU DO FOR UPPER ELEMENTARY CHILDREN?

The preceding chapters end with questions to consider, but rather than raise more questions, it is more appropriate to consider actions that teachers, administrators, teacher educators, and parents can take to keep the joy in upper elementary classrooms. Some of these actions can be taken individually, whereas others necessitate working collaboratively. Addressing the issues both individually and collaboratively will make the incremental changes that will benefit children.

Developmentally Appropriate Practice

1. Join networks of upper elementary teachers to support and advocate for developmentally appropriate practice. Start a discussion group at your school or use grade level or team planning time to explore what developmentally appropriate practice should look like.
2. Stay current on research on best practice, and use it to advocate for state or district curricular decisions that meet the needs you see in your classroom.
3. View testing as a constraint, not as an excuse, and continue to teach what you know is right for your children. Remember why you became a teacher, and use your confidence to do what you know is best for your students. Involve students and parents on your side to lobby for use of testing as a means of tracking progress, not as an end in itself.
4. Work with teacher educators and other researchers to compile and disseminate research on best practices for upper elementary grades.

Professional Identity for Upper Elementary Teachers

1. Support the formation of a professional organization (national, state, and local) targeted to the needs of upper elementary teachers.
2. Support teacher educators who pressure accrediting agencies to balance knowledge of children and knowledge of content in setting program accreditation standards.
3. Support colleagues who start vehicles (e.g., journals, Web sites, organizations) that identify and encourage research and discussion of best practice focused on upper elementary.
4. Work with organizations like the National Board for Professional Teaching Standards, your teacher union, or Phi Delta Kappa to promote a professional identity for upper elementary teachers that balances understanding and valuing the students and content.

Advocacy

1. Support higher education colleagues who work to establish vehicles through organizations such as the American Educational Research Association or the Society for Research on Child Development to compile research on upper elementary children, teaching, and school and classroom environment and to develop a research agenda.
2. Join groups to advocate for consideration of the direct or unintended effect of policies on upper elementary children and teachers. Contact legislators and policy-makers and let them know your opinions of legislation or policies.
3. Encourage school board or city council members to include upper elementary children in intervention programs rather than targeting them exclusively to young children or adolescents.
4. Join other professional upper elementary teachers to challenge current definitions of "highly qualified" teachers; insist that knowledge of and affinity with students be a critical component of any definition of a highly qualified teacher.
5. Remain in the profession and continue to have fun with your students. Their joy will be your joy.

References

Ackerman, D. B. (2003). Taproots for a new century: Tapping the best of traditional and progressive education. *Phi Delta Kappan, 84,* 344–349.

Adler, P. A., & Adler, P. (1998). *Peer power: Preadolescent culture and identity.* New Brunswick, NJ: Rutgers University Press.

Ainsworth, L. & Viegut, D. (2006). *Common formative assessments: How to connect standards-based instruction and assessment.* Thousand Oaks, CA: Corwin Press.

American Educational Research Association (AERA). (2007). *About AERA.* Retrieved October 1, 2007, from http://www.aera.net. About AERA Annual Meeting Program. Washington, DC: American Educational Research Association.

America's Promise Alliance. (2006). *Every child every promise: Turning failure into action.* Retrieved November 21, 2006, from http://www.americaspromise.org/ECEP.aspx?id=208

Anderson, L. W., Krathwohl, D. R., Airasian, P. W., Cruikshank, K. A., Mayer, R. E., Pintrich, P. R., et al. (2001). *A taxonomy for learning, teaching, and assessing: A revision of Bloom's Taxonomy of Education Objectives.* New York: Longman.

Artiles, A. J., Klingner, J. K., & Tate, W. F. (2006). Race, class, and disproportionality: Reevaluating the relationship between poverty and special education placement. *Educational Researcher, 35*(6), 3–5.

Au, W. (2007). High-stakes testing and curricular control: A qualitative metasynthesis. *Educational Researcher, 36,* 258–267.

Bali, V. A., Anagnostopoulos, D., & Roberts, R. (2005). Toward a political explanation of grade retention. *Educational Evaluation and Policy Analysis, 27,* 133–155.

Bariaud, F. (1988). Age differences in children's humor. In P. E. McGhee (Ed.), *Humor and children's development: A guide to practical applications* (pp. 15–46). New York: The Haworth Press.

Barrett, L. F., & Salovey, P. (Eds.). (2002). *The wisdom of feeling: Psychological processes in emotional intelligence.* New York: Guilford Press.

Baumrind, D. (2005). Patterns of parental authority and adolescent development. *New Directions for Child and Adolescent Development, 2005,* (108). 61–69.

Berk, L. E. (2003). *Child development* (6th edition). Boston: Pearson Education, Inc.

Berry, B., Raspberry, M., & Byrd, A. (2007, February). Supporting and staffing high-needs schools: Recommendations from South Carolina's National Board Certified Teachers. *National Education Association and Center for Teaching Quality.* Retrieved April 17, 2007, from http://www.thescea.org/policy.pdf

Boocock, S. S., & Scott, K. A. (2005). *Kids in context: The sociological study of children and childhoods*. Lanham, MD: Rowman & Littlefield.

Bourdieu, P. (1986). The forms of capital. In J. G. Richardson (Ed.), *Handbook of theory and research for Sociology of Education* (pp. 241–258). New York: Greenwood Press.

Borland, M., Laybourn, A., Hill, M., & Brown, J. (1998). *Middle childhood: The perspective of children and parents.* London: Jessica Kingsley Publishers.

Borman, G. D., & Overman, L. T. (2004). Academic resilience in mathematics among poor and minority students. *The Elementary School Journal, 104*(3), 177–195.

Bowles, S., & Gintis, H. (1976). *Schooling in capitalist America.* New York: Basic Books.

Boy Scouts of America (2007). Scouting for all ages. *The Boy Scouts of America.* Retrieved March 22, 2007, from http://www.scouting.org/cubscouts/about/boys/scouting.html

Bredekamp, S., & Copple, C. (1997). *Developmentally appropriate practice in early childhood programs* (Rev. ed.). Washington, DC: National Association for the Education of Young Children.

Brizendine, L. (2006). *The female brain.* New York: Morgan Road Books.

Bryant, B. K. (1994). How does social support function in childhood? In F. Nestmann & K. Hurrelmann (Eds.), *Social networks and social support in childhood and adolescence* (pp. 23–35). Berlin, Germany: Walter de Gruyter.

Carnoy, M., & Levin, H. M. (1985). *Schooling and work in the democratic state.* Palo Alto, CA: Stanford University Press.

Causgrove Dunn, J., Dunn, J. G. H., Bayduza, A. (2007). Perceived athletic competence, sociometric status, and loneliness in elementary school children. *Journal of Sports Behavior, 30,* 249–269.

Cazden, C. B. (1988). *Classroom discourse: The language of teaching and learning.* Portsmouth, NH: Heinemann.

Center for Mental Health in Schools. (2006). *Grade retention: What's the prevailing policy and what needs to be done?* Los Angeles: Center for Mental Health in Schools.

Center on Education Policy. (2007). *Answering the question that matters most: Has student achievement increased since No Child Left Behind?* Washington, DC: Center on Education Policy.

Center on Education Policy. (2006). *From the capital to the classroom: Year 4 of the No Child Left Behind Act.* Washington, DC: Center on Education Policy.

Civil Rights Project. (2002). Mission statement. *The Civil Rights Project at Harvard University.* Retrieved February 9, 2007, from http://www.civilrightsproject.harvard.edu/aboutus.php

Cohen, D. K., McLaughlin, M. W., & Talbert, J. E., (Eds.). (1993). *Teaching for understanding: Challenges for policy and practice.* San Francisco: Jossey-Bass.

Cole, M. (1996). *Cultural psychology: A once and future discipline.* Cambridge, MA: Belknap Press of Harvard University Press.

Collins, W. A. (Ed.). (1984). *Development during middle childhood: The years from six to twelve.* Washington, DC: National Academies Press.

Collins, W. A. (2005). Contextualizing middle childhood: Beyond 1984. In C. R. Cooper, C. T. García Coll, W. T. Bartko, H. Davis, & C. Chapman (Eds.), *Developmental pathways through middle childhood: Rethinking contexts and diversity as resources.* (pp. ix–xi). Mahwah, NJ: Lawrence Erlbaum Associates.

Commins, N. L., & Miramontes, O. B. (2006). Addressing linguistic diversity from the outset. *Journal of Teacher Education, 57*(3), 240–246.

Connell, J. P. (1990). Context, self, and action: A motivational analysis of self-system processes across the life span. In D. Cicchetti & M. Beeghly (Eds.), *The self in transition: Infancy to childhood* (pp. 61–97). Chicago: University of Chicago Press.

Cooper, C. R., García Coll, C. T., Bartko, W. T., Davis, H., & Chatman, C. (Eds.). (2005). *Developmental pathways through middle childhood: Rethinking contexts and diversity as resources*. Mahwah, NJ: Lawrence Erlbaum Associates.

Council for Exceptional Children (CEC). (2007). *Policy and Advocacy*. Retrieved November 5, 2007, from http://www.cec.sped.org/AM/Template.cfm?Section=Policy_and_Advocacy&Template=/TaggedPage/TaggedPageDisplay.cfm&TPLID=1&ContentID=2014

Council for Exceptional Children (CEC). (2006). *Giftedness and the gifted: What's it all about?* Retrieved November 17, 2006, from http://www.cec.sped.org/AM/Template.cfm?Section=Gifts_and_Talents&Template=/TaggedPage/TaggedPageDisplay.cfm&TPLID=37&ContentID=5628

Creitz, R. (2007). *Time and timing in the classroom: The cornerstone of any child's education*. West Conshohocken, PA: Infinity.

Darling-Hammond, L. (1997). *The right to learn: A blueprint for creating schools that work*. San Francisco: Jossey-Bass.

Davis, G. A., & Rimm, S. B. (2004). *Education of the gifted and talented* (5th ed.). Needham Heights, MA: Allyn & Bacon.

Davis, L. J. (1997). Constructing normalcy. In L. J. Davis (Ed.), *The disability studies reader* (pp. 9–28). New York: Routledge.

Delgado-Gaitan, C. (1994). Socializing young children in Mexican-American families: An intergenerational perspective. In P. M. Greenfield & R. R. Cocking (Eds.), *Cross-cultural roots of minority child development* (pp. 55–86). Hillsdale, NJ: Lawrence Erlbaum Associates.

Delpit, L. (2006). Lessons from teachers. *Journal of Teacher Education, 57*(3), 220–231.

Delpit, L. (1995). *Other people's children: Cultural conflict in the classroom*. New York: New Press.

Dewey, J. (1990). The school and society and the child and the curriculum. Chicago: University of Chicago Press. (Original work published 1900)

Dickens, W. T., & Flynn, J. R. (2001). Heritability estimates versus large environmental effects: The IQ paradox revolved. *Psychological Review, 108*(2), 346–369.

Driscoll, A., & Nagel, N. G. (2005). *Early childhood education, birth-8: The world of children, families, and educators* (Rev. ed.). Boston: Allyn & Bacon.

Duffett, A. & Johnson, J. (2004). All work and no play? Listening to what kids and parents want from out of school time. *Public Agenda*. Retrieved March 21, 2007, from www.publicagenda.org/research/pdfs/all_work_no_play_exec_summary.pdf

Dweck, C. S. (2002). Beliefs that make smart people dumb. In R. J. Sternberg (Ed.), *Why smart people can be so stupid* (pp. 24–40). New Haven, CT: Yale University Press.

Dweck, C. S. (2006). *Mindset: The new psychology of success*. New York: Random House.

Education Alliance at Brown University (2004, Fall). *Implementing for success: An analysis of five CSR models: Accelerated School summary.* Providence, RI: Brown University.

Education Trust (2006, September). Yes we can: Telling truths and dispelling myths about race and education in America. *The Education Trust.* Retrieved November 7, 2006, from http://www2.edtrust.org/EdTrust/Press+Room/Yes+We+Can.htm

Emerick, S., Hirsch, E., & Berry, B. (2004). Does highly qualified mean high-quality? *Infobrief,* 39. Alexandria, VA: Association for Supervision and Curriculum Development.

Erickson, E. H. (1968). *Identity, youth, and crisis.* New York: Norton.

Fashola, O. S. (Ed.). (2005). *Educating African American males: Voices from the field.* Thousand Oaks, CA: Corwin Press.

Fenning, P., & Rose, J. (2007). Overrepresentation of African American students in exclusionary discipline: The role of school policy. *Urban Education, 42,* 536–559. Retrieved October 26, 2007, from http://uex.sagepub.com/cgi/content/abstract/42/6/536

Ferguson, A. A. (2000). *Bad boys: Public schools in the making of black masculinity.* Ann Arbor, MI: University of Michigan Press.

Ferguson, R. F. (2002). *What doesn't meet the eye: Understanding and addressing racial disparities in high-achieving suburban schools.* The Achievement Gap Initiative at Harvard University. Retrieved October 26, 2007, from http://www.agi.harvard.edu/

Finn, C. E., & Ravitch, D. (2007). Why liberal learning. In C. E. Finn & D. Ravitch (Eds.), *Beyond the basics: Achieving a liberal education for all children* (pp. 1–10). Washington, DC: Thomas B. Fordham Institute.

Finn, J. D., & Rock, D. A. (1997). Academic success among students at risk for school failure. *Journal of Applied Psychology, 82*(2), 221–234.

Finnan, C. (1982). The ethnography of children's spontaneous play. In G. Spindler (Ed.), *Doing the ethnography of schooling: Educational anthropology in action* (pp. 356–380). New York: Holt, Rinehart & Winston.

Finnan, C. (2000). *Implementing school reform models: Why is it so hard for some schools and easy for others?* Paper presented at the annual meeting of the American Educational Research Association, April, New Orleans, LA. ED#: 446356. Retrieved April 13, 2007, from http://www.eric.ed.gov/ERICDocs/data/ericdocs2/content_storage_01/0000000b/80/23/4a/fb.pdf

Finnan, C., Bartel, V., & Knight, M. (2004). *Teaching upper elementary students.* Unpublished manuscript. College of Charleston, Charleston, SC.

Finnan, C., & Meza, J. (2003). The Accelerated Schools Project: Can a leader change the culture and embed reform? In J. Murphy & A. Datnow (Eds.), *Leadership lessons from comprehensive school reforms* (pp. 83–109). Thousand Oaks, CA: Corwin Press.

Finnan, C., Schepenel, K. C., & Anderson, L. W. (2003). Powerful learning environments: The critical link between school and classroom cultures. *Journal of the Education for Students Placed At Risk, 9,* 391–418.

Finnan, C., & Swanson, J. D. (2000). *Accelerating the learning of all students: Cultivating culture change in schools, classrooms, and individuals.* Boulder, CO: Westview Press.

Florio-Ruane, S. (1989). Social organization of classes and schools. In M. Reynolds (Ed.), *Knowledge base for the beginning teacher* (pp. 163–172). New York: Pergamon Press.

Florio-Ruane, S. (1994). Anthropological study of classroom culture and social organization. In T. Husen & T. N. Postlethwaite (Eds.), *International encyclopedia of education research and studies* (2nd ed.). (pp. 796–803). Oxford: Pergamon.

Frankenberg, E., Lee, C., & Orfield, G. (2003). A multiracial society with segregated schools: Are we losing the dream? *The Civil Rights Project, Harvard University.* Retrieved January 29, 2007, from http://www.civilrightsproject.harvard.edu/research/reseg03/resegregation03.php

Freud, S. (1959). *Collected papers.* New York: Basic Books.

Fryer, R. G., & Levitt, S. D. (2006). Testing for racial differences in the mental ability of young children. *The Achievement Gap at Harvard University.* Retrieved November 8, 2006, from http://agi.harvard.edu/events/download.php?id=93

Fullan, M. (2007). *The new meaning of educational change* (4th ed.). New York: Teachers College Press.

Gardner, H. (1993). *Frames of mind: The theory of multiple intelligences.* New York: Basic Books. (Original work published in 1983)

Gardner, H. (1999). Are there additional intelligences? In H. Gardner (Ed.), *Intelligence reframed* (pp. 47–66). New York: Basic Books.

García Coll, C. G., & Szalacha, L. A. (2004). The multiple contexts of middle childhood. Children of immigrant families. *The Future of Children.* 14(2), 81–97. Retrieved January 20, 2007, from www.futureofchildren.org/usr_doc/Vol_14No2_no_photos.pdf

García Coll, C. G., & Szalacha, L. A., Palacios, N. (2005). Children of Dominican, Portuguese, and Cambodian immigrant families: Academic attitudes and pathways during middle childhood. In C. R. Cooper, C. T. García Coll, W. T. Bartko, H. Davis, & C. Chapman (Eds.), *Developmental pathways through middle childhood: Rethinking contexts and diversity as resources.* (pp. 207–234). Mahwah, NJ: Lawrence Erlbaum Associates.

Gilligan, C. (1982). *In a different voice: Psychological theory and women's development.* Cambridge, MA: Harvard University Press.

Ginsburg, K. R. (2007). The importance of play in promoting healthy child development and maintaining strong parent-child bonds. *American Academy of Pediatrics.* Retrieved on March 23, 2007, from http://pediatrics.aappublications.org/cgi/reprint/119/1/182

Girl Scouts of America (2007). Girl Scout programs. *The Girls Scouts of America.* Retrieved March 22, 2007, from http://www.girlscouts.org/program/

Girls Inc. (2007). *Inspiring all girls to be strong, smart, and bold.* Retrieved March 22, 2007, from http://girlsinc.org/ic/

Girls Only (2007). Ask Dr. M. and Molly. *Girls Only.* Girl Scouts of America. Retrieved March 22, 2007, from http://www.gogirlsonly.org/girltalk/askdrm/friends/friends_22.asp

Graue, E., Hatch, K., Rao, K., & Oen, D. (2007). The wisdom of class-size reduction. *American Educational Research Journal, 44,* 670–700.

Greenfield, P. M. (1994). Independence and interdependence as developmental scripts: Implications for theory, research, and practice. In P. M. Greenfield &

R. R. Cocking (Eds.), *Cross-cultural roots of minority child development* (pp. 1–37). Hillsdale, NJ: Lawrence Erlbaum Associates.

Gurian, M., Henley, P., & Trueman, T. (2001). *Boys and girls learn differently!* San Francisco: Jossey-Bass.

Hale, J. E. (1994). *Unbank the fire: Visions for the education of African American children.* Baltimore: Johns Hopkins University Press.

Haney, W. (1993). Testing and minorities. In L. Weis & M. Fine (Eds.), *Beyond silenced voices: Class, race and gender in United States schools.* Albany, NY: SUNY Press.

Harris, J. R. (1995). Where is the child's environment? A group socialization theory of development. *Psychological Review, 102,* 458–489.

Harris, J., (2006). *No two alike: Human nature and human individuality.* New York: W.W. Norton, Co.

Hart, B., & Risley, T. R. (1995). *The social world of children learning to talk.* Baltimore: Brookes Publishing Co.

Harter, S. (1998). The development of self-representations. In W. Damon (Series Ed.) & N. Eisenberg (Vol. Ed.), *Handbook of child psychology: Vol. 3. Social, emotional, and personality development* (5th ed.). (pp. 553–617). New York: Wiley.

Hartup, W. W. (1996). *The company they keep: Friendship in childhood and adolescence.* New York: Cambridge University Press.

Heath, S. B. (1983). *Way with words: Language, life, and work in communities and classrooms.* Cambridge, UK: Cambridge University Press.

Hetherington, E. M., Stanley-Hagan, M., & Anderson, E. R. (1989). Marital transitions: A child's perspective. *American Psychologist, 44,* 303–312.

Hirsch, E. D. (2007). What do they know of reading who only reading know? Bringing liberal arts into the wasteland of the "literacy block." In C. E. Finn & D. Ravitch (Eds.), *Beyond the basics: Achieving a liberal education for all children* (pp. 17–24). Washington, DC: Thomas B. Fordham Institute.

Hopfenberg, W., & Levin, H. M., and Associates (1993). *Accelerated Schools resource guide.* San Francisco, CA: Jossey-Bass.

Humphrey, D. C., Koppich, J. E., & Hough, H. J. (2005). Sharing the wealth: National Board Certified Teachers and schools that need them the most. *Educational Policy Analysis Archives, 13*(18).

Huston, A. C. (Ed.). (1994). *Children in poverty.* Cambridge, UK: Cambridge University Press.

Jackson, P. (1968). *Life in classrooms.* New York: Holt, Rinehart, & Winston.

Jacob, R. T. (2004). The instructional response to high stakes accountability trends in test preparation and content emphasis in mathematics and reading, 1994–2001. In J. Nagaoka & M. Roderick (Eds.), *Ending social promotion: The effects of retention* (pp. 31–55). Chicago: Consortium on Chicago School Research.

James, A. N. (2007). *Teaching the male brain: How boys think, feel, and learn in school.* Thousand Oaks, CA: Corwin Press.

James, A., Jenks, C., & Prout, A. (1998). *Theorizing childhood.* New York: Teachers College Press.

Jarolimek, J. D., Foster, C. D., & Kellough, R. D. (2005). *Teaching and learning in the elementary school.* Upper Saddle River, NJ: Prentice Hall.

Jehlen, A. (2007). Testing: How the sausage is made. *NEA Today.* Retrieved August 17, 2007, from http://www.nea.org/neatoday/0704/coverstory1.html?mode=print

Jennings, N. E. (1998). Reforming practice in urban schools of poverty: Lessons from the field. Paper presented at the annual meeting of the American Educational Research Association, April, San Diego, CA.

Jensen, E. (1998). *Teaching with the brain in mind.* Alexandria, VA: Association for Supervision and Curriculum Development.

Kappa Delta Pi (2007). International honor society in education. *Kappa Delta Pi.* Retrieved September 13, 2007, from http://www.kdp.org/

Kennedy, M. M. (2005). *Inside teaching: How classroom life undermines reform.* Cambridge, MA: Harvard University Press.

Kluckhohn, C. (1949). *Mirror for man: The relationship of anthropology to modern life.* New York: Whittlesey House.

Knapp, M. S., Adelman, N. E., Marder, C., McCollum, H., Needles, M. C., Padilla, C., Shields, P. M., Turnbull, B. J., & Zucker, A. A. (Eds.). (1995). *Teaching for meaning in high-poverty classrooms.* New York: Teachers College Press.

Knowles, T., & Brown, D. F. (2000). *What every middle school teacher should know.* Portsmouth, NH: Heinemann.

Kohlberg, L. (1969). Stage and sequence: The cognitive-developmental approach to socialization. In D. A. Goslin (Ed.), *Handbook of socialization theory and research* (pp. 347–480). Chicago: Rand McNally.

Kowaleski-Jones, L., & Duncan, G. J. (1999). The structure of achievement and behavior across middle childhood. *Child Development, 70*, 930–943.

Kozol, J. (1991). *Savage inequities: Children in America's schools.* New York: Crown.

Kozol, J. (2005, December). Confections of apartheid: A stick-and-carrot pedagogy for the children of our inner-city poor. *Phi Delta Kappan, 87*(4).

Krappmann, L. (1989). Family relationships and peer relationships in middle childhood: An exploratory study of the associations between children's integration into the social network of peers and family development. In K. Kreppner & R. M. Lerner (Eds.), *Family systems and life-span development* (pp. 93–104). Hillsdale, NJ: Lawrence Erlbaum Associates.

Ladd, H., & Hansen, J. (1999). *Making Money Matter: Financing America's Schools.* Washington, DC: National Academies Press

Ladd, H. F., Sass, T. R., & Harris, D. N. (2007). *The impact of national board certified teachers on student achievement in Florida and North Carolina.* Report prepared for the National Academies Committee on the Evaluation of the Impact of Teacher Certification by NBPTS.

Ladson-Billings, G. (2006a). It's not the culture of poverty, it's the poverty of culture: The problem with teacher education. *Anthropology and Education Quarterly, 37*(2), 104–109.

Ladson-Billings, G. (2006b). From the achievement gap to the education debt: Understanding achievement in U.S. schools. *Educational Researcher, 35*(7), 7–12.

Ladson-Billings, G. (1994). *The dreamkeepers: Successful teachers of African American children.* San Francisco: Jossey-Bass.

Lamb, S., & Brown, L. M. (2006). *Packaging girlhood: Rescuing our daughters from marketers' schemes.* New York: St. Martins Press.

Landry, D. (2006). Teachers' (K–5) perceptions of student behaviors during standardized testing. *Curriculum and Teaching Dialogue, 8*, 29–40.

Lareau, A. (2003). *Unequal childhoods: Class, race, and family life.* Berkeley, CA: University of California Press.

Lee, J. C., & Williams, M. (Eds.). (2006). *School improvement: International perspectives.* New York: Nova Science Publishers, Inc.

Levine, A. E. (2006). *Educating school teachers.* Washington, DC: Education Schools Project.

Levine, M. (2002). *A mind at a time.* New York: Simon & Schuster.

Lewis, A. E. (2003). *Race in the schoolyard: Negotiating the color line in classrooms and communities.* New Brunswick, NJ: Rutgers University Press.

Lewis, J. (2004–2005, Winter). Risk, resilience, and attitudes toward learning. *WCER Research Highlights, 16*(4), 3–4.

Lorsen, D. J., & Orfield, G. *Racial inequity in special education.* Cambridge, MA: Harvard Education Publishing.

Maccoby, E. E. (1984). Middle childhood in the context of the family. In W. A. Collins, (Ed.), *Development during middle childhood* (pp. 184–239). Washington, DC: National Academies Press.

Maccoby, E. E. (1990). Gender and relationships: A developmental account. *American Psychologist, 45*(4), 513–520.

Maccoby, E. E. (1992). The role of parents in the socialization of children: An historical overview. *Developmental Psychology, 28,* 1006–1017.

Maccoby, E. E., & Jacklin, C. N. (1987). Gender segregation in childhood. E. H. Reese, (Ed.), *Advances in child development and behavior, 20,* 239–287. New York: Academic Press.

Mahoney, J. L., Lord, H., & Carryl, E. (2005, July/August). An ecological analysis of after-school program participation and the development of academic performance and motivational attributes for disadvantaged children. *Child Development, 76*(4), 811–825.

Marzano, R., & Kendall, J. (1998). *Content knowledge.* Aurora, CO: Mid-continent Regional Educational Laboratory.

McColl, M. S., Hauser, C., Cronin, J., Kingsbury, G. G., & Houser, R. (2006, November) *Achievement gaps: An examination of differences in student achievement and growth.* Lake Oswego, OR: Northwest Evaluation Association. Retrieved January 23, 2007, from http://www.nwea.org/research/gap.asp

McDermott, R., Goldman, S., & Varenne, H. (2006). The cultural work of learning disabilities. *Educational Researcher, 35*(6), 12–17.

McDevitt, T. M., & Ormrod, J. E. (2002). *Child development and education.* Upper Saddle River, NJ: Merrill Prentice Hall.

McGhee, P. E. (1988). Introduction: Recent developments in humor research. In P. E. McGhee (Ed.), *Humor and children's development: A guide to practical applications* (pp. 1–12). New York: The Haworth Press.

McLanahan, S., & Booth, K. (1989). Mother-only families: Problems, prospects, and politics. *Journal of Marriage and the Family, 51,* 557–580.

McMurrer, J. (2007). *Choices, changes, and challenges: Curriculum and instruction in the NCLB era. Center on Education Policy.* Retrieved July 25, 2007, from http://www.cep-dc.org/index.cfm??fuseaction=Page.viewPand&pageID=495&parented=481

McQuillan, P. J. (1998). *Education opportunity in an urban American high school: A cultural analysis.* Albany, NY: State University of New York Press.

Mehan, H. (1979). *Learning lessons: Social organization in the classroom.* Cambridge, MA: Harvard University Press.

Meier, D. (1995). *The power of their ideas: Lessons for American from a small school in Harlem.* Boston: Beacon Press.

Murdoch, S. (2007). *IQ: A smart history of a failed idea.* Hoboken, NJ: John Wiley & Sons, Inc.

Mueller, C. M., & Dweck, C. S. (1998). Intelligence praise can undermine motivation and performance. *Journal of Personality and Social Psychology, 75,* 33–52.

Nagaoka, J., & Roderick, M. (2004). *Ending social promotion: The effects of retention.* Consortium on Chicago School Research. Retrieved February 21, 2007, from http://ccsr.uchicago.edu/content/publications.php?pub_id=12.

National Association for the Education of Young Children (NAEYC). (2007). *About NAEYC.* Retrieved July 17, 2007, from http://www.naeyc.org/about/

National Association for Gifted Children. (2005). *State of the states: A report by the National Association for Gifted Children and the Council of State Directors of Programs for the Gifted.* Washington, DC: National Association for Gifted Children.

National Board for Professional Teaching Standards (NBPTS). (2007). *Every child deserves a great teacher.* National Board for Professional Teaching Standards. Retrieved September 25, 2007, from http://www.nbpts.org

National Board for Professional Teaching Standards (NBPTS). (2001). *Middle childhood/generalist standards* (2nd ed.). National Board for Professional Teaching Standards. Retrieved January 12, 2007, from http://nbpts.org/the_standards/standards_by_cert

National Center for Education Statistics (2006). National Assessment of Educational Progress Data Explorer. *National Center for Education.* Retrieved February 15, 2007, from http://nces.ed.gov/nationsreportcard/naepdata/

National Economic and Social Rights Initiative. (2007). Deprived of dignity: Degrading treatment and abusive discipline in New York city and Los Angeles public schools. *National Economic and Social Rights Initiative.* Retrieved November 5, 2007, from http://www.nesri.org/fact_sheets_pubs/index.html

National Education Association (NEA). (2007). NEA student program. *National Education Association.* Retrieved September 2, 2007, from http://www.nea.org/student-program/membership/index.html

National Education Association (NEA). (2006, July). ESEA: It's time for a change! *National Education Association.* Retrieved May 7, 2007 from http://www.nea.org/esea/posagendaexecsum.html

National Middle School Association (NMSA). (2005). National Middle School Association's position statement on curriculum, instruction, and assessment. *National Middle School Association.* Retrieved September 1, 2006, from http://www.nmsa.org/AboutNMSA/PositionStatements/Curriculum/tabid/767/Default.aspx

National School Board Association (2003). *GAO: NCLB testing will cost $1.9 billion.* Retrieved August 6, 2007, from http://www.nsba.org/site/print.asp?TRACKID=&VID+58&ACTION=PRINT&CID=1063

National Technical Assistance Center on Positive Behavior Interventions and Supports (2007). What is PBIS? *National Technical Assistance Center on Positive Behavior Interventions and Supports.* Retrieved April 17, 2007, from http://www.pbis.org/schoolwide.htm

Nelson, C. A., de Haan, M., & Thomas, K. M. (2006). *Neuroscience of cognitive development: The role of experience and the developing brain.* Hoboken, NJ: John Wiley & Sons.

Newmann, F. M., Bryk, A. S., & Nagaoka, J. K. (2001, January). Authentic intellectual work and standardized tests: Conflict or coexistence? *Consortium on*

Chicago School Research. Retrieved February 24, 2007, from http://ccsr.uchicago.edu/publications/p0a02.pdf

Newmann, F. M., et al.. (1996). *Authentic achievement: Restructuring schools for intellectual quality.* San Francisco: Jossey-Bass.

Nieto, S. (2000). *Affirming diversity: the sociopolitical context of multicultural education* (3rd ed.). White Plains, NY: Longman.

Noblit, G. W. (1993). Power and caring. *American Educational Research Journal, 30*(1), 23–38.

Noddings, N. (1984). *Caring: a feminine approach to ethics and moral education.* Berkeley, CA: University of California Press.

Noddings, N. (1992). *The challenge to care in schools.* New York: Teachers College Press.

Noddings, N. (2005). What does it mean to educate the whole child? *Educational Leadership, 63*(1), 8–13.

Noguera, P. A. (2002). The trouble with black boys: The role and influence of environmental and cultural factors on the academic performance of African American males. *In Motion Magazine, May 13.* Retrieved October 26, 2007. from http://www.inmotionmagazine.com/er/pntroub1.html

Noguera, P. A., & Wing, J. Y. (2006). Introduction: Unfinished business: Closing the achievement gap at Berkeley High School. In P. A. Noguera & J. Y. Wing (Eds.), *Unfinished business: Closing the racial achievement gap in our schools* (pp. 3–28). San Francisco: Jossey-Bass.

Oakes, J. (1985). *Keeping track: How schools structure inequality.* New Haven, CT: Yale University Press.

Oakes, J., Wells, A. S., & Datnow, A. (1997). Detracking: The social construction of ability, cultural politics, and resistance to reform. *Teachers College Record, 98,* 482–510.

Olson, S. (2002). *Mapping human history: Genes, race, and our common origins.* Boston: Houghton Mifflin.

Opie, I. & Opie, P. (1987). *Lore and language of schoolchildren.* New York: Oxford University Press.

Pace Marshall, S., & Price, H. B. (2007). *The learning compact redefined: A call to action.* Alexandria, VA: Association of Supervision and Curriculum Development. Retrieved March 16, 2007, from http://ascd.org/ASCD/pdf/Whole%20Child/WCC%20Learning%20Compact.pdf

Pass, S. (2004). *Parallel paths to constructivism: Jean Piaget and Lev Vygotsky.* Greenwich, CT: Information Age Publishing.

Payne, R. K. (2005). *A framework for understanding poverty* (Rev. ed.). Highland, TX: AHA! Press.

Peace Games (2007). About us. *Peace Games.* Retrieved on May 6, 2007, from http://www.peacegames.org/About.shtml

Pellegrini, A., & Bohn, C. (2005). The role of recess in children's cognitive performance and school adjustment. *Educational Researcher, 34*(1), 13–19.

Perlstein, L. (2007). *Tested: One American school struggles to make the grade.* New York: Henry Holt, & Co.

Peterson, K. D., & Deal, T. E. (1998). How leaders influence the culture of schools. *Educational Leadership, 56,* 28–30.

Phares, V., Steinberg, A. R., Thompson, J. K. (2004). Gender differences in peer and parental influences: Body image disturbance, self-worth, and psychological functioning in preadolescent children. *Journal of Youth and Adolescence, 33,* 421–429.

Phelan, P. A., Davidson, A. L. & Cao, H. T. (1992). Speaking up: Students' perspectives on school. *Phi Delta Kappan, 73,* 695–704.

Phi Delta Kappa (2007). About Phi Delta Kappa. *Phi Delta Kappa.* Retrieved September 3, 2007, from http://www.pdkintl.org/

Piaget, J. (1952). *The origins of intelligence in children* (Rev. ed.). International Universities Press. New York. (Original work published in 1936)

Piaget, J., & Inhelder, B. (1969). *The Psychology of the Child.* New York: Basic Books.

Pogrow, S. (2000, January). Success for all does not produce success for students. *Phi Delta Kappan, 82,* 67–80.

Pomerantz, E. M., & Eaton, M. M. (2000). Developmental differences in children's conceptions of parental control: "They love me, but they make me feel incompetent." *Merrill Palmer Quarterly, 46,* 140–167.

Portes, A., & Rumbaut, R. (2001). *Legacies: The story of the immigrant second generation.* Berkeley, CA: University of California Press.

Powell, S. D. (2005). *Introduction to middle school.* Boston: Pearson.

Power, C., Higgens, A., & Kohlberg, L. (1989). The habit of the common life: Building character through democratic community schools. In L. Nucci (Ed.), *Moral development and character education: A dialogue* (pp. 125–143). Berkeley, CA: McCutchan Publishing Corporation.

Raina, M. K. (1997). 'Most dear to all the muses': Mapping Tagorean networks of enterprise—A study in creative complexity. *Creativity Research Journal, 10*(2/3), 153–174.

Renchler, R. (2000). Grade span. *ERIC Research Roundup, 16*(3). Retrieved on July 20, 2005, from http://eric.uoregon.edu/publications/roundup/soohtml

Reid, D. K., & Knight, M. G. (2006). Disability justifies exclusion of minority students: A critical history grounded in disability studies. *Educational Researcher, 35*(6), 18–24.

Renzulli, J. S. (1986). The three ring conception of giftedness: A developmental model for creative productivity. In R. J. Sternberg & J. E. Davidson (Eds.), *Conceptions of giftedness* (pp. 53–92). New York: Cambridge University Press.

Rich school, poor school: Suburbs face great school spending divide. (2004, February 1). *Chicago Tribune.* Retrieved February 7, 2004, from http://www.chicagotribune.com/news/local/chicago/chi-0702040055feb04,1,3512404.story?ctrack=1&cset=true

Rigby, K. & Johnson, B. (2006/07, fall/winter). Playground heroes. *Greater Good.* Retrieved March 17, 2007, from http://greatergood.berkeley.edu/greatergood/current_issue/rigbyjohnson.html

Roberts, D. F., Foehr, U. G., Rideout, V. J., & Brodie, M. (1999). *Kids & media @ the new millennium: A comprehensive national analysis of children's media use.* Menlo Park, CA: The Henry J. Kaiser Family Foundation.

Roderick, M. (1993). *The path to dropping out: Evidence for intervention.* Plymouth, NH: Greenwood.

Rogoff, B. & Chavajay, P. (1995). What's become of research on the cultural basis of cognitive development? *American Psychologist, 50*, 859–877.

Rogoff, B., Mistry, J., Göncü, A., & Mosier, C. (1993). Guided participation in cultural activity by toddlers and caregivers. *Monographs of the Society for Research in Child Development, 58*(8), V–179.

Rong, X. L., & Preissle, J. (1998). *Educating immigrant students: What we need to know to meet the challenges.* Thousand Oaks, CA: Corwin Press.

Roscigno, V. J., & Ainsworth-Darnell, J. A. (1999). Race, cultural capital, and educational resources: Persistent inequalities and achievement returns. *Sociology of Education 72*(3), 158–178.

Rossi, A. S., & Rossi, P. H. (1990). *Of human bonding: Parent-child relations across the life course*. New York: Aldine de Gruyter.

Rothstein, R. (2004). *Class and schools: Using social, economic, and educational reform to close the Black-White achievement gap.* Washington, DC: Economic Policy Institute.

Rothstein, R. & Jacobsen, R. (2006). The goals of education. *Phi Delta Kappan, 88.* Retrieved January 12, 2007, from http://www.pdkintl.org/kappan/k_v88/k0612rot.htm

Rothstein, R., Jacobsen, R., & Wilder, T. (2006, November). Proficiency for all: An oxymoron. Prepared for symposium Examining America's Commitment to Closing Achievement Gaps: NCLB and its Alternatives sponsored by the Campaign for Educational Equity, Teachers College, Columbia University, New York. Retrieved November 17, 2006, from www.epi.org/webfeatures/viewpoints//rothstein_20061114.pdf

Rueda, M. R., Fan, J., McCandliss, B. D., Halparin, J. D., Gruber, D. B., Lercari, L. P, et al. (2004). Development of attentional networks in childhood. *Neuropsychologia, 42*, 1029–1040.

Runco, M. A. (2007). *Creativity: Theories and themes: Research, development, and practice.* Boston: Elsevier Academic Press.

Sadker, M., & Sadker, D. (2002). The miseducation of boys. In *The Jossey-Bass reader on gender in education* (pp. 182–203). San Francisco: Jossey-Bass.

Salkind, N. J. (2004). *An introduction to theories of human development.* Thousand Oaks, CA: Sage.

Sarason, S. (1996). *Revisiting "The culture of the school and the problem of change."* New York: Teachers College Press.

Scales P. C., Sesma, A., & Bolstrom, B. (2004). *Coming into their own: How developmental assets promote positive growth in middle childhood.* Minneapolis, MN: Search Institute.

Schëin, E. (1992). *Organizational culture and leadership* (Rev. ed.). San Francisco: Jossey-Bass.

Schneider, W. & Pressley, M. (1989). *Memory development between 2 and 20.* New York: Springer-Verlag.

Scherer, M. M. (2006). Teaching the tweens. *Educational Leadership, 63,* 7.

Schram, T. (1994). Playing along the margin: Diversity and adaptation in a lower track classroom. In L. Spindler & G. Spindler (Eds.), *Pathways to cultural awareness: Cultural therapy with teachers and students.* Thousand Oaks, CA: Corwin Press.

Sergiovanni, T. J. (2006). *Rethinking leadership: A collection of articles.* Thousand Oaks, CA: Corwin Press.

Shaw, P., Greenstein, D., Lerch, J., Clasen, L., Lenroot, R., Gogtay, N., Evans, A., Rapoport, J., et al. (2006). Intellectual ability and cortical development in children and adolescents. *Nature, 440,* 676–579.

Siegel, D. L., Coffey, T. J., & Livingston, G. (2001). *The great tween buying machine: Marketing to today's tweens.* Ithaca, NY: Paramount Market Publishing, Inc.

Siegler, R. S. (1996). *Emerging minds: The process of change in children's thinking.* New York: Oxford University Press.

Skinner, E. A., & Belmont, M. J. (1993). Motivation in the classroom: Reciprocal effects of teacher behavior and student engagement across the school year. *Journal of Educational Psychology, 85,* 571–581.

Smith, S. J. (1997). Observing children on a school playground: The pedagogics of child-watching. In A. Pollard, D. Thiessen, & A. Filer (Eds.), *Children and their curriculum: The perspective of primary and elementary school children* (pp. 143–161). Bristol, PA: Falmer Press.

Smith, T. J., & Paul, J. L. (2000). Sharing space, negotiating power, and creating meaning in the classroom. In J. L. Paul & T. J. Smith (Eds.), *Stories out of school: Memories and reflections on care and cruelty in the classroom* (pp. 1–14). Stamford, CT: Ablex Publishing Corporation.

Solomon, R. P. (1992). *Black resistance in high school: Forging a separatist culture.* Albany, NY: State University of New York Press.

South Carolina Department of Education (2006). *Third Grade Science Standards.* Retrieved August 13, 2007, from http://ed.sc.gov/agency/offices/cso/standards/science/

South Carolina Department of Education (2005). *Fourth Grade Social Studies Standards.* Retrieved August 13, 2007, from http://ed.sc.gov/agency/offices/cso/standards/ss/

Spear-Swerling, L., & Sternberg, R. J. (1996). *Off track: When poor readers become "learning disabled."* Boulder, CO: Westview Press.

Spillane, J. P., & Diamond, J. B. (Eds.). (2007). *Distributed leadership in practice.* New York: Teachers College Press.

Spindler, G. D. (1997). Beth Anne – A case study of culturally defined adjustment and teacher perceptions. In G. D. Spindler (Ed.), *Education and cultural process: Anthropological approaches,* (3rd ed.) (pp. 246–261). Prospect Heights, IL: Waveland Press, Inc.

Stanton-Salazar, R. D. (1997). A social capital framework for understanding the socialization of racial minority children and youth. *Harvard Educational Review, 67,* 1–40.

Sternberg, R. J. (1985). *Beyond IQ: A triarchic theory of human intelligence.* New York: Cambridge University Press.

Sternberg, R. J. (1997). *Successful intelligence.* New York: Plume.

Sternberg, R. J., Birney, D., Kirlik, A., Stemler, S., Jarvin, L, & Grigorenko, E. L. (2006). From molehill to mountain: The process of scaling up educational interventions (firsthand experience upscaling the theory of successful intelligence). In M. A. Constas & R. J. Sternberg (Eds.), *Translating theory and research into educational practice: Developments in content domains, large-scale reform, and intellectual capacity* (pp. 205–221). Mahwah, NJ: Lawrence Erlbaum Associates.

Sternberg, R. J., & Subotnik, R. F. (Eds.). (2006). *Optimizing student success in school with the other 3 R's: Reasoning, resilience, and responsibility.* Charlotte, NC: Information Age Publications.

Stevenson, K. R. (2006). *Educational facilities within the context of a changing 21st century America.* Retrieved April 16, 2007, from http://www.eric.ed.gov/ERICDocs/data/ericdocs2/content_storage_01/0000000b/80/32/79/34.pdf

Strachota, B. (1996). *On their side: Helping children take charge of their learning.* Turner Falls, MA: Northeast Foundation for Children (NEFC).

Sullivan, T. (2007). *Adventures in the darkness: Memoirs of an eleven-year-old blind boy.* Nashville, TN: Nelson Books.

Sussman, G. L. (2006). The violence you don't see. *Educational Leadership, 63.* Retrieved June 7, 2007, from http://www.ascd.org/portal/site/ascd/template.MAXIMIZE/menuitem.459dee008f99653tb8

Swadener, B. B., & Lubeck, S. (1995). The social construction of children and families "at risk": An introduction. In B. B. Swadener & S. Lubeck (Eds.), *Children and families "at promise": Deconstructing the discourse of risk* (pp. 1–16). Albany, NY: State University of New York Press.

Taylor, G., Shepard, L., Kinner, F., & Rosenthal, J. (2002). *A survey of teachers' perspectives on high-stakes testing in Colorado: What gets taught, what gets lost.* ERIC Digest #475139. CSE Technical Report. Center for the Study of Evaluation, UCLA.

Teach for America. (2007). *Teach for America.* Retrieved November 1, 2007, from http://www.teachforamerica.org/mission/index.htm

Thompson, C. L., & Cunningham, E. K. (2000). *Retention and social promotion: Research and implications for policy.* ERIC Digest #161/ED449241: Retrieved June 30, 2006 from http://www.ericdigests.org/2001-3/policy.htm

Thorne, B. (2005). Unpacking school lunchtime: Structure, practice, and the negotiation of differences. In C. R. Cooper, et al. (Eds.), *Developmental pathways through middle childhood: Rethinking contexts and diversity as resources* (pp. 63–88). Mahwah, NJ: Lawrence Erlbaum Associates.

Thorne, B. (1993). *Gender play.* New Brunswick, NJ: Rutgers University Press.

Toch, T. (2007, July 24). In testing, the infrastructure is buckling. *Education Week.* Retrieved July 26, 2007, from http:www.edweek.org/ew/articles/2007//07/23/44toch_web.h26.html?print=1

Tollefson, K. & Osborn, M. K. (2008). *Cultivating the learner-centered classroom: From theory to practice.* Thousand Oaks, CA: Corwin Press.

Tomlinson, C. A. (2003). *Fulfilling the promise of the differentiated classroom: Strategies and tools for responsive teaching.* Alexandria, VA: Association for Supervision and Curriculum Development.

Tomlinson, C. A., & McTighe, J. (2006). *Integrating Differentiated Instruction and Understanding by Design.* Alexandria, VA: Association for Supervision and Curriculum Development.

Tough, P. (2006, November 26). What it takes to make a student. *The New York Times.* Retrieved November 27, 2006, from www.nytimes.com/2006/11/26/magazine/26tough.html

Trumbull, E., Greenfield, P. M., & Quiroz, B. (2003). Cultural values in learning and education. In B. Williams (Ed.), *Closing the achievement gap: A vision for changing beliefs and practices* (2nd ed.) (pp. 67–98). Alexandria VA: Association for Supervision and Curriculum Development.

Tyack, D., & Cuban, L. (1995). *Tinkering toward utopia: A century of public school reform.* Cambridge, MA: Harvard University Press.

Tyler, K. M., Boykin, A. W., & Walton, T. R. (2006). Cultural considerations in teachers' perceptions of student classroom behavior and achievement. *Teaching & Teacher Education: An International Journal of Research and Studies, 22*(8), 998–1005.

United States Census Bureau. (2006, April 3). National spending per student rises to $8,287. Retrieved May 7, 2007, from http://www.census.gov/Press-Release/www/releases/archives/economic_surveys/006685.html

United States Department of Education (2007). *Executive Summary of No Child Left Behind. Retrieved* October 10, 2007, from http://www.ed.gov/nclb/overview/intro/execsumm.html

Valli, L., & Buese, D. (2007). The changing roles of teachers in an era of high-stakes accountability. *American Educational Research Journal, 44*, 519–558.

Vygotsky, L. S. (1978). *Mind in society.* Cambridge, MA: Harvard University Press.

Wang, M. C., & Finn, J. D. (2000). *How small classes help teachers do their best.* Philadelphia: Laboratory for Student Success.

Wang, X. H., & Yang, B. Z. (2003). Why competition may discourage students from learning? A behavioral economic analysis. *Education Economics 11*(2), 117–128.

Warner, L., & Sower, J. (2005). *Educating young children from preschool through primary grades.* Boston: Allyn & Bacon.

Wasley, P. A., Hampel, R. L., & Clark, R. W. (1997). *Kids and school reform.* San Francisco: Jossey-Bass.

Weinstein, C., Curran, M., & Tomlinson-Clarke, S. (2003). Culturally responsive classroom management: Awareness into action. *Theory Into Practice, 42*(4), 269–276.

Weinstein, R. S. (2002). *Reaching higher: The power of expectations in schooling.* Cambridge, MA: Harvard University Press.

Weis, H. B., Dearing, E., Mayer, E., Kreider, H., & McCartney, K. (2005). Family involvement: Who can afford it and what does it afford? In C. R. Cooper, C. T. García Coll, W. T. Bartko, H. Davis, & C. Chatman (Eds.), *Developmental pathways through middle childhood* (pp. 17–40). Mahwah, NJ: Lawrence Erlbaum Associates.

West, M. (2007). Testing, learning, and teaching: The effects of test-based accountability on student achievement and instructional time in core academic subjects. In C. E. Finn & D. Ravitch (Eds.), *Beyond the basics: Achieving a liberal education for all children* (pp. 45–63). Washington, DC: Thomas B. Fordham Institute.

Wiggins, G., & McTighe, J. (1998). *Understanding by Design.* Alexandria, VA: Association for Supervision and Curriculum Development.

Williams, B. (2003). What else do we need to know and do? In B. Williams (Ed.), *Closing the achievement gap: A vision for changing beliefs and practices* (2nd ed.) (pp. 13–24). Alexandra, VA: Association for Supervision and Curriculum Development.

Willis, J. (2007, May). Special Section Educating the Whole *Child. Educational Leadership 64*(8), 8–79.

WINGS for kids. (2007). Programs. *WINGS for kids.* Retrieved May 6, 2007, from http://www.wingsforkids.org/

Wolfe, P., & Brandt, R. (1998). What do we know from brain research? *Educational Leadership, 56*(3), 13–18.

Zebrowitz, L. A., Hall, J. A., Murphy, N. A., & Rhodes, G. (2002). Looking smart and looking good: Facial cues to intelligence and their origins. *Personality and Social Psychology Bulletin, 28*(2), 238–249.

Zuckerman, D. (2001). When little girls become women: Early onset of puberty in girls. Retrieved December 4, 2006, from http://www.center4research.org/children11.html

Index

The Corwin Press logo—a raven striding across an open book—represents the union of courage and learning. Corwin Press is committed to improving education for all learners by publishing books and other professional development resources for those serving the field of PreK–12 education. By providing practical, hands-on materials, Corwin Press continues to carry out the promise of its motto: **"Helping Educators Do Their Work Better."**